Card Games
Made Easy

Card Games
Made Easy

by

Arnold Marks and Jacqueline Harrod

Contents

Dedication

For card lovers everywhere.

Introduction

Games using playing cards have evolved over many centuries and in many countries. There are accounts of cards being used in Egypt, China, India, and by the Romans who came with Caesar to Britain. In all probability the only reason why the Stone Age Britons did not play was the difficulty in shuffling the stones!

All card games have one feature in common – luck, and it is not difficult to see why. Put two people in different rooms, each with a pack of cards, tell them to mix the cards thoroughly and take the top 13 cards (a quarter) off the pack. The odds against the top 13 in one room being the same as the top 13 in the other room are in excess of 620,000,000,000 to 1.

Whereas luck is apportioned between everybody in shares affected by the whims of the Goddess of Fate, the amount of skill each person displays has an influence which is just as important to the chances of winning. This book will tell you not only how specific card games should be played according to their rules, it will also comment on those areas of each game in which skill can be exercised to a player's advantage. If skill cannot be used in a game, i.e. if the game is 100% chance, you will not find it in this book.

As you go through the book you may find a game described which has some differences from the way you remember having played it in the past. This is because there are very few games where the rules have been codified completely and accepted universally. Local, Regional, and National differences abound in the rules of many card games so, in order to avoid having to write a series of volumes, I have attempted to limit my descriptions to the fewest possible variations of each game. I have also omitted some games which are known to very few. There is little point in being the best in the world at "Inverted Duplicate Rummy" if you and your wife are the only people in the world who play it. By the way, what exactly is "Inverted Duplicate Rummy"?

It is likely that the readers of this book will fall into one of the following categories:

1. Those whose knowledge of cards consists of being able – just – to recognise a pack for sale on a shop shelf.
2. Those who have played games which they have been shown, but who have little idea of the rules and even less conception of how to apply skill in their play.
3. Card players seeking to extend their existing knowledge of games they play, and to add new games to their repertoire.
4. Those who wish to settle arguments by consulting rules.

There is a broad gulf between those in either of the first 2 categories and those in the latter 2. The majority of people in the first 2 need to be introduced gradually into card games. They should read through the book, chapter by chapter, and resist the temptation to go straight to a chapter which deals with a game that interests them. It would be a grave mistake, for example, for them to think along these lines: "Mrs Jones at number 43 plays Bridge. Mrs Jones is a leading contender for the title 'moron of the year'. If Mrs Jones can play Bridge then so can I. I will start my reading with the chapters on Bridge." This is akin to a would-be driver taking his first driving lesson on a frosty night in a fast sports car.

This book is designed to build knowledge for those without any, and still be complete enough in each chapter to satisfy the requirements of those with some knowledge. So, please advance with caution, and absorb the basics before making great leaps into the unknown. Your patience will be rewarded.

1

Definitions

If you already play one or more of the games described in this book it is possible that you are not in need of the information in this chapter – but read it all the same please, some of it may be new to you.

The Pack

This consists of fifty-two cards divided into 4 "suits", each of which has 13 cards. The suits are ♠ ("Spades"), ♥ ("Hearts"), ♦ ("Diamonds"), and ♣ ("Clubs"). The names have no significance; they are merely a form of "shorthand" for descriptive purposes. After all, it is easier to say "I have 2 Hearts in my hand" than "I have 2 of those red cards with heart-shaped symbols on them."

The cards in each suit are A ("Ace"), K ("King"), Q ("Queen"), J ("Jack", or, as it is also known, "Knave"), then 10 down to 2. Unless the rules of the particular game state otherwise the pecking order is as above; an Ace is more important than a King; both are more important than a Queen; a Jack is less important than the 3 cards above it but more important than all those below it . . . and so on, down to the little 2, which has no-one to bully.

When playing card games a number of terms may be used. I give below the most common of terms and their definitions.

"Cutting" and "Shuffling"

Imagine a card-table, preferably square and large enough to avoid the risk of bloodshed but small enough to enable the cards to be reached from any point. A game which requires 4 players would have a player seated at each side of the table. For convenience we can allocate compass points to each side of the table, so that one player is sitting as North, the next as East and so on. Many articles, books etc., name the players as "North", "East", "South" and "West", and so shall I where it is easiest for descriptive purposes.

Before a game starts the pack will be placed face down in the middle of the table. Each player in turn lifts a small section off and displays the card at the bottom of the section. This is "cutting", and will decide who will "deal" (generally the player who has cut the highest card, i.e. according to the "pecking" order described above). An alternative method of cutting for deal is to fan the cards face down across the table and for each player to select one. In most games the cards are then "shuffled", in other words mixed at random so that no one can know the order in which they finish in the shuffled pack. The act of shuffling may also be known as "making". The cards next pass, still face down, to the player on the dealer's right, who cuts them into two sections, the bottom section being placed on the top by the dealer. The cards are then ready to be dealt.

Etiquette

Many people give the impression that they regard etiquette as the most important aspect of a card game. If the right person doesn't shuffle, or the right person doesn't cut, it is looked upon as an offence in respect of which capital punishment should be reintroduced as soon as possible. In some games, although only one pack is in use at a time, in order to keep the game moving quickly one person deals while another shuffles a second pack in preparation for the next deal. For example, while North is dealing South shuffles the alternate pack. Once shuffled he places it face down on East's left, ready when it becomes East's turn to deal, for him to ask North to cut it to him prior to the deal.

For this purpose 2 different colour packs may be used, possibly in order to give the etiquette fiend the opportunity to point it out to the dealer should he be committing the sacrilege of

16

dealing with the wrong colour pack. To keep the peace it is best to pay tribute to the God of etiquette so that you can get on with the serious business of playing.

Dealing

Let's look at an example, inventing a game as we go along, to be played by Messrs. North, East, South and West.

Assume that everything has been done correctly and that of the 4 players in the game North is going to deal. Assume also that the rules of the game state that each player is to receive 9 cards, dealt one at a time. North deals by placing one card at a time face down in front of each of the players in a clockwise fashion, starting with the player on his left. A bird now enters through the window and flies around peeking at the cards. This is what the bird sees:-

N (North)
♠ 8 4
♥ K 3 2
♦ —
♣ Q 9 6 4

W (West)
♠ 7 2
♥ 4
♦ A K 8 5 2
♣ 2

E (East)
♠ 5
♥ Q 10 6
♦ 6 4 3
♣ A J

S (South)
♠ 6
♥ 9 7 5
♦ —
♣ K 10 8 5 3

Description of the "Hands"

North's "hand", i.e. the cards that he is holding in such a way that only he and the bird can see them, is:- two ♠ (a "double-ton"), three ♥, no ♦ (a "void"), and four ♣ (3 or more cards in a suit are sometimes described as "times", i.e. "3 times", "4 times" etc.).

East has one ♠ (a "singleton"), 3 times ♥, 3 times ♦, and

17

"Ace doubleton" ♣, i.e. a doubleton containing an Ace.

South has a singleton ♠, 3 times ♥, a void ♦ and 5 times ♣. West has a doubleton ♠, singleton ♥, "Ace, King five times", ♦, and a singleton ♣.

These descriptions are common usage but you won't be thrown out of the game if you forget them.

The "Lead" and "following suit"

Another assumption now is that as is normal in many games East, because he is the next player on dealer's left, is going to "lead". He is going to choose a card to place face upwards in the middle of the table; that is the "lead" – the first card actually played face-up on the table. For no good reason – possibly a Chinese superstition he connects with the 5 of Spades (5 ♠) – he leads that card – 5 ♠.

Under our rules, and also under the rules of many games, a player whose turn it is to play must play a card in the same suit as that which has been led provided he has a card in that suit, in other words must "follow suit", which South does by placing 6 ♠ face upwards in the middle of the table. West plays 7 ♠ and North plays 8 ♠.

"Tricks"

North has played the highest of the 4 cards; the 4 together constitute a "trick" and by playing the highest North has won that trick. He picks up all 4 cards, carefully arranges them into a little block and places that block face down in front of him – his trick.

Having won (also known as "made" or "taken") the trick it is North's responsibility to play the first card to the next trick. Flushed with the success of his 8 ♠ he plays 4 ♠. East has not got a Spade. If he had a Spade he would have to follow but as he can't follow he must play a card in a different suit, i.e. he must "discard". South must also discard, but West has to follow with 2 ♠. Again North will have won the trick. Note that neither East nor South could elect not to play a card when it was their turn. Their choices were limited to "follow" or "discard".

I'll leave you to work out the rest of the play for yourself.

"Trumps"

The word trump comes from the French word "triomphe". The trump suit is a suit which triumphs over the other three. In most games as stated above it is necessary to follow suit if you can; if you can't follow, and the game includes trumping, you may either discard or use a trump. In other words you may choose to "trump" an opponent's card and may thereby win the trick. The term "ruff" means the same thing.

There are a number of different ways in which the trump suit can be chosen, in fact some games are almost built around the method of deciding upon the trump suit. One way, and we can assume it was the way chosen for the game I am illustrating, is to have an extra cut of the cards before they are cut for the deal, the suit revealed by the card cut being the trump suit for that hand.

Let's look again at the deal illustrated above and assume this time that in a cut before the cut for deal the trump suit became ♦. Go back to the second trick, the one which North won with the 4 ♠. East now has a choice of card to play because (unlike some games which stipulate that a player must trump if he cannot follow) our game allows him to discard a ♥ or a ♣ or, if he wishes, to trump with a ♦. Let's say that he decides to play the 3 ♦. He will win the trick because South cannot "over-trump" (play a higher ♦) because he has no ♦, and nor can West who must follow to the card first led, i.e. a ♠.

If more than one trump is played in the course of a trick, or the card led was a trump, the highest trump played wins the trick.

Sometimes the selection of the trump suit is determined before the first hand for the whole of the game. A sort of rota system might be applied to each hand in turn, e.g. ♠, then ♥, then ♦, then ♣, and then perhaps "No Trumps". This means exactly what it says, i.e. that in that hand there will be no trump suit . . . just like our first hand before Diamonds were introduced as trumps.

2

Skill

Skill in the actual play of the cards comes easier to some than to others, but all people come to the card-table for the first time with the most essential piece of equipment – a brain. Most card games have the same fundamental skills in common, a little memory, a little mathematics, and a little common sense. Some games, particularly those involving partnerships, require methods of communication – enabling one partner somehow to impart information to the other without making pointed remarks, or foot tapping, or eyebrow lifting etc.

Memory

It is a common complaint that "I can't remember the cards that have already been played". The reason is usually that the complainant has not really watched the cards that have been played. Here is a simple illustration of how memory should work.

Messrs. North, East, South and West sit clockwise around a table. North deals one card at a time to each player until all 52 cards have been dealt. The "rules" of the game that they are playing are very simple:- they will play out all 13 tricks; each player in turn will lead to the next trick, irrespective of who may have won the trick just played; there will be no trump suit. In tabular form, with the card led being marked *, the play of the first 5 tricks proceeds as follows:

Trick	N		E		S		W	
1	♠	A*	♠	2	♠	4	♠	5
2	♥	A	♥	K*	♥	3	♥	2
3	♥	6	♥	8	♥	Q*	♥	5
4	♠	3	♦	2	♠	8	♠	K*
5	♠	Q*	♦	3	♣	2	♠	10

If each player has been watching what has been played then everyone should know these facts about the Spade suit:

1. North and West started with 10 Spades between them.
2. East only had 1 Spade to start with and South only had 2.
3. 9 Spades have been played so far, therefore North and West still have 4 between them.
4. The highest remaining Spade is the Jack.
5. As West played the 10 under North's Q at trick 5, unless he is messing about the probability is that at most he only has the Jack left. Given a choice of cards to play to a trick which a player knows he will lose it is a natural tendency to play the lowest card that he has in the suit, retaining the higher card for a subsequent trick. Accordingly it is fair to assume that North has 3, or all 4 of those that are left.

Most of the time you can get by if you look for the high cards particularly; count the number actually played; and note who cannot follow. The more a player tries to do this the easier it becomes, until he reaches the point when doing so becomes subconscious.

Mathematics

The above example also takes us into the realm of mathematics. For example, take the statement that North and West started with 10 Spades between them; how do you know? Because East couldn't follow to the second Spade played, and South couldn't follow to the third played, which means that they only had 3 between them. As each suit has 13 cards that leaves 10 between the other two players. Most card mathematics are as simple as that.

Common Sense

The example also shows how common sense is used. I have already pointed to the probability that West has either the Jack or no Spades left. The logic is that if a player has a choice, must follow suit but cannot play a card higher than one already played, he will play the smallest card he has in the suit unless he is trying to convey a message to a partner. In the above game there were no partners, so when West played the 10 ♠ under the Q ♠ the inference to be drawn is that he either still holds the Jack or has none left.

Extend the reasoning to Hearts. South has already won the third trick by playing the Queen, the Ace and King already having been played on trick 2. The other 3 players played the 6 (North); the 8 (East); the 5 (West). The 2 and 3 were played on trick 2. Who is most likely to have the 4? The answer is South because each of the others played higher cards when they had the opportunity to play the 4. And why do I bother with an example concerning a little 4? Because the reasoning is the same no matter what the value of the card may be. Knowing that South has the 4 may prove to be the knowledge that will win the game.

Equally, North, South or West may have the 7, because each played a lower card or cards to previous tricks.

Of course players make mistakes, or play wrong cards purposely to put opponents off, but common sense dictates that one should try and use whatever information becomes available because it will lead one to the right conclusion more often than not. Isn't that just common sense?

In the following chapters you will see how the above fundamental skills are used and extended, and how the use of skill can make each game more enjoyable.

3

Whist and Friends

The Whist family of card games is extensive and extremely popular. It ranges from simple 2 handed variations right through to the aristocrat – Contract Bridge. Whist is also a very old game ... C. S. Forrester fans will recall that it was the favourite game of Hornblower during the Napoleonic wars.

Universal Rules and Objects
All the variations have the following rules and objects in common:-

1. The shuffle and cut procedures prior to the deal are as explained in Chapter 1;
2. With 2 players each takes turn in dealing; with more than 2 each fresh hand is dealt by the next player, going clockwise around the table; the cards are shuffled after each hand;
3. The first card is led by the player on the dealer's left (his opponent if only 2 are playing);
4. The winner of each trick leads to the next trick;
5. A player must follow suit if he can;
6. The object is to win more tricks than the other player(s).

Simple 2 handed Whist
If you have mastered the definitions in Chapter 1, and the fundamentals of skill in Chapter 2, you are already well on your way to being able to play Whist. First a 2 handed version.

The Preliminaries

Our friends North and South decide to play one hand of 7 card Whist, with trumps being selected by a preliminary cut, and the dealer being the player who then cuts the highest card. North wins the cut for dealer; he shuffles the complete pack of 52 cards and South cuts it; North then deals 7 cards to each of them, one card at a time, starting with South's first card.

The Play

Let's assume Spades are trumps and that the players have:-

N		S	
♠	A 3	♠	–
♥	8 6 4	♥	J 10 9
♦	7	♦	A 3 2
♣	Q	♣	7

Tabulating the play, with South leading to the first trick and the winner of each trick playing first to the subsequent trick, the cards played to each trick are:-

Tricks	N		S	
1	♥	4	♥	J*
2	♥	6	♥	10*
3	♥	8	♥	9*
4	♦	7	♦	A*
5	♠	3*	♦	3
(North trumps)				
6	♠	A*	♦	2
7	♣	Q*	♣	7

The winning cards are marked *. South wins by taking 4 tricks to North's 3.

This simple procedure could be adopted by more than 2 players, perhaps dealing out all 52 cards.

Knock Out Whist

An entertaining but still simple variation of Whist is ''Knock Out''. In this game the number of cards dealt to each player, after an initial deal following the normal cut and shuffle procedure, reduces hand by hand, with the winner of the previous hand dealing and choosing trumps. In the event of a tie for the number of tricks won in a hand the winner is decided on a cut.

The complete pack is used, and it is usual, but not mandatory, for each player to receive 7 cards, dealt 1 at a time, from the first deal. A player is "knocked out" if he fails to make a trick in a hand. The game can be played by several players or only 2, and the eventual winner is the one who survives after all others have fallen by the wayside.

Example of "Knock Out"
North and South agree that the game of simple 2 handed Whist they played above was the first in a game of Knock Out. As South won that hand he deals and chooses trumps. Assume that in the second hand South wins 4 of the 6 tricks that can be taken. He deals again for the third hand and the cards are:-

N		S	
♠	8 6 4	♠	10
♥	Q	♥	—
♦	2	♦	—
♣	—	♣	5 4 3 2

He chooses Clubs as trumps and poor North does not make a trick. North is knocked out and South wins the game.

German Whist
German Whist is a variation which uses the whole of the pack throughout the play, and is the most skilful of the games of Whist for 2 players. There are 26 tricks to be taken and the object is to win 14 or more, i.e. over half of them.

Preliminaries
After the usual cut and shuffle procedure the cards are dealt face down one at a time until each player has 13. The pack is then placed face down in the centre of the table with the then top card

turned face-upwards on the top. The suit of the card displayed is the trump suit for the whole of the game.

The Play

The dealer's opponent leads to the first trick. The winner of the trick takes into his hand the faced-up top card; the loser takes the next card, keeping it concealed from his opponent. The new top card in the remainder of the pack is turned face-up on top of the pack. The winner of the first trick plays first to the second trick. The winner of that second trick takes into his hand the top card; the loser taking the next card . . . and so on until the cards in the middle are exhausted, at which point the remaining 13 cards held by each player are played for the last 13 tricks.

Example Game

North has dealt and the top card turned over to view is Q ♥. Hearts will therefore be trumps throughout the 26 trick game. The cards held are:-

N					S			
♠	A	J	4	3	♠	Q	8	2
♥	8	6	5	2	♥	A	K	4
♦	K	10			♦	9	8	5	3
♣	Q	J	4		♣	10	6	5

It is South's lead as North dealt. Obviously the Q ♥ is a card well worth having; South already has the A ♥ and K ♥ so the Q ♥ is bound to be a trick-winning card later on in the game. South wishes to win the trick and, to make sure, he leads A ♥. North follows with 2 ♥. South takes the Q ♥ into his hand. North takes the next card from the pack (keeping it concealed from South) and finds it to be 9 ♣. The next card is turned over and is revealed as being the A ♦. Another very good card and again South wishes to win the trick. He plays K ♥ and North follows with 5 ♥. South takes the A ♦ and North finds that his new card taken from the top of the pack is 7 ♥. The next card is turned over. It is 2 ♦. South does not want it – the card which is under it is likely to be better. South therefore plays the 3 ♦ and North is forced to take the trick with the 10 ♦. And so it continues until all 26 tricks have been divided between the 2 players. The player who wins over half the tricks wins the game.

Skill

Obviously luck plays a large part in German Whist but, assuming equal luck, the more skilful player will generally win. The longer the game goes on the more important it becomes to have a good idea of the cards that have been played and the cards that your opponent is known to have won from the top of the pack. In the above example North should remember that South took the A ♦ from the top of the pack; his own K ♦ is the second highest Diamond and he may lose it under South's A ♦ if he plays it as a lead to a new trick. He should remember that 4 trumps have already been played, including the A and K.

Tactics have already been demonstrated in the example by South's lead of the A of trumps in order to make sure of winning the Q of trumps, by his play of the K ♥ to make sure of winning the A ♦ and by his subsequent play of 3 ♦ to force North to win a card which neither player wanted.

By the time the first 13 tricks have been taken a very good player will remember all the cards that have been played and will be able to work out exactly which cards his opponent has. He will be able to judge the best order in which to play his own cards and thereby win as many tricks as possible. This is where common sense comes in; there are no rules to follow, only those dictated by the actual situation at the time. Even if the game is obviously a lost cause there is enjoyment to be had in squeezing out every possible trick ... including the ''impossible'' ones!

German Whist is a very good learning game. There are no rules governing the number of hands to be played, or for scoring points; you can make these up for yourself. For example you could decide to play 3 hands, with the eventual winner being the player who has taken the most tricks over all 3.

Partnership Whist

It's time now to turn to Partnership Whist. As its name indicates, 2 players play against another 2. In our example North and South will play against East and West.

The Preliminaries

Among 4 players the partners are usually decided on a cut unless for example family rivalry decrees who plays with whom. (At a Whist drive, where several partnerships all will be playing against each other, the pairs swap round during the drive according to a complicated "movement" procedure – of no interest at this time – see later description in Chapter 8.) The trump suit for each deal may be decided by a cut or by agreement on the rota system described in Chapter 1. All 52 cards are dealt out, one at a time, after the normal cut for deal, shuffle, and deal procedure (see page 16).

The object of the game is the same as all other versions of Whist, i.e. to win the most tricks out of the available number, in this case 7 or more out of 13. The tricks won by each partner count towards the partnership total.

Skill

Communication is the main element of skill in Partnership Whist. To obtain maximum enjoyment from the game it is essential that the partners communicate. This does not mean that as they play an Ace they can lean across the table and whisper "I also have the King", nor does it mean that nods of approval, or scowls of disapproval are permitted by the rules, or that they can have a secret code. For example, if the partners have decided that the play of a 2 is meant to indicate that the player playing that card has or has not got certain other specific cards, all 4 players seated at the table must be equally aware of the special meaning intended. By the way, that is known as a "signal", of which more later.

Communication takes place in part by the card which is led, in part by the card the partner plays on the card led and in part by the discards made during the game.

The first lead (the "opening lead")

The lead of a specific card is generally understood to promise, or to deny, the holding of other specific cards in the suit led. At the end of this chapter you will find a table of leads which shows the recognised card to be led from a holding in a suit, if that suit is chosen for the first lead in the game. It doesn't matter which suit

28

you choose – the card you play in that suit should give your partner an idea of the remaining cards you have in the suit. For example, in a no trump game, having decided to lead a card from Q J 10 4 3, the recognised lead according to the table would be the Queen. That is known as the "top of a sequence". If the cards held had been the J 10 9 4 3, the correct lead would be the Jack. In the first instance the partner will expect the person on lead to have the J and 10 to back his Queen (or J and 9); in the second instance he will expect 10 and 9 to be backing up the Jack.

Signals

The card the partner of the person on lead plays to the first trick should, if possible, be a "signal". There are many systems of signals in use, but the easiest to remember and the one most widely used is "High-Low". All that means is that if the partner of the person on lead plays a fairly high card (if possible higher than a six) he likes the suit led; in other words he has some good cards in that suit which may win tricks. If on the other hand he plays a low card, he does not like the suit led. These signals are not "commands"; they are intended to inform, not instruct.

Discards

If a good player is unable to follow suit at any time during the play he will try to pass a message with the card chosen as his discard.

Many systems for discarding exist, but again the easiest and most commonly used is "High-Low". A high card discarded means . . . "I am interested in this suit partner", a low card discarded means . . . "I'm not interested in this suit partner." The partner of the player making a discard, having been given information by his partner, will use his own judgment in deciding which of his own cards he will discard when he has to, which he will retain, and which he will play if it becomes his lead. Again the message given by such a discard is generally only a message, not a command. Having said which, if partner, being forced to discard on your play of the highest Club, discarded the Ace of Spades, would you expect to leave the room alive if you had a Spade but failed to lead it in an early opportunity? Could partner have made his passionate desire for you to lead a Spade more clear?

Counting

A further element of skill arises out of "counting", a spin-off from memory. To take a very simple example, suppose you start with A K Q 2 of a suit in your hand and lead the Ace, to which all follow suit; then you play the King and again all follow suit; then you play the Queen to which both your opponents follow suit, but upon which your partner discards. By this time you should have counted that 11 cards in the suit have been played. One of your opponents still has a card left in the suit which must be higher than your 2. By using counting, discards, and signals, good players can paint a picture in their minds of all three of the other hands, and will engineer the play of the last few cards to their own advantage. This ability comes after a lot of practice but anyone who wishes to acquire it has only to persevere.

Example of Partnership Whist

N (North)
♠ A J 5
♥ 8 6
♦ K Q 8 7
♣ A 9 8 7

W (West)
♠ 6 4
♥ Q J 9 7 3
♦ 10 4 2
♣ K 6 4

E (East)
♠ K Q 10 3 2
♥ A K 4
♦ 6 3
♣ 5 3 2

S (South)
♠ 9 8 7
♥ 10 5 2
♦ A J 9 5
♣ Q J 10

North has dealt, and there are No Trumps.

In tabular form, with the winning card of each trick marked *, the play proceeds as follows:-

Trick	E	S	W	N
1	♠ K*	♠ 7	♠ 4	♠ 5
2	♥ A*	♥ 2	♥ 9	♥ 6
3	♥ K*	♥ 5	♥ 3	♥ 8
4	♥ 4	♥ 10	♥ J*	♦ 8
5	♣ 2	♠ 8	♥ Q*	♣ 7
6	♦ 3	♦ 9	♥ 7*	♣ 8
7	♠ 10	♠ 9	♠ 6	♠ A*
8	♦ 6	♦ 5	♦ 2	♦ K*
9	♣ 3	♦ J	♦ 4	♦ Q*
10	♣ 5	♦ A*	♦ 10	♦ 7
11	♠ 2	♣ Q	♣ K	♣ A*
12	♠ 3	♣ J*	♣ 4	♣ 9
13	♠ Q	♣ 10*	♣ 6	♠ J

If you are in difficulty following the above I suggest you sort the hands out with a pack of cards, play them in the order shown, and go along with me now in this commentary:-

Trick 1 – The King of Spades is the correct lead from this combination. The 4 ♠ from West is simply a low card denoting a lack of interest. The 5 ♠ from North was a "waiting card"; the A ♠ is not going to run away in No Trumps and he can afford to wait and see how the rest of the play develops.

Trick 2 – The A ♥ is played because partner does not like Spades. The 9 ♥ is an encouraging card.

Trick 3 – Self-evident after trick 2; partner encouraged East to continue playing Hearts and he obliges.

Trick 4 – The 8 ♦ from North suggests to South that Diamonds might be a good suit in which to make tricks.

Trick 5 – The 2 ♣ from East says "no interest in Clubs partner".

Trick 6 – The 3 ♦ from East says "I haven't got these either". The 9 ♦ from South agrees North's signal at Trick 4.

Trick 7 – The 6 ♠ from West says without words "you led

Spades partner; at trick 5 you told me you had no interest in Clubs; at trick 6 you told me that you had no interest in Diamonds; I'm not stupid. So, as you want Spades . . . have a Spade." The 10 ♠ from East confirms that Spades are exactly what he wants; as it happens East's Q ♠ will never have the chance to come good in this hand but he couldn't have known that when he expressed his desire.

Tricks 8-13 – should be self-evident after the previous exchanges of signals.

North/South win by 7 tricks to 6. They did so with the aid of legitimate signals used throughout the game.

Table of Opening Leads
Before the first card is led the suit from which it is led has to be chosen. The card to be led will most often be in a suit which, to that player, seems to represent the best chance for making tricks. This is known as an "attacking" lead. However, sometimes the person on lead will not like to lead the suit which seems strongest; it may appear to be better to hope that partner or opponents will play that suit. For example to choose a card from K J 9 7 may give tricks to opponents. In such a case a "passive" lead may be selected from another suit.

As a result of the thinking of many good players in the past an accepted table of leads has evolved that is generally used by all such players. Each specific card that is chosen for a lead by an expert player sends a message to his partner: "I have chosen this card because (1) I have (may have) 'this or that' in the suit; or (2) I do not want you to think that I have 'whatsit or thingyme-bob'; or (3) rightly or wrongly I think this is the best suit from which I should lead a card".

The complete table is shown below and the novice player should make every effort to memorise it. It is not as difficult as it looks – it falls into easily recognisable groups. For example in a trump game if an expert player chooses an Ace to lead, his partner will expect him to have at least the King of the same suit; if the expert chooses a 10 his partner will assume that the 10 is the highest card he has in the suit.

In each case the table that follows shows the card which

should be led from a selected suit with holdings as illustrated. Note the differences in selection if a game is played in which a trump suit has been agreed, against a game in which there are no trumps. The symbol x is used to denote small cards of little value.

Cards in chosen suit				A Trump game	No Trump game
A	K	Q	J	A	A
A	K	Q	xxx	A	A
A	K	Q	xx	A	A
A	K	Q	x	A	A
A	K	x		A	A
A	K			K	A
A	K	J	10	A	A
A	K	J	xxxx	A	A
A	K	J	xx	A	x
A	K	J	x	A	x
A	K	xxxx		A	x
A	K	xxx		A	x
A	K	10	9 x	A	10
K	Q	J	xx	K	K
K	Q	10	xx	K	K
K	Q	xxx		K	x
Q	J	10	xx	Q	Q
Q	J	9	xx	Q	Q
Q	J	xxx		x	x
Combinations headed by					
J	10	9		J	J
10	9	8		10	10
xxx				the highest	the highest

The leads against a trump game could be made from the actual trump suit, or any one of the others.

If possible the undershown suits in the next page of the table should not be chosen in a trump game. If this cannot be avoided the selected cards to be led in a trump game are as shown in the first column.

However, in a No Trump game the cards to lead from the chosen suit are those shown in the second column.

Cards in chosen suit	A Trump game	No Trump game
A Q J xx	A	Q
A Q 10 9 x	A	10
A Q xxxx	A	x
A J 10 xx	A	J
K J 10 xx	J	J
Q 10 9 xx	10	10
A xx	A	x
K xx, Q xx, or J xx	x	x

Note: when leading a small card from a suit with 4 or more cards but without one of the combinations commented upon above in either part of the table, it is usual to play the card which is the 4th highest (from the top).

Please turn to Chapter 8 if you wish to learn about Whist drives and how they are organised.

4

Solo and Napoleon

Solo Whist ("Solo") is a game for 4 people, although there are some 3 handed variations. It is a gambling game usually for money stakes, as is Napoleon ("Nap"). Solo incorporates a fair amount of skill and is extremely popular, although not as popular as it once was, having been overtaken by Bridge.

SOLO

The Preliminaries
The 4 players sit around a table in the normal fashion, i.e. 1 player at each side. After deciding who is to deal, usually on a cut of the cards, the 52 cards are shuffled by the dealer and dealt out face down until all 4 players have 13 cards in their hand. The sequence of deal is 3 cards to each player for 4 rounds followed by 1 card each. The dealer turns his own last card face upwards on the table. That card shows in the first instance which is to be the trump suit for that hand and remains exposed on the table until an "Auction" has been completed. The dealer takes the card back into his hand before the play.

The Auction
Bids ("calls") are made in the auction by the players in turn, starting with the player on the dealer's left. The bids shown below are listed in order of strength, with the least important first.

A player who would like to say something other than "pass" cannot do so if his call would be lower than one already made.

With 2 exceptions dealt with shortly, each player is only allowed one bid opportunity in the auction, i.e. when it is his turn to call.

"Pass" – "Count me out of this auction please". (If all 4 "Pass", cards go to next player to shuffle and re-deal.)

"Prop" – Short for "I propose". This is an offer to combine with one of the other players to make 8 tricks in partnership.

"Cop" – The acceptance of a Prop. This can only be made after a Prop and provided no other player has already made a stronger call. With one exception, detailed later, you cannot call "Cop" if you have already said "Pass".

"Solo" – An undertaking to make 5 tricks; the trumps being as already shown by the faced up card.

'Misère" – An undertaking to make no tricks at all. If this call is made the trump suit is *cancelled* and the hand is played without a trump suit.

"Abondance" – An Abondance caller has to make 9 tricks, provided the trump suit is *changed* to his choice.

"Abondance in Trumps" – Usually, but not necessarily, made after someone else has called an Abondance. The call states that the trump suit will remain as shown. 9 tricks are still required.

"Misère Ouverte" – Otherwise known (in 'fractured' French) as "misère-évère"; this differs from Misère in as much as the caller must lead the first card and then expose the rest of his cards face upwards on the table. He must still make no tricks with the trump suit cancelled.

"Abondance Déclarée" – Requires the caller to make all 13 tricks without a trump suit. Again the caller must lead the first card.

If a player calls "Prop" and the other 3 players decline to call "Cop" or make a call of greater strength, then subject to exception (2) below the situation becomes the same as if all had said "Pass" and the cards go to the next player for a new deal. A call is always superseded by a call of greater strength being made.

The exceptions to the rule that each player has only one call are:-

1. If the player making the first call (i.e. the player to the left of the dealer) says "Pass" he can still accept a Prop made by another player which neither of the other 2 has accepted. For example, North deals and the calls proceed:

   > East – "Pass"
   > South – "Prop"
   > West – "Pass"
   > North – "Pass"
   > East – "I'll take you". The expression "I'll take you" is often used instead of "Cop".

2. If the player making the first call says "Prop" and each of the other 3 Pass, the first player then has the option of changing his call to a "Solo". For example, North deals:-

   > East – "Prop"
   > South, West and North each "Pass'.

   East can either throw in his cards, or call "Solo". If he decides not to call " Solo" then, as his original "Prop" was not accepted, the cards pass on for a new deal as already noted.

Example Auctions

1. The dealer is North. His last card is the 2 ♣, which is placed face-upward on the table. Clubs are going to be the trump suit.

   > East – "Prop"
   > South – "I'll take you" ("Cop")
   > West – "Pass"
   > North – "Pass"

   East and South are to make 8 tricks together in partnership, Clubs being trumps. North was the dealer so East will lead to the first trick, following normal Whist rules.

2. Dealer East; trump card is 4 ♥.

> South – "Pass"
> West – "Prop"
> North – "Solo"
> East – "Pass"

North's call supersedes that of West. North must make at least 5 tricks; trumps will be Hearts and South is to lead.

3. Dealer South; trump card Q ♠.

> West – "Pass"
> North – "Solo"
> East – "Pass"
> South – "Misère"

South must avoid making a trick. There is no trump suit and West will lead.

4. Dealer West; trump card A ♦.

> North – "Misère"
> East – "Abondance"
> South – "Pass"
> West – "Abondance in Trumps"

West has to make 9 tricks and the trump suit will remain Diamonds. (Note that when East called "Abondance" he did not state immediately what his intended trump suit would be ... in fact it would have been against the rules for him to do so until it had been established that his call was highest in the auction. That is the moment it has to be done.) North must lead to the first trick.

At this point it is worth noting that some Solo "Schools" permit 3 more exceptions to the calling rules I have set out above. They are:-

1. A player whose call of "Solo" has been superseded by a call of "Misère" or "Abondance" can increase his call to "Abondance in Trumps".
2. A player whose call of "Misère" has been superseded by "Abondance" or "Abondance in Trumps" can increase his call to "Misère Ouverte".

3. A player whose call of "Abondance" has been superseded by "Abondance in Trumps", or whose call of "Abondance in Trumps" has been exceeded by "Misère Ouverte", can increase his call to "Abondance Déclarée".

Skill in the Auction

The skill in calling is not great. All that is required is an assessment of the value of the cards in one's hand, coupled with a reappraisal, if it seems to be necessary, following a call by a previous player. Three examples illustrate:-

1. North deals and a small Spade is turned over. East passes and South is looking at this collection –

   ♠ 10 x x x x x (x = a card of little value)
   ♥ A J x
   ♦ x
   ♣ x x x

   South's reasoning is as follows: "The other players have 7 cards between them in the trump suit and the best distribution I can look for is a 2:2:3 split. The most I can expect in the way of tricks from the trump suit is 3 so my hand is worth a maximum of 4 tricks. I will say 'Prop' because my hand, played in partnership with another with some high cards outside the trump suit, has a good chance of producing 8 tricks." Why 3 tricks in trumps? If the adverse trumps *are* distributed 2:2:3 and trumps are led 3 times, opponents' trumps will be exhausted after the third round, and South will be left with the last 3, each of which will be worth 1 trick.

2. On the same deal West has –

   ♠ K Q J x
   ♥ K Q x x
   ♦ x x
   ♣ x x x

West's reasoning: "South has said 'Prop' so, assuming he has either A ♠ or A ♥ my hand can produce 4 tricks in partnership with his. If his hand can produce 4 more we will reach our target of 8 tricks. A fair chance – I will say 'Cop'.

3. On the same deal North has –

♠ A
♥ x x x x
♦ A K Q x
♣ A K Q x

North's reasoning: "I have all these high cards – how pretty! If each of the other 3 players has at least 2 cards in both of the Diamond and Club suits (which seems a reasonable distributional chance) I can make 4 tricks plus my Ace of trumps. If either suit is split 3:3:3 between my opponents I should have 3 tricks in that suit and only need 1 from my other A K Q. Either of those distribution patterns will see my contract home, so I will call a Solo."

I make no apology for using the word "reasoning" in the 3 examples. The chances of the non-reasoning player being a consistent winner are similar to the chances of survival of a blind jaywalker.

Order of Play
The order of play is as follows:-

1. Except where "Misère Ouverte" or "Abondance Déclarée" has been called, when the caller has to lead to the first trick, the lead always comes from the person to the left of the dealer.
2. Following normal Whist rules, the play proceeds throughout in a clockwise direction on each trick. The winner of each trick plays the first card to the next trick.

3. The players must follow suit whenever possible. If they cannot do so they may discard or, if the suit played is not the trump suit, use a trump as they wish; there is no rule compelling them to use a trump if they cannot follow.

4. Each hand may end when the declarer (the person or partnership making the highest call in the Auction) concedes defeat, or the opponents accept that they cannot win instead by preventing declarer reaching his objective – not necessarily waiting till all the cards have been played. There is a variation of this rule played in some Solo Schools whereby extra tricks ("over-tricks") win more, e.g., if a "Solo" is worth 2p from each player then perhaps a 6th trick gains an extra 1p from each player. We will discuss example stakes after looking at using skill.

Skill in the Play
Leads
Much of the skill in the play of Solo evolves from the opening lead. There are a number of recognised lead situations, all of which can be illustrated using the following hand:-

♠ J 7 4
♥ A J 6 4 3
♦ 7 4
♣ Q J 10

You are the lucky person holding the above and are sitting in the East position in every case, North having dealt.

1. Hearts are trumps. Your deliberations led you to the conclusion that in partnership with a hand of equal or nearly equal strength the combined hands stood a good chance of producing 8 tricks. If your partner has 3 trumps, including either or both of the King or Queen of trumps, that suit alone will produce 4 or even 5 tricks. You said "Prop", and one of the other players accepted your proposition. The probability is that your partner's acceptance is based on high cards in 1

or more of the other suits rather than in trumps. You have 5 trumps, so statistically the odds are against him having many. To make your 8 tricks together you need him to make tricks in the "outside" suits, which means that you must minimise the danger of your opponents trumping his high cards. You play A ♥ and continue with Hearts. Thus you draw out the opponents' trumps before they might do you damage.

2. Spades are trumps and 2 of the other players have formed a "Prop" and "Cop" partnership. Your best chance of making some tricks lies in the Heart suit. Perhaps your partner in "defense" (i.e. also trying to beat the "Prop and Cop" duo out of making their required 8 tricks) has the King; perhaps as you have 5, he may only have 1 or 2 and can then make (i.e. win with) a small trump. Again you lead A ♥.

3. Spades are trumps and South makes what proves to be the highest call of "Solo". If you are leading as here, immediately before the player calling a Solo, you are said to be sitting "in front" of him. In that position it is almost always best to lead a high card from your longest suit – the longer the better. Imagine that the distribution of the Heart suit is as follows:-

N
9 8 7 5

W
2

E
A J 6 4 3

S
K Q 10

If you lead A ♥ and follow with a small Heart South may not make a single Heart trick, which he might have been relying on in order to make his Solo. West hopefully will trump South's K ♥, and if North can obtain the lead (i.e. win a trick) while West still has another trump he will be able to play another heart and West will be able to trump South's Q ♥.

It would be exactly the same if the Hearts held by North and East were:-

> **N**
> A 8 7 5
>
> **E**
> J 9 6 4 3

Again the play of the Heart may result in South making no trick in that suit. Try it and see.

4. Spades are trumps and North's "Solo" was the highest bid. You are now in the opposite position to that of hand 3, behind, or "below", the Solo aspirant. Here it generally pays to lead a card from your shortest suit.

    Imagine that the distribution of the Diamond suit is:-

> **N**
> 8 6
>
> **W**   **E**
> A K Q 9 3   7 4
>
> **S**
> J 10 5 2

You lead 7 ♦, West plays A ♦ and wins the trick. He then plays K ♦, wins the trick, and plays Q ♦. If North trumps the third round of Diamonds with any card lower than your Jack of Spades you will be able to over-trump him; if he trumps with a higher card then your Jack will be converted into the third highest trump left. Again that may lead to the defeat of the Solo.

5. One of the other players is the highest bidder with "Misère". You and the other 2 have to force him into winning a trick. Clearly the suit which holds out the least hope of that in your hand is the Club suit. Imagine that it is South who called Misère and that the 4 hands are:-

N
- ♠ 10 9 6
- ♥ Q 8
- ♦ K Q J 5
- ♣ K 8 7 2

W
- ♠ A K Q
- ♥ K 10 9 7
- ♦ A 10
- ♣ A 9 6 3

E
- ♠ J 7 4
- ♥ A J 6 4 3
- ♦ 7 4
- ♣ Q J 10

S
- ♠ 8 5 3 2
- ♥ 5 2
- ♦ 9 8 6 3 2
- ♣ 5 4

Seeing all the cards it becomes obvious thinking it through that South's most vulnerable suit is the Club suit, but even that seems perfectly safe in view of your Q J 10. However, if you can discard 2 or 3 of your Clubs before the suit is even played the situation will be very different.

If you lead the highest card of your shortest suit, i.e. 7 ♦, West and North should continue to play that suit. West will win the first with the A ♦ and North the next 3 with his remaining 3 Diamonds. You will be able to discard 2 of your 3 Clubs. Next North should play K ♣, your last Club will fall and West will play his Ace on North's King. If West now plays his 3 ♣, and North his 2 ♣, South will be forced to win with his remaining Club and will be defeated. So against a Misère, lead the highest card of your shortest suit.

6. One of the other players calls Abondance and, it having proved to be the highest call, announces before the first card is played (as the rules require) that his trump suit will be Diamonds. Very often a player who calls Abondance hopes to make some of the 9 tricks he needs from a suit outside the trump suit he names. For example 12 of his 13 cards may be 7 cards in the trump suit and 5 in another. Timing is critical for him; he must exhaust his opponents' trumps but still retain enough to get back to his hand in time to take his final tricks in his second suit.

In an attempt to destroy such a plan the person on lead should try to make the caller use his trumps earlier than he intended. For example if one of the "defending" players called a Solo earlier, or two of you Propped and Copped, then the original trump suit is one that the Abondance caller can be expected to be short in and thus it would be the one to play. However, if there are no indications to the contrary the player on lead against an Abondance should lead his longest suit, in this case therefore East should lead his A ♥.

Memory and Reasoning
The other skills in Solo all relate to memory and reasoning. Remembering cards that have been played is easier than most people think, and gets easier with practice. Start by trying to remember the high cards played, and go on from there to remember *how many* cards have been played in a suit. What is most important is to try; the more you try the more you will succeed.

Reasoning? Well, "reason" it out. What did A call? What didn't he call? What is he likely to have as a result of his call; his failure to call; his lead? What did B . . .? What didn't B . . .? And so on. You won't always get it right, but it's so satisfying when you do!

The Stakes
Stakes are always agreed before play commences. They are paid by the losers to the winners in agreed units per call. Each hand is won either by the declarer if successful, or by the opposition when they defeat him and thus he loses his stake. For example you might decide that for "Prop and Cop", 1p to each winner is to be paid out between the losing pair; for "Solo", 2p from each player is to go to a successful caller (or 2p to each player from a defeated caller); on the same basis stronger calls might be agreed at "Misère" 3p, "Abondance" or "Abondance in Trumps" 4p, "Misère Ouverte" 5p, "Abondance Déclarée" 6p. It is usual to have a Kitty, i.e. a pool into which each player pays an agreed amount whenever all 4 players "Pass". A player

45

who then makes a successful individual call (i.e. "Prop and Cop" excluded) wins the money in the Kitty; a player who fails to make his call doubles the Kitty.

The Kitty works separately and in addition to the normal agreed stakes and can get quite large if there is a succession of hands which are "passed out" with no call made, or there is a succession of calls which are defeated. If the Kitty gets too large for the appetite of the players it may be split into parts, so that no player can win or lose too much all in 1 hand. The players agree at the time if and how the Kitty may be split; there are no rules to guide them.

"Goulash" Variation
In some schools an entertaining variation on the rule that following 4 calls of "Pass" the cards are shuffled and dealt by the next player is played; instead the cards are stacked together, cut, and dealt by him without a shuffle. This produces some very unusual distributions which add to the excitement of the game.

Three Handed Variations
The two most popular 3 handed variations of Solo are:-

1. Playing with 39 cards only by taking out a complete suit. In this variation the Prop and Cop possibility is cancelled, and a Solo requires 6 tricks in place of the normal 5. All the other calls remain the same. In addition a second round of calling is added if all 3 pass on the first round. In this each player is given the opportunity (if it reaches his turn) to call a Solo, this time with the trump suit being one of his choice. When this happens the money in the Kitty at the time remains unaltered, it cannot be won or doubled.

2. Playing with an extra (4th) hand. All 52 cards are dealt with the extra hand included to the dealer's right. Before the auction commences the dealer has the right to exchange his hand with that of the 4th ("dummy") hand, taking the risk that it will turn out to be better. In this variation a Solo call requires 5 tricks and there is no second round of calling. Again there are no "Prop" and "Cop" calls, and the other calls remain the same.

Solo Drives
Rather like Whist drives, these enjoyable sessions are described in Chapter 8.

NAPOLEON ("NAP")

Nap is another of the games based on Whist which are primarily gambling games. The rules state that it can be played by any number from 2 to 8, but it is probably most enjoyable with 4 or 5 players.

Dealing
The complete pack of 52 cards is used and the usual cut, shuffle and deal formalities apply. The dealer gives each player 5 cards, 1 at a time. The remaining cards are placed face down on the table until they are wanted for the next deal. A short auction follows.

The Auction
Commencing with the player on the dealer's left each player can make 1 bid only. The Auction ends after each of the players has made his single bid. The bids in ascending order of strength are:-

"**Pass**" – "I do not wish to participate in this auction."

"**Two**" – "I undertake to make 2 tricks; my choice of trump suit will be made known if I win the auction."

"**Three**" – I undertake to make 3 tricks . . . etc."

"**Misère**" – "I commit myself to making no tricks." If this bid is the highest in the Auction there will be no trump suit.

"**Four**" – "I will make 4 tricks . . . etc."

"**Nap**" – "I will make all 5 tricks . . . etc."

"**Wellington**" – "I will make all 5 tricks, and, if defeated, will pay double the stakes set for Nap."

A player who would like to say something other than "Pass" cannot say it if his bid would be lower than one already made by another player. If all players say "Pass" the cards are shuffled (re-introducing those that were left face down on the table), and re-dealt by the player whose turn it is to deal next.

Each bid represents a specific gamble on success. We discuss the (bid-related) stakes last (p. 50). Not only must you balance the chances of winning what you gamble against the potential loss of your stake, the matter can also be considered in the light of winning via the defeat of an opposing bid.

Example Auction with 4 players
North deals and the hands are:-

N
♠ A 7 3 2
♥ K
♦ —
♣ —

W
♠ 10 9
♥ —
♦ 8
♣ J 4

E
♠ 8
♥ Q J 10
♦ —
♣ K

S
♠ —
♥ —
♦ A J 4
♣ Q 10

The auction could well be:

E	S	W	N
2	3	Pass	4

With only 20 cards having been dealt out of the 52 East hopes that his Hearts and K ♣ could provide 2 tricks if Hearts are trumps. South is more optimistic about the possibilities of his Diamond suit, backed by his Clubs and bids 3. West is not remotely interested and passes. North has high hopes of his Spade suit and bids 4.

The Play

The highest bidder always leads to the first trick and, unless the call is Misère, he must lead a card from his designated trump suit. From that point on the winner of each trick plays first to the next trick. A player must follow suit if he can; if he cannot follow suit he may choose any discard convenient to him, or, if the suit which he cannot follow is not the trump suit, he may use a trump.

Skill

Skill in Nap is really a matter of valuation, i.e. correctly assessing the trick-taking potential of a hand, although sometimes working out the best chances may require a little tactical thinking.

For example, in a game for 4 players the other 3 say "Pass" and you call "Three" with:-

♠ K
♥ K
♦ A Q J
♣ —

Your trump suit is Diamonds and the play proceeds as follows:-

South (You)	West	North	East
A ♦*	x ♠	x ♠	x ♦
Q ♦	x ♠	x ♠	K ♦*
J ♦*	10 ♠	Q ♣	A ♣

(* = the winning card)

What card do you play in order to win your third trick? Think about this:-

1. West said "Pass" but with 3 Spades and an Ace would surely have said "2" or even "3". He has no Ace.
2. North would surely have called "2" or even "3" if he had A ♠, i.e. starting with A x x. He might have A ♥ but not A ♠.
3. East also said "Pass" but would have made a bid if he had an Ace in addition to the A ♣ and K ♦ that he has already played. He has no Ace.

49

Conclusion? No-one has A ♠ so you play K ♠ for your third winning trick.

The Stakes

Stakes are always agreed before the game commences and usually follow the number of tricks promised by a bid – with Misère being paid at the same rate as paid for 3. Thus, if the stakes were in penny units 2p would be paid for 2, 3p for 3 (and Misère), 4p for 4 etc. Each other player pays the going rate to a successful bidder. If he fails to make the number of tricks bid for, the bidder must pay out the staked amount to every other player instead, remembering the proviso that the stakes for a defeated ''Wellington'' are doubled.

5

Contract Bridge

Part One

Background to the game, and Opening Bids

The most widely played game of the Whist family is Bridge, and the most widely played version is "Contract Bridge". Historically the game of Contract was preceded by a simpler game called "Auction Bridge"; I shall be taking the latter out of historical context by dealing with it second in the next chapter. In this chapter on Contract I shall use the popular title of "Bridge". For those interested in Tournament Bridge please turn to Chapter 8.

Bridge is a partnership game for 4 players which can be very skilful indeed, but it can also be enjoyed on a fairly simple level. Many good books have been written on Bridge, including complete books just to initiate the beginner into its mysteries. It would be extremely presumptuous of me to try to do more than sketch out the basics in the short space I have available. Before you start, please pause for a short commercial.

Author's Warning: attempting to understand Bridge without prior understanding of the previous chapters of this book may be injurious to your brain!

Object

The object of the game is to be the winning partnership as the result of scoring the most points in the course of a "Rubber". A Rubber consists of 2 "Games", each separate Game being won by the side first scoring 100 points below the line on the Score Sheet.

The Score Sheet
The Score Sheet looks like this:-

The horizontal line is to separate scores towards Games from Penalty and Bonus scores. "Game going" scores, i.e. scores on individual hands earned in the manner in which I shall shortly be describing, are scored (written) below the line; points earned as Penalties or from Bonuses (details later) are scored above the line.

Earning Game Going Scores
Game going scores are earned as a result of making in the play of the cards the specific number of tricks contracted for in an Auction which precedes the play.

The Preliminaries
The game commences after the partners have been selected (perhaps by a cut of the cards, perhaps by pre-arrangement). A cut is made to decide who will deal, and then all 52 cards are shuffled and dealt, one at a time, in a clockwise direction so that each has 13. At this point you may need to recall Chapter 1 on the subject of Etiquette, particularly on who shuffles, who cuts, who sits where etc. The cards are dealt face down and retained unexposed by each player for the time being. It is now time for the Auction.

The Auction
The players make their "Bids" in the Auction in clockwise rotation commencing with the dealer. Bidding continues until

one of the players makes a bid with which the other 3 signify that they do not wish to compete any further. For example, without worrying for the time being about what the bids are supposed to mean, an Auction might proceed:-

	N (the dealer)	E	S	W
1st round:	1 Spade	2 Clubs	3 Hearts	4 Diamonds
2nd round:	No Bid	No Bid	No Bid	

West has made the highest bid in this Auction which ended in 2 rounds. The other 3 having each said "No Bid" in round 2 thereby surrendered the Auction to West. West does not need to say any more having already "bought the contract" with the highest bid.

Every bid made in the course of an Auction is an undertaking to make a specified number of tricks between the player's own hand and that of his partner, either with a trump suit or with no trump suit, as stated by that player when making the bid.

There is a lot of "shorthand" (my description) used in making bids; none of the bids made in an Auction means exactly what it seems to mean to start with because of "the Book". The Book is a base of 6. For example, a bid of 1 Club means: "I am ready to contract for making 7 tricks between my partner's hand and that of my own, provided Clubs are trumps" (1 + the book of 6 = 7). A bid of 3 ♠ would mean: "I am ready to contract to make 9 tricks between the 2 hands with Spades as trumps" (3 + the book = 9). A bid of 2 No Trumps would mean: "I am ready . . . etc . . . etc . . . 8 tricks . . . etc . . . etc . . . there being no trump suit".

Bidding cannot start below the level of "one", i.e. it's not permitted to make a bid contracting for 6 tricks of less. If the player whose turn it is to bid does not wish to bid he says "No Bid".

For bidding purposes the suits in Bridge have a power ranking which, starting with the weakest suit, is Clubs, Diamonds, Hearts, Spades, with a bid of No Trumps being regarded as the highest. Apart from No Trumps the suits are thus ranked in alphabetical order from the weakest. The effect of this pecking order is that a bid of 1 ♦ ranks as more powerful than a bid of 1 ♣. A bid of 1 ♠ is more powerful than a bid of 1 ♥ and both of these are more powerful than bids of 1 in the Club or Diamond suits.

If a player wishes to make a bid more powerful than that already made in a higher ranking suit he must make a bid which undertakes to make more tricks. For example to make a bid in Clubs higher than a bid of 2 ♥, already made by one of the other players, requires a bid of 3 ♣ (or more). Incidentally, it is illegal to make a bid knowing it to be insufficient, i.e. ranking below a bid already made by another player.

Point Value of Bids
To re-cap: the object in Bridge is to win a Rubber. A Rubber is won by the first partnership to win 2 Games. To win a Game a partnership has to be the first to score 100 points or more below the line. Each score below the line represents the point scoring value of a bid which has been contracted for and made. For example a contract of 3 ♥ is, as already noted, one that requires 9 tricks to be made with Hearts as trumps; that contract, if it is fulfilled, will be worth a score of 90 points below the line. Such points are earned according to a standard scoring scale as follows:-

Provided the contract is made or exceeded, then, below the line:

For every trick that is both contracted for and made in the Club or Diamond suits (the "minors"), you earn 20 points.

For every trick both contracted for and made in the Heart or Spade suits (the "majors"), 30 points.

For the first trick that is both contracted for and made in No Trumps, 40 points; for each successive trick in No Trumps, 30 points.

Remember "trick contracted for" means a trick in excess of the Book, i.e. a contract of 1 equals a commitment to make 7 tricks. The scale means, for example, that a contract of 3 ♦, if the 9 tricks needed are made, will be worth a score of 60 points below the line; a contract of 2 ♥, if the 8 tricks are made, will equally be worth 60 points below the line.

Notice that the scale is so arranged that to score 100 points or more in one hand requires a contract at the level of 5 (11 tricks) in a Minor suit (Clubs or Diamonds), a contract of 4 in a Major (10 tricks – Hearts or Spades), or a contract of 3 in No Trumps (9 tricks).

A typical Score Sheet, just before the Rubber was won, could arise as follows:

On hand 1 North/South bid and made 3 ♠.
On hand 2 East/West bid and made 2 No Trumps.
On hand 3 East/West bid and made 3 ♣.
On hand 4 North/South bid and made 2 ♥.
On hand 5 East/West bid and made 3 ♦.

	We (N/S)	They (E/W)	
	90		Hand 1
		70	Hand 2
		60	Hand 3
(First game to E/W . . .)			
	60		Hand 4
		60	Hand 5

Note that after the East/West score on hand 3, giving them a total of more than 100 points, a line was drawn indicating that a Game had been won. Neither those extra points over the 100 nor the North/South score of 90 on hand 1 are carried forward to the next Game.

At the stage that has been reached above East/West have 1 Game towards Rubber and both sides have 60 points towards a new Game. If N/S earn another 40 or more points before E/W

55

they will win the second Game, and a third Game will have to be completed. If E/W earn the 40 or more points first they will win the Rubber.

Once a side has succeeded in making 100 points or more below the line – i.e. has won its first Game, it is said to be "Vulnerable"; if a side has not yet scored 100 points it is "Non Vulnerable". In the example above the East/West partnership is now Vulnerable; the North/South partnership is still Non Vulnerable. The importance of this is that Bonuses and Penalties are both larger if a partnership is Vulnerable. If both sides win a Game, both are Vulnerable.

Bonuses

There are a number of bonus points which can be earned and which are scored above the line:

1. For each trick made above the contract level in a *suit* (each "over-trick") – the same number of points as each contracted trick scores below the line. For example, if the contract is 4 ♠ and 11 tricks are made the score below the line is 120 (4 x 30), and there is a bonus of 30 above the line (1 x 30). The bonus for each over-trick in a *No Trump* contract is 30.

2. For winning the Rubber while the other side is still Non Vulnerable, a bonus of 700.

3. For winning the Rubber when both sides are Vulnerable a bonus of 500.

4. For bidding and making 12 tricks when Non Vulnerable a bonus of 500. A trick contract is known as a "small slam".

5. For bidding and making a small slam when Vulnerable a bonus of 750.

6. For bidding and making all 13 tricks when Non Vulnerable a bonus of 1000. This contract is known as a "grand slam".

7. For bidding and making a grand slam when Vulnerable a bonus of 1500.

8. For holding in one hand 4 of the top 5 cards in the trump

suit a bonus of 100. This is known as having 4 of the "honours".

9. For holding all 5 of the honours in the trump suit in one hand, or all 4 Aces in a No Trump contract, a bonus of 150.

Note: in order to earn the bonus for having honours it is not necessary to be the partnership which bid the contract. The bonus must be claimed (for example "100 for Honours") between the time the last card is played and the re-deal for the next hand.

If a Rubber is not completed by the time play for the session ends a bonus of 300 points is earned by a partnership which is Vulnerable.

A bonus of 50 points is earned by the only side to have scored partly towards a game if both sides are Non Vulnerable, or partly towards a second game if both sides are Vulnerable. The latter are known as "part score" bonuses. These incomplete-rubber bonuses recognise the advantage one side may have gained over the other.

There are more bonuses to be described later, but for now let's look at a score sheet which includes some of the above:-

On hand 1 North/South bid 2 ♠ and made 9 tricks.
On hand 2 East/West bid 2 No Trumps and made 10 tricks.
On hand 3 North/South bid and made a small slam in No Trumps.
On hand 4 East/West bid and made 1 ♣. West had A K Q 10 ♣.
On hand 5 East/West bid 3 No Trumps and made 10 tricks.
On hand 6 North/South bid 4 ♠ and made 12 tricks. North had A K Q J ♠.

Before I translate the above onto a score sheet why don't you have a try? When doing so, note how the scores would have changed if both sides had made bids which were equivalent to the number of tricks they proved able to make in the course of the subsequent play. This should lead you to the correct conclusion that it is often very important to bid up to the full value of the combined hands.

We	They	
N/S	E/W	
30		The over-trick, hand 1.
	60	2 over-tricks, hand 2.
500		Small slam bonus, hand 3.
	100	4 of the honours, hand 4.
	30	The over-trick, hand 5.
60		2 over-tricks, hand 6.
100		The honours, hand 6.
500		The Rubber bonus.
60		2 Spades bid, hand 1.
	70	2 No Trumps bid, hand 2.
190		6 No Trumps bid, hand 3.
(The 1st Game)		
	20	1 Club bid, hand 4.
	100	3 No Trumps bid, hand 5.
(Second Game)		
120		4 Spades bid, hand 6.
(Rubber)		

North/South win by scoring 1560 points in all to 380. BUT, if East/West had bid 3 No Trumps on hand 2 the Rubber would have ended with hand 5, and a win to East/West by 880 points to 780.

The above framework describes the main bonuses to know about, preferably committed to memory; there are more and there are penalty scores, all of which we will discuss, under the general headings of Doubles and Redoubles later, but it's time to consider what a player must take into account when making bids during the Auction.

Bidding

There are *Opening* bids, *Responding* bids, *Intervening* bids, and *Re-bids* all to consider separately but first we will take a look at Opening bids.

The questions to be answered are:- How do you decide that

with the hand you hold it may be worth making a bid? What then do you bid? How do you know how to assess your partner's hand? Will the responsibility to play the hand make any difference? (In the course of an Auction one partner will have been the first to make a bid in the suit in which the final bid was made; this player will, as you will see, become the "Declarer" and bear that responsibility, the effects of which will be discussed in some detail when we reach the sections on Play in Part Three.)

Bidding is a form of communication which can be in a number of different "languages", or, more correctly, systems. That most commonly used in the U.K. (and the one upon which these notes will be based) is "Acol", a system designed before the 2nd World War and improved and extended in the years since. In attempting to reach the best contract, both partners will use the Acol system and you will see how doing so enables them to communicate with each other. The knowledge exchanged via the bidding is crucial to the fun of bridge; that knowledge together with the information which can be exchanged by the play of specific cards at specific times provides the basis of much of the fascination the game holds for so many.

As you work your way through the Acol system you will probably ask yourself from time to time, "why that bid, and not another?" Remembering that each bid has to convey a message, you can see that any system of bidding is in practice an edifice of coded messages. Each separate bid has its part in that system and even an expert has to work his way through a complete system before he can understand the reasoning behind some of the rules. Acol took many years to develop. Experts constantly devise "improvements" and, in the course of time, some of those improvements are adopted by average players. As a result there are always 3 versions of Acol in use: (1) out of date, (2) used by the majority of players, (3) not yet in general use. Version (2) rules are described here. The best way for the novice to develop understanding and fluency in bidding is to accept and absorb the rules, taking them on trust in the learning stage. As facility in use grows with practice, understanding will, I promise you, dawn, with a degree of comprehension that endless question-ing too early can never reveal.

OPENING BIDS

Worth a bid?
A pack of cards has 4 Aces, 4 Kings, 4 Queens and 4 Jacks. Give the Aces a value of 4 points each, the Kings a value of 3 each, the Queens 2 and the Jacks 1. The pack now has a total value of 40 "high card points", 10 in each suit. This is the "Milton Point Count", so named after its American inventor.

"High Card Points"
If the pack has 40 points an average hand would have 10. Imagine that you have a hand in which the high card points add up to 13; the other 3 players have 27 between them. If you are lucky your partner will have 9 or more of that 27, so you and your partner could easily have 22 points between you. If you do have 22 then your opponents can only have 18 – a difference of 4 in your favour. An Ace is worth 4 high card points, and if your combined hands are an Ace better than your opponents' hands you should have a good chance of making 7 tricks to their 6. Conclusion – with 13 high card points or more you have a hand on which you should make a bid if no-one else has yet done so, and perhaps even if they have. In practice you will make many bids with 12 high card points or even less, but the above should illustrate the general theory adequately. Here are two examples:-

1. ♠ A K Q x
    ♥ A x x   13 high card points
    ♦ x x x   – a bid should be made.
    ♣ x x x

2. ♠ A x x
    ♥ A K Q x   16 high card points
    ♦ K x x   – a bid should be made.
    ♣ x x x

"Distribution Points"

It is possible, and certainly advisable, to value a hand on an extended basis, i.e. more than on a simple high card point count alone. Look at these 2 hands:-

(a) ♠ A x x   (b) ♠ Q x x
    ♥ A K Q x   ♥ A K Q x x x
    ♦ x x x   ♦ x x
    ♣ x x x   ♣ x x

Which hand will produce the most tricks with Hearts as trumps assuming the remaining Hearts happen to be evenly distributed between the other 3 players? Hand (a) should produce 4 Heart tricks and the Ace ♠ – a total of 5 tricks. (If the top 3 Hearts are played first the little x will be the only one left and it, and the A ♠, will be the 4th and 5th tricks.) Hand (b) will produce 6 Heart tricks if the remaining 7 Hearts are taken away by playing the top 3. So hand (b) is better than hand (a) even though it has 2 high card points fewer.

The distribution points which should be taken into account are 1 extra point for every card in excess of 4 cards in the desired trump suit. Thus hand (b) is better regarded as worth 13 points, i.e. 11 high card points, and 2 "distribution" points. However, this basis is *only* used when valuing a hand if (1) you are the dealer and as such are the first to bid, or (2) players whose turn it was to bid before you all said "No Bid".

What to Bid?

Let's look first at the hands in which no suit has more than 4 cards. Most of the hands will be "flat".

A hand which has a distribution pattern of either 4:3:3:3, or 4:4:3:2, is flat. An alternative description which is often used is "balanced". If you had a flat hand with 13 points it might look like this:-

♠ A x x   ♠ A x
♥ K Q x   or even ♥ K Q x
♦ Q J x   ♦ Q J x x
♣ J x x x   ♣ J x x x

Neither hand contains a suit which looks particularly promising as a trump suit. If your partner has a similarly shaped hand, perhaps with his longer suit or suits being one or both of your shorter suits, then it would seem best to avoid any contract which involves having a trump suit. Ideally, at least at first sight, you would prefer to play the hand in a No Trump contract.

However, the above chain of reasoning does not necessarily conclude with the statement that the opening bid should be in No Trumps. Other factors we go on to deal with in the rest of this chapter may have to overrule such a decision, so read on.

No Trump Opening Bids

I stated a little earlier that the most widely used system in the United Kingdom is the Acol system. I now have to expand that statement a little by saying that it is possible to vary requirements for any opening bid within the Acol system. This is done by partnership agreement which the partners *must* adhere to, and the existence of which must be made known to the opponents before the game starts. The most frequent variations are those which concern No Trump opening bids – others are a little beyond the scope of beginners.

The usual variations from which the partners make their selection in No Trump opening bids are:-

1. An opening bid of 1 No Trump promises that the player making the bid has a balanced hand with 12 to 14 high card points not all of which are in only 1 suit. This is a "weak" No Trump bid.

2. As 1, but with 13 to 15 points. This is also a "weak" No Trump bid.

3. As 1, but with 15 to 17 points. This is a "strong" No Trump bid.

4. As 1, but with 16 to 18 points. This is also a "strong" No Trump bid.

5. Variable No Trump: You can choose to vary the strength of an opening No Trump bid according to the vulnerability of the partnership at the time. In this case the hand will be understood to have either of the weak bids (as specifically agreed) when the partnership is non vulnerable, and

either of the strong bids (again as specifically agreed) whenever the partnership is vulnerable.

These selections are known as : "weak throughout" – 12 to 14 or 13 to 15 as agreed (1 and 2 above); "strong throughout" – 15 to 17 or 16 to 18 as agreed (3 and 4 above); or "variable", i.e. "weak" when non vulnerable and "strong" when vulnerable (5 above).

It follows that it is essential to agree with your partner before starting to play on what basis you would open the bidding in No Trumps and to exchange such information with your opponents.

Once you have agreed to use a specific range you *must* stick precisely to that range. This means that even though you may have a hand which appears to be ideal insofar as its "shape" and point count is concerned, if that point count is only slightly more or less than the limits you have agreed upon you *must not* open the bidding with one No Trump. You must instead make an opening bid in your best suit, just as you would if you had the agreed number of points but not the right shape. If you open the bidding with 1 NT partner will be relying on you to have described your hand accurately. If you err chaos will ensue.

For the purposes of this book I am going to assume that we are agreed that an opening bid of 1 No Trump promises 13 to 15 high card points in a balanced hand, irrespective of vulnerability – "weak throughout", as in 2 above. As you gain experience, and as you go on to read the really comprehensive books that will (hopefully) attract you after my short description, you are bound to decide to vary the parameters to suit different company or whatever, but for now . . . 13 to 15 points.

Opening Bids in a Suit
We will deal with strong hands (worth 8 tricks or more) in a moment; meanwhile I shall discuss more modest hands which are still strong enough for you to make an opening bid. Let's assume you have become the lucky possessor of a hand with 13 or more points, and have decided that the hand is not suitable for an opening bid in No Trumps (unbalanced perhaps, or without high card points in 2 of the suits – see foregoing); you will have

to make your opening bid at the level of one in a suit. Some definitions must of necessity come first:-

1. Reminders . . . Spades and Hearts are the "majors", Diamonds and Clubs are the "minors", and the pecking order of ranking (weakest first) of the suits is Clubs, Diamonds, Hearts, Spades.
2. "Adjoining", or "touching" suits in this ranking are Spades and Hearts; Hearts and Diamonds; Diamonds and Clubs.
3. "Divided" suits are Spades and Diamonds; Hearts and Clubs. Spades and Clubs are a special case (see no. 4 below).

The elementary rules for selection of a suit for an opening bid must be taken on trust as explained earlier, and memorised.

They are:

1. Always open the bidding with a suit which is longer than any other, for example with:-

     ♠ Q 5 4 3 2
     ♥ A K J 2
     ♦ K 3 2
     ♣ 2

the correct bid is 1 Spade.

However, you can exercise a little discretion (but only a very little). For example, with –

     ♠ 6 5 4 3 2
     ♥ A K Q J
     ♦ K 3 2
     ♣ 2

open the bidding with 1 Heart (and subsequently stoutly maintain that you thought the black 2 of Spades was the red

64

2 of Hearts). Why? Because although the rule states that the longer suit should be opened first, for all practical purposes the Spade suit above may be valueless. It is more sensible to bend the rules in such a case.

2. With 2 suits which both have 4 cards, open with the higher ranking suit unless one of the suits is Spades, in which case open with the other suit.

3. With 2 suits which are touching and which are of equal length, each having more than 4 cards, open with the higher ranking suit. For this purpose you must regard the ranking as proceeding upwards: Clubs, Diamonds, Hearts, Spades, Clubs, Diamonds, etc.

4. With 2 suits which are divided by 1 of the remaining 2 suits and which are of equal length, each having more than 4 cards, 1 of those remaining suits will be longer than the other. The opening bid should be made in the suit which is ranked below the shorter of the other 2 suits. For example:-

With ♠ A Q x x x   and with ♠ A Q x x x
     ♥ x   ♥ Q x
     ♦ A Q x x x   ♦ A Q x x x
     ♣ Q x   ♣ x

open with 1 Diamond   open with 1 Spade (see above).

5. With 3 suits only, 2 of which are longer than the third, divided and of equal length, open the bidding in whichever of the 2 longest suits is nearest below the suit in which you have no cards, i.e. the suit ranking below the "void". For example, with a void in Clubs and with equal length Spades and Diamonds, your bid should be made in Spades; if the void had been in Hearts you would bid in Diamonds.

6. If the distribution is a singleton in 1 suit and 4 cards in each of the other 3 suits then (1) with a singleton Spade open in Diamonds; (2) with a singleton Heart or Diamond open in Clubs; (3) with a singleton Club open in Hearts. For example:-

With	With	With	With
♠ A J x x	♠ K Q x x	♠ x	♠ K J x x
♥ A J x x	♥ x	♥ A x x x	♥ A Q x x
♦ x	♦ A J x x	♦ K Q x x	♦ A x x x
♣ A J x x	♣ A J x x	♣ A J x x	♣ x

Open 1 Club   Open 1 Club   Open 1 Diamond   Open 1 Heart

Stronger Opening Bids

When you are fortunate enough to pick up a hand which is much stronger than the average hand on which you would open at the level of one, you must try to take the fullest possible advantage of it with a bid that gives your partner the good news. Being thus made aware of your good hand you should avoid the possibility of your partner making no initial response to your opening bid. Apart from the No Trump type of hand (for which see below) and a hand where your strongest suit happens to be Clubs (for reasons which will become clear soon), the simplest way of getting the message across to your partner is to make your opening bid at 1 level higher than you would normally make it. For example 2 Hearts instead of the more usual 1 Heart.

This higher level bid is taken to promise that even if your partner's hand is an unmitigated disaster your hand is strong enough by itself to make 8 tricks, provided that the suit you have named becomes the trump suit.

For example:-

With	♠ A Q x x		♠ A K Q x x x
	♥ K Q x	whereas with	♥ A K Q
	♦ x x x		♦ x x
	♣ x x		♣ x x

you open 1 Spade   you would open with 2 Spades

Opening Bid of 2 No Trumps

Opening 2 No Trumps generally means that the hand is both balanced and has 20 to 22 high card points ("generally" because a partnership may agree to 19 to 21). For example:-

$\spadesuit$ A Q 10
$\heartsuit$ K Q x x
$\diamondsuit$ A K x
$\clubsuit$ Q J 10

21 points – a balanced hand – open 2 No Trumps.

Opening Bid of 2 Clubs

In the Acol system although the Club suit is the lowest ranked suit in Bridge, the opening bid of 2 Clubs is the strongest bid in common use. It is *not* intended to convey any message about the Club suit as such; it is a "conventional" bid, i.e. a bid which does not mean what it says.

The opening bid of 2 $\clubsuit$ promises either 23, or more, high card points, or a hand with which the opener is satisfied that he will be able to make a game contract (worth 100 points or more) with no assistance at all from his partner. For example, with either of the hands shown below it would be correct in Acol to open the bidding with 2 $\clubsuit$.

$\spadesuit$ A K Q $\spadesuit$ A K Q J x
$\heartsuit$ A K x $\heartsuit$ A K Q J x
$\diamondsuit$ A Q x $\diamondsuit$ x x
$\clubsuit$ Q J 10 x $\clubsuit$ x

The first hand qualifies because it contains more than 23 points; with the second, 10 tricks (worth a game) should not be difficult in either major. Therefore . . . bid 2 $\clubsuit$ to open. As you will see later on, the partner of the player making the bid of 2 $\clubsuit$ must *not* say "No Bid", so that there is no danger of 2 $\clubsuit$ becoming the actual contract.

Pre-emptive Bids

Although opening bids at the 2 level are made on strong hands, opening bids at the 3, or even 4, level in a suit are made on much weaker hands. The purpose of this kind of bid is to pre-empt the bidding (thus "Pre-emptive"). Deliberately opening the bidding at an unusually high level at the first opportunity can make it very difficult for opponents to find their best contract. If they wish to bid they will be forced to enter into the bidding at an inconveniently high level, thereby making communication between them very difficult, and reducing their chances of bidding their best contract.

The pre-emptive opening bid is usually made on a hand which contains no less than 6, and not more than 9, high card points, and has a suit which contains at least 7 cards. In making such a bid (before his partner has had his chance to bid) the player must not have 4 cards in a major suit as well as the 7 card suit he is bidding. The sort of hand which would justify a pre-emptive bid would be:-

♠ A Q J 9 7 5 2
♥ 8
♦ Q 10 2
♣ 5 2

The hand is worth an opening bid of 3 ♠. One more little Spade instead of the singleton Heart would justify an opening bid of 4 ♠ because the extra Spade would be worth an extra trick.

INTERVENING BIDS

A bid which is made by a player after an opponent has made an opening bid is known as an "Intervening" bid. For example, if North deals and bids 1 Heart anything which East says other than "No Bid" is an intervening bid. Similarly, if, after North's bid of 1 Heart both East and South were to say "No Bid" then a positive bid made by West would be an intervening bid.

An intervening bid can be made in a suit or in No Trumps.

If the bid is made in a suit and at the minimum level, e.g. 1 Spade over 1 Heart, or 2 Diamonds over 1 Heart (the lowest permitted levels in the suits selected), it does *not* promise that the player making the bid has enough points for a normal opening bid (he may have but that is not what the bid promises). It promises only that a good suit is held, one which, given reasonable luck, will produce 5 tricks or more. In the hand below, 2 ♦ would be a good intervening bid after an opening bid of 1 Spade:-

♠ x x
♥ J 10 x x
♦ A K J x x x
♣ x

An intervening bid in a suit made at a higher level than absolutely necessary promises a strong hand with a very good suit. For example alter the above hand to:-

♠ x x
♥ J 10 x x
♦ A K Q x x x
♣ A

and the intervening bid over 1 Spade should be 3 ♦.

(If the opening bid had been 1 Club the intervening bid would be 2 ♦, again one level higher than necessary.)

An intervening bid in No Trumps, i.e. 1 No Trump over a suit bid made by an opponent, should promise the point count needed to open a strong No Trump, although some partnerships agree to make the bid with lower values or in a variable manner . . . just as they may agree to do when opening the bidding in No Trumps (as was discussed earlier). The most frequently adopted range is from 15 to 17 high card points. The bid also promises that some good cards are held in the suit opened by the other side. For example, after an opening bid by an opponent of 1 Spade, this hand would merit a fair intervening bid of 1 No Trump:-

♠ A J 10
♥ K Q x
♦ K 10 x
♣ Q 9 8 x

OTHER BIDS

There are other types of opening bid and many other types of intervening bid. Some are conventional with names given to them by their inventors; some form part of the Acol system beyond the scope of the beginner. However, I believe that I have given enough data to enable an opening bid to be made on the vast majority of hands which do in fact qualify for an opening bid, and a sufficient basis of knowledge for making intervening bids.

If you absorb the bids which I have described so far you are well on your way to understanding the game of Bridge. For the aspiring Life Master there are innumerable books to lead you on in due course to more subtle or complicated bidding routines.

Part Two

Responding Bidding

How does the auction progress? How does a player "reply" to his partner's bid . . . if at all?

Let's assume North has opened the bidding and it is up to South. For the time being we will assume that there has been no intervening bid. The bid made by South in reply to North's opening bid is called a "response". It is, as far as possible, the message he needs to convey to his partner in reply to the message passed to him by means of the opening bid. We will examine the responses to opening bids of 1 No Trump first.

Responses to 1 No Trump
It is generally accepted that a combined strength of 26 high card points between two hands makes a 3 No Trump contract an odds on probability (i.e. a chance to earn a game in one hand); 25 points is good enough in the majority of cases. Remembering the agreed range of a 1 No Trump opening made by North (13 to 15 high card points – see page 63), South may wish to:-

1. Leave the contract in 1 No Trump by saying "No Bid";
2. Make a bid which may enable the partnership to play in what seems to be a safer contract;

3. Invite a game contract in No Trumps;
4. Bid a game contract in No Trumps;
5. Investigate other possibilities.

South's response will be intended to make North aware of his wishes.

"Passing" 1 No Trump

If South has a balanced hand but it is impossible for the partnership to have a combined strength of 25 points, South will say "No Bid". With our range of 13 to 15 high card points this means that South will not have to think for long before taking option number 1 if his own points are less than 10.

The "Weak Take-out"

If South's hand is unbalanced, has less than 10 points, and has a long suit, he may wish to try to retreat to a 2 level contract in that suit, on the grounds that it will be a safer contract, i.e. more likely to succeed, than 1 No Trump. The Acol system allows him to do this in any suit *other* than Clubs (the reason will be explained later). It is the second of the above options, for example:-

♠ A x x x x
♥ K x
♦ Q x x x
♣ x x

The hand is only worth 9 points (remember please that the "distribution" points described in the previous part of this chapter can only be taken into account by a player making a bid before partner had made a bid, or after his partner had already said "No Bid" – in other words only for the purpose of making an opening bid). The maximum number of points between the two partners will only be 24, but the hand may easily produce a few more tricks if Spades are trumps.

South should bid 2 ♠ over North's 13 to 15 point 1 No Trump opening. This kind of hand is known as a "Weak Take Out", and it is imperative that the 1 No Trump opener should say "No

Bid" without hesitation when it is his turn to bid again, even if his best suit happens to be the same suit named by partner. In effect his partner is saying "I believe we will make at least one more trick if the trump suit is the one I have named and you may not even make 7 tricks in 1 No Trump – please do not try to make matters better as it is more likely you will make them worse!" Look closely at the above hand and try to visualise the result of any ambition by North holding:-

♠ Q x x x
♥ J 10 x x
♦ A K x
♣ Q J

Imagine that East has A K 10 xxx in Clubs and West has A Q in Hearts. In a No Trump contract the first 8 tricks may be lost, i.e. 6 Clubs and 2 Hearts, whereas in a Spade contract East will only be able to make 2 tricks in Clubs because his next Club will be trumped by either the North or South hand.

"Limit" Bids in No Trumps
The third option can be used where it is theoretically possible for the partnership to have a total of 25 high card points between the two hands, for example, when South has a hand such as:-

♠ A 10 9 2		♠ A J 4 3
♥ K 10 8	or	♥ K 4 3
♦ Q 9 7		♦ Q 4 3
♣ J 9 8		♣ J 4 3

South should bid 2 No Trumps. This raise is known as a "Limit" bid in as much as it describes the hand held by the partner of the opening No Trump bidder within specific limits.

In the case of a bid of 2 No Trumps over partner's 1 No Trump the Limit bid means: "I do not have enough points to be certain that our best contract will be 3 No Trumps, but it will be if your hand is at or near its maximum for your opening bid of 1 No Trump. I therefore invite you to bid 3 No Trumps." The opener may either accept the invitation by bidding on, or reject it by saying "No Bid" when it is his turn.

If it appears certain that 25 or 26 points are there South should bid 3 No Trumps directly, for example with a balanced 12 point hand (12 + a minimum of 13 = 25). This Limit bid denies any interest in a contract other than 3 No Trumps. In effect it says "I have enough to make 3 No Trumps the right contract but no more than enough."

Note that the numeric ranges of response vary according to the agreed range of opening No Trump; for example, 10 points justify a 2NT (No Trumps) response opposite a 13 to 15 point range, whereas 11 points are needed opposite a 12 to 14 range bid.

We now look at the 5th and last of South's options. Because he has one of the following types of hands he wishes to look into other possibilities before settling for a game in No Trumps.

1. ♠ A K J x x 2. ♠ A K x x 3. ♠ A Q J x
   ♥ Q x x   ♥ K Q x   ♥ A Q J x
   ♦ Q x x   ♦ A J x   ♦ x x x
   ♣ x x   ♣ Q x x   ♣ x x

With (1) South can see that if North has 3 or 4 Spades, possibly headed by the Queen, the best contract could be 4 ♠; if North is weak in Spades the best contract will be 3 No Trumps. South should bid 3 ♠. This North should take as a command to bid when it is his turn either 4 ♠ or 3 No Trumps according to the value of his holding in Spades.

With (2) South can see that the partnership has at least 32 points between the 2 hands. If there happen to be 33 or 34 points held, then the opposition has at the most one Ace, and there should be a very good chance of making 12 tricks . . . a small slam. South should bid 4 No Trumps. This is another Limit bid; it is an invitation to North, with a good 14 point hand, or with 15 points, to bid 6 No Trumps. With less all that North has to do when it is his turn is to say "No Bid".

Hand (3) is ideal for the use of the "Stayman Convention" (named after a Mr Stayman of the USA although also claimed as the invention of a well known British player, Mr Benjamin). "Stayman", although not strictly part of the Acol system, is used by almost all serious Acol players, and can be treated as though it has been adopted by Acol. In its simplest form this is how it works.

The Stayman Convention

South can visualise that if North has either 4 Spades or 4 Hearts the 2 hands may combine to produce 10 tricks with a major suit as trumps more easily than they might do to produce 9 tricks in a No Trump contract. South is not allowed to ask North directly if he has 4 cards in a major suit, but can do what amounts to the same thing by bidding 2 ♣.

2 ♣, bid directly over his partner's opening 1 No Trump, says: "Do you have 4 cards in a major suit partner?" The replies are:-

2 Diamonds	–	"No, I do not have a 4 card major."
2 Hearts	–	"I have 4 Hearts; it's not possible for me to tell you in the same bid if I also have 4 Spades."
2 Spades	–	"I have 4 Spades. Incidentally, I do not have 4 Hearts."

If a responder re-bids 2 No Trumps in the sequence:-

N	S
1 NT	2 ♣
2 ♦	2 NT

the re-bid of 2 No Trumps is a Limit bid, i.e. promising 10 points and inviting partner to bid 3 No Trumps if he has a maximum, or near maximum 1 No Trump opening hand. The convention has thus improved the partnership's chances of reaching the best contract by enabling them to explore other possibilities as in option 5 and still revert to option 3.

The Stayman Convention is very useful. Beginners love it. However, a mistake which is often made is to make the bid of 2 ♣ when one of the 3 answers could be very embarrassing. If that could prove to be the case the bid should not be made, and an alternative bid should be found. Let us examine a typical situation where the beginner will often go wrong.

On hand (3) above there is no problem because if North bids 2 ♦ South will simply bid 3 No Trumps. But, if South had a hand similar to the following:-

♠ A x x x
♥ A x x x
♦ x x x
♣ x x

a bid of 2 ♣, hoping to play in 2 ♥ or 2 ♠, would be very bad. What can South do if North bids 2 ♦? Any bid that South makes after 2 ♦ bid by North could be a catastrophe, and South should never have courted disaster in the first place by bidding 2 ♣.

Beginners also tend to confuse the Stayman 2 ♣ bid with an opening bid of 2 ♣. They have very different meanings, the key being that Stayman is a conventional *response*, whereas an opening bid of 2 ♣ is an Acol *opening bid* promising a very strong hand (see page 67).

Responses to an Opening Bid of 1 Spade or 1 Heart

The Acol system makes considerable use of "*Limit Bids*". The direct raise of 1 No Trump to 3; the invitational bids of 2 No Trumps and 4 No Trumps over 1 No Trump; these are all Limit Bids. Each is intended to give a precise description of the point limits of the hand, i.e. "not more than . . . or less than . . ." The same principle applies when responding to opening bids in a suit, particularly if that suit is one of the majors, Spades or Hearts.

In responding, it is first necessary for the responder to decide whether or not he has "support" for his partner's suit. Support is defined as being 4 or more cards in partner's suit, or 3 cards, provided they include 2 from the Ace, King, and Queen.

If the responder has support for partner's suit he can reassess his hand by adding points for *shortages* in the other suits on the scale of 1 point if a suit has only 2 cards in it; 2 points if a suit has only a singleton; 3 points if there is a suit void (without any cards in it). The responder cannot add anything to the value of his high card points for length in a suit.

Points for shortages are the responder's "distribution"

points. There are fewer tricks to be lost in a suit in which the responder has a shortage, whereas length in a suit may duplicate partner's hand, or be in a suit in which his partner has no interest. They do not exist if responder does not have support for partner's suit because without sufficient trumps in the same hand there is no advantage in the shortage.

The majority of the "Limit" responses to an opening bid at the 1 level in a major suit are contained in the following:-

1. With less than 6 points – No Bid.
2. With support for partner's suit raise the opening of 1 by Limit Bids as follows:-
   > to the 2 level with 6 to 9 points
   > to the 3 level with 10, or a balanced 11 (or a flimsy looking balanced 12) points
   > to the 4 level with an unbalanced 11 or 12 points.
3. With support for partner's suit and 13 to 15 points, bid a new suit – and bid 4 in partner's suit on the next round. (This is known as a "delayed game raise".)
4. With support for partner's suit and 16 points or more bid a new suit one level higher than necessary and bid in partner's suit on the next round.
5. With 6 or 7 points and no support for partner's suit bid 1 Spade over 1 Heart if there are 4 or more cards in the Spade unit, otherwise bid 1 No Trump.
6. With 8 to 15 points and without support for partner, bid in your longest suit at the lowest level but, if you have fewer than 5 Hearts, or a very poor looking suit of your own, bid 1 No Trump with 8 to 10 points; 2 No Trumps with 11 points (a good 10 or a poor 12); 3 No Trumps with 12 to 15 points.
7. With 16 or more points but without support bid a new suit one level higher than necessary.

Responses to an Opening Bid of 1 in a Minor Suit

1. With less than 6 points the responder should always say "No Bid".

   Subject to 2. below, the same scale of Limit Bids applies to responses to minor suit opening bids as applies to major suits.

2. With 6 points or more the responder should use considerable discretion. Remember that to bid a contract in either Clubs or Diamonds which, when made, will constitute a game requires an 11 trick contract, i.e. a contract at the 5 level, whereas a major suit game contract only needs 10 tricks, and a game contract in No Trumps only needs 9 tricks. Accordingly it is important to bid in such a way as to give the maximum information possible about values held in suits other than the suit bid by partner. For example:-

1. ♠ A x x x	2. ♠ K J x	3. ♠ K x
♥ x x x	♥ Q x x	♥ Q x x
♦ x x	♦ K x x	♦ x x x x
♣ A x x x	♣ x x x x	♣ A x x x

On hand 1, although the 4 Clubs would constitute support if partner has opened 1 Club, if your partner also has 4 Spades (quite possible) a Spade contract will be more valuable than a Club contract, fewer tricks resulting in as many or more points (8 tricks in Spades are worth as many points as 9 in Clubs).

On hand 2 over a 1 Club opening, the values held in the other 3 suits justify a bid of 1 No Trump in preference to a Limit Bid in Clubs.

On hand 3 the cards in the 3 suits other than Diamonds are good enough to warrant a response of 1 No Trump if the opening bid was 1 Diamond but the hand would probably play better in Clubs if partner opened 1 Club. A Limit Bid in Clubs would then be better than 1 No Trump.

Responses to a 2 Level Opening Bid in a Suit

If a player makes an opening bid at the 2 level in a suit other than clubs (see page 67) his partner should try to keep the bidding open for one round. In practice this means that even if No Bid would have been the reply to an opening in a suit at the 1 level, a bid of 2 No Trumps should be made to an opening at the 2 level. If the responder has less than 3 cards in partner's suit and would have responded to an opening at the 1 level by making a bid in No Trumps or in a suit, then the same response should be made, at 1 level higher of course. With a *good* suit of his own, responder should always bid in that suit.

With 6 or more points, 3 or more cards in partner's suit, and without a good suit of his own, the responder is expected to bid in his partner's suit:-

1. At the level of 3 if his cards contain any of the 4 Aces or a void in one of the other 3 suits.
2. At the level of 4 without an Ace or a void.

The lower (3 level) response with a stronger hand makes an extra round of bidding available to the opener for further investigation, if he so desires.

Responses to 2 No Trumps

If partner opens the bidding with 2 No Trumps, showing a balanced hand with 20 to 22 points (see page 66), it is clear that very little is needed to make a game. Without a fair major suit but with 4 or more points the opening of 2 should be raised to the game contract level of 3 No Trumps. With a fair major suit there are a number of different ways in which the hand can be bid, the easiest of which is to follow the Stayman convention, here adapted to begin at the higher level. Thus, you would bid 3 ♣ over 2 No Trumps to enquire about partner's major suit holding. (The Stayman convention is described on page 74.) There are no "Weak take-out" bids over 2 No Trumps; a bid other than 3 Clubs or 3 No Trumps shows a good hand and/or suit, and insists that an appropriate game, or possibly slam contract must be bid.

Responses to a 2 Club Opening

It is very important to realise that if partner opens the bidding with 2 ♣ he may not wish to play the hand in anything less than a game contract. Accordingly, with only 1 exception, the bidding has to be kept open (i.e. "No Bid" cannot be said) until a game contract has been reached. The partner of the opening bidder must value his hand on the basis that if he does *not* have one or other of the undershown types of holding he must make a "negative" bid of 2 ♦. The holdings are:-

1. An Ace and a King, possibly in 2 different suits.
2. A King and Queen in 1 suit and a King in another.
3. Three Kings.
4. A hand containing various honour cards with a combined 7 or more high card points.

Any response to 2 ♣ other than 2 ♦ is a "positive" response and promises, at the very least, one of the above.

If the opening bidder replies (re-bids) to your negative response of 2 ♦ with a bid of 2 No Trumps he is describing his hand as being balanced and containing 23 or 24 high card points. If you have anything worth showing at all, you must now bid it. However with a very poor hand indeed (for example less than 2 points) you can here say No Bid when it is your turn. The one exception referred to above applies. It is the *only* exception to that rule allowed.

If he re-bids after your negative "2 Diamonds" in anything other than the 2 No Trumps just described, you are again obliged to bid (at the minimum level of uplift) unless your hand is just a collection of old tram tickets. If you do have such an appalling hand you bid 2 No Trumps (or 3 if need be) as a 2nd negative but one which still allows game at least to be reached.

Examples: South has one of the following hands after North has opened 2 Clubs:-

1. ♠ x x x x   2. ♠ x x x x   3. ♠ A J x x x
   ♥ K x   ♥ x x x x   ♥ x x x
   ♦ x x   ♦ x   ♦ x x
   ♣ A x x x x   ♣ x x x x   ♣ x x x

With (1) South has a positive hand and will bid 3 Clubs. With (2) he has a negative hand and bids 2 Diamonds. If North now bids 2 No Trumps South will be able to say "No Bid", but he will have to make the second negative of 2 No Trumps over 2 Hearts or 2 Spades from North, or 3 No Trumps over 3 Clubs or 3 Diamonds. With (3) South will bid 2 Diamonds over 2 Clubs but will bid his Spade suit, at the lowest possible level, over any bid that North makes – including a re-bid by North of 2 No Trumps.

Remember a game level contract must be reachable between the two hands.

Responses to a Pre-emptive Bid

Opposite a pre-emptive bid there is no point in responding in a different suit unless the responder is 100% certain that his hand is better, and that his suit is better than the best his partner might have. Similarly there is no point in bidding in No Trumps unless the responder has 2, or preferably 3 cards in his partner's suit together with good values in the un-bid suits. If he bids No Trumps without 2 cards in his partner's suit and finds that he cannot gain entry to his partner's hand during the play he has only himself to blame. This will become clearer in Part 3 of this chapter concerning the play of the cards, but be warned now!

A pre-emptive bid should not be raised unless the responder has a minimum of 3 quick and certain tricks, e.g. three Aces or an Ace and King in one suit and an Ace in another. Those tricks need not be in the opener's suit; he should be able to take care of that suit himself, after all he must have had at least 7 cards in that suit to start with, in order to make his pre-emptive bid.

Strong Responses

There are a number of types of hand which, when responding (other than to a pre-emptive opening bid as above), merit bids which will inform your partner that you have more values than a weaker bid might have conveyed. These hands are – possibly without support for partner's suit, *but*:

1. With 16 or more high card points if the responder has not yet had an opportunity to bid, *or*
2. A hand with which the responder has already said "No Bid" although it very nearly justified an opening bid in a suit other than that now bid by his partner.

The responder gets his message across by making his response in a new suit (not No Trumps) at a level one higher than was necessary. For example, a 2 Spades response over a 1 Heart opening, or 3 Clubs over 1 Diamond etc.

Examples:

♠ A K x x x   Over partner's opening bid of
♥ Q x x   1 in a suit other than Spades,
♦ A K x   respond 2 Spades
♣ x x

or, having already said No Bid with –

♠ A K x x x   Respond 2 Spades to an
♥ x x x   opening of 1 in one of the
♦ A x x   other 3 suits
♣ x x

RE-BIDS BY THE OPENER

One of the beauties of the Limit Bid method of the Acol system is that the opener is under no compulsion to make another bid if his partner has made a limit response unless that response clearly leads to a better contract. For example, with:-

♠ A K x x x
♥ K J x
♦ K 10 x
♣ x x

having opened the bidding with a bid of 1 Spade, and having received a limit response of 2 Spades, the opener can see that the 10 tricks needed for a game are unlikely and can say "No Bid". How can he "see" that? The Limit Bid of 2 Spades made by his partner has shown a maximum of 9 points, in which case opponents seem very capable of making 4 or more tricks with the minimum of 17 high card points they have between them. However, if the response had been 3 Spades the opener would bid 4 Spades. In the first case, including a distribution point for the fifth Spade, opener has 15 points opposite a maximum of 9, whereas in the second case there is a minimum of 10 in responder's hand and a game should be bid on the strength of the combined 25 points between the two hands (see page 70).

Change of suit by responder

What if the responder changes suit? The rule here is that if partner has already said ''No Bid'' before you come to open the bidding then, should he change suit in response to your opening bid, you are entitled to follow this with ''No Bid'' if the change is acceptable to you.

For example:-

N	E	S	W
No Bid	No Bid	1 Spade	No Bid
2 Hearts	No Bid	No Bid	No Bid

South's partner did not have a hand good enough to open the bidding so the possibilities are limited. South says ''No Bid'' over 2 Hearts.

However, if partner had not already had an opportunity to bid, this minimum level change of suit might have been made on a hand with as many as 15 points. (A change of suit also at a raised level would indicate even more points – see Strong Responses above.) In either event the opener is therefore obliged to bid again in order to continue the search for the best contract.

Put another way . . . if you open the bidding before partner has had a chance to bid then you guarantee that if he changes the suit when it is his turn you will make another bid in either your original suit, or a new suit, or in No Trumps, or your partner's suit. This guarantee does not operate if partner's response was in No Trumps as that is also taken as a Limit Bid response, describing his hand within precise limits (see foregoing, page 76).

Strong re-bids

There are 2 types of strong re-bid by the opening bidder, one of which shows that he expects to make 7 tricks without help provided the named suit is the trump suit; the other shows that the opener has 16 or more points.

The first (known as a "7 trick playing hand") is shown by a re-bid in that suit at the 3 level (but only if partner has not made a *supporting* limit bid). For example:-

N	S
1 ♠	2 ♥
3 ♠	

The second of these strong re-bids is known as a "Reverse". It is a difficult concept for the beginner to grasp and you will have to study the technicalities closely. The bids have the effect of raising the level of bidding sharply and arise as follows:-

1. The opener makes his opening bid in a suit at the 1 level.
2. The responder replies at the lowest level possible in a different suit or in No Trumps, or in the opener's suit at the minimum limit bid level of 2.
3. There are no intervening bids by the opposition.
4. The opener re-bids in a new suit at a level which means that if the responder wishes to re-bid in the opener's first named suit he will have to do so at the level of 3 or above. The responder may have no desire to re-bid in the opener's original suit but that does not alter the meaning of the message.

For example:-

N	S		N	S
1 ♦	1 ♥	or	1 ♠	2 ♥
2 ♠			3 ♣	

In either case if South re-bids in North's original suit he must do so at the 3 level.

Reverse bids are known as "forcing for 1 round". The partner of the player making the reverse bid is "forced" to make another bid – not necessarily in either of his partner's two named suits.

DOUBLES AND RE-DOUBLES

The bids which can be made in the course of the Auction include "Double" and "Re-Double". Either of these is automatically cancelled if there is a subsequent ordinary bid. In theory, when a player says "Double" over his opponent's bid, he is gambling that his opponent will not be able to make his contract. In practice there are also some conventional meanings to consider too but we shall return to them shortly. If the doubler is right and the contract is defeated the side making the bid of "Double" will gain greater Penalty scores above the line. If the doubler is wrong the declarer will earn extra points for his side, both above and below the line (see below). If the Double is the last bid in the Auction the contract is described as "... Doubled". For example:-

N	E	S	W
1 No Trump	Double	No Bid	No Bid
No Bid			

The contract to be played by North is 1 No Trump Doubled.

If your partnership's contract has been doubled and you are super-confident about the contract you can call "Re-Double" – the potential bonuses are then much greater – though, be warned, so are the penalties!

N	E	S	W
1 Spade	No Bid	4 Spades	Double
Re-Double	No Bid	No Bid	No Bid

The contract to be played by North above is 4 Spades Doubled and Re-Doubled. If East (or any of the others) had become unhappy about the increased risks inherent in North's Re-Double, they would have had to bid up from 4 Spades in order to cancel it and so reduce the total number of points at stake.

Penalty scores

Penalties are paid for being defeated in a contract. They also increase if the side having to pay is Vulnerable, and even further if the contract has been Doubled or Re-Doubled:-

(1) Un-Doubled Penalties

Non Vulnerable – 50 points to be added to the opponents' score above the line for each trick short.

Vulnerable – 100 points away for each trick short.

(2) Doubled

Non Vulnerable – 100 points away for the first trick short; 200 points away for each subsequent trick short.

Vulnerable – 200 points away for the first trick short; 300 points for each subsequent trick short.

(3) Re-Doubled

If the contract has been Re-Doubled and is defeated, each of the "Double" penalties is multiplied by 2, which can be very expensive if you are playing for money!

Bonuses when Doubled or Re-Doubled

The Bonuses which are earned by making a doubled contract are the doubling of the normal score below the line, plus 50 points above the line for the "insult", plus, –

100 points above the line for each over-trick when Non Vulnerable.

200 points above the line for each over-trick when Vulnerable.

Apart from the "insult" Bonus, which remains 50 points, each of the others is multiplied by 2 if the contract has been Re-Doubled and is successful.

Conventional Meanings of "Double"

I mentioned that, in practice, a bid of "Double" can also be intended to mean a number of different things. The most usual of these are (1) "Take-out" Doubles; (2) "Protective" Doubles; and (3) "Penalty" Doubles. The meaning, i.e. the message conveyed by the Double, varies according to the bidding up to the time the bid is made.

(1) Take-out Doubles

If a player doubles an opening bid in a suit which has been made at the level of 1 or 2, before the partner of the doubler has had an opportunity to bid (e.g. North deals and bids 1 Spade and East doubles), it is meant to be a "Take-out" Double. The player making the double is promising his partner that he has good values in the un-bid suits and is asking his partner to bid the one of those suits in which he has the best cards. His partner must bid, unless (1) the next player makes a bid, in which case the command to bid does not apply, or (2) in the honest opinion of the partner the doubled contract is most unlikely to be success-ful, given all the good cards *he* happens to have in that suit.

(2) *Protective Doubles*

If the bidding has started with an opening bid in a suit made at the level of 1 or 2 and the next 2 players have both said "No Bid", a double made by the player sitting in the 4th position is a "Protective" Double. It is very similar to a Take-out Double but differs in as much as it can be an acceptable bid even if the hand upon which it is made is not as good as one upon which a Take-out Double would have been made. The fourth player to bid thus keeps the bidding open and invites his partner to respond exactly on the same lines as he would have done opposite a Take-out Double.

(3) *Penalty Doubles*

In Acol a Double of an opening bid of 1 No Trump is always a Penalty Double, as is any Double which does not fit the criteria of a Take-out or Protective Double. It announces the belief that the contract will be defeated.

With X as the symbol for "Double" examples of sequences in which the different types of Double feature are:-

N	E	S	W	
1 ♠	X			. . . Take-out Double

N	E	S	W	
1 ♠	No Bid	No Bid	X	. . . Protective Double

N	E	S	W	
1 ♠	No Bid	3 ♠	No Bid	
No Bid	X			. . . Penalty Double

THE CONTINUING AUCTION

We have now dealt with Opening Bids, Responses, Intervening bids, and Re-bids, but the auction does not end until 3 players in succession have said "No Bid" and that point may not yet have been reached.

One particular area in which special meanings are attached to a responder's bids, and which may directly affect all subsequent bids, is that following an intervening "Take-out Double". Those meanings can best be illustrated by the following:-

   N   E S

1. 1 ♣* X 2 ♣ = "I have Club support but would have said 'No Bid' if East had not doubled."

2. 1 ♥* X 3 ♥ = "I would have said '2 Hearts' if East had not doubled."

3. 1 ♦* X 2NT = "I would have said '3 Diamonds' if East had not doubled."

4. 1 ♠* X XX   (Redouble) = "I have a fairish hand but do not have support; perhaps we can double their final contract!"

each of the suits bid and supported in the examples could have been in any of the other 3 suits.

Bids 1 and 2 above are designed to raise the level of bidding in order to make it more difficult for opponents to reach their best contract; bid 3 is necessary because bid 2 has taken away the normal meaning of a 3 level Limit Bid response – the opener can now bid the suit at the 3 level or make any other bid which seems justified.

The specialised meanings of bids in the Acol system become fewer as the auction progresses and, to a large extent, are replaced by bids which call for commonsense interpretations rather than having conventional meanings. For example in a competitive auction:-

N	E	S	W
1 ♥	X	2NT	3 ♠
No Bid	4 ♠	No Bid	No Bid
5 ♥	X	No Bid	No Bid
No Bid			

The first double is a "Take-out" double and the bid of 2 No Trumps is equivalent to a normal Limit Bid response of 3 Hearts. The remaining bids have their common sense meanings; North obviously thinks he will lose less points by being defeated in his Heart contract than he will if his opponents play in 4 Spades, and the final double is a penalty double.

There are conventional bids in the Acol system that go beyond the point we have reached, and many experienced players also use conventional bids borrowed from other systems. However, all such bids are beyond the scope of this chapter – they are delights still to come for the keen student.

Skill in the Bidding

Bearing in mind that all the above falls some way short of being a complete description of the Acol system, and that there are other systems, I nevertheless believe a thorough understanding of the foregoing should be enough to enable most hands to be bidded to a reasonable contract. Accordingly I am going to end the bidding saga with some comments on the skill factors.

First and foremost it is imperative to stick to the system of bidding agreed upon by the partnership whenever possible. For example, if it has been argued to use a 13 to 15 point one No Trump range, irrespective of the Vulnerability, it would be completely wrong to open 1 No Trump with 12 points, or with 16 points . . . "it looked the best thing to do . . ."

With 12 points the partnership could land in an impossible 3 No Trump contract; with 16 points the partnership could stay out of an unbeatable 3 No Trump contract – because in each case the response will be based upon faulty data given by the opening bid.

The Limit bid ranges when support is held are also very important. Again, if these are not adhered to exactly the partnership may well end in the wrong contract.

Each partner must listen to the bidding. Every bid made is a message passed – even a "No Bid" – and, too often, the wrong contract is reached because a player does not take the time to decode the messages correctly, including the messages that he himself is passing to his partner by his own bids.

Finally, if your hand does not seem to fit the system and yet it is obvious that a bid should be made, use some imagination, being careful to ensure that your partner is likely to understand what is meant. For example, sitting in the West position you have:-

♠ A K x x
♥ A K x x
♦ A K x x
♣ x

North bids 1 Club; your partner says "No Bid", and South bids 2 Clubs. It seems utterly wrong not to make a bid, even though it is highly probable that your partner has very little indeed. Perhaps his hand is:-

♠ x x x
♥ x x x
♦ x x x x x
♣ x x

How do you find out? How about bidding 3 Clubs? Your partner cannot possibly believe that you seriously mean to play in a Club contract, not after both opponents have bid Clubs. He will be forced to bid his best suit, even though he hates it, and either he will be left to play in the 3 Diamonds which he will have to bid with the above hand, or, if your opponents decide to compete further, you will have a nice juicy penalty Double to make next time it is your turn to bid.

Part Three

The Play

As a derivative of Whist, the rules of play of Bridge generally follow those of Whist but with a few important differences. The procedure is as follows:-

1. The person who, in the side which made the highest bid in the Auction, first bid the suit in which the contract is to be played is known as the Declarer and the player to his left leads the first card. He has a free choice of which card to lead.

Dummy, as seen by Declarer

2. When the first card has been led the partner of the Declarer places his cards face upwards on the table, arranged with each separate suit in a row facing the Declarer. The trump suit should be positioned on the left as seen by the Declarer. From that point on the cards of Declarer's partner constitute the "dummy" hand, and he is "dummy".

3. The play proceeds in a clockwise fashion throughout, the winner of each trick playing the first card to the next trick.

4. Exactly as in Whist, each player must follow suit if he can but, if unable to follow, may discard or use a trump as he sees fit.

5. The Declarer has the task of playing both his own hand and that of the dummy. Each card played from the dummy hand when it is the turn of the dummy to play (e.g. immediately after the first card led) is called for by the Declarer. Alternatively he may actually pull the card required into the centre of the table. (The latter practice is permitted in the United Kingdom but is against the rules in some countries.) The dummy must not question the Declarer's decision – unless the Declarer calls for a card which isn't there, or instructs dummy to revoke (fail to follow to a suit when he can), or plays a card out of turn. In the latter 3 cases the Declarer must correct his instructions and follow the rules of play.

To illustrate the foregoing, following this bidding:-

N	E	S	W
1 ♠	No Bid	2 ♥	No Bid
4 ♥	No Bid	No Bid	No Bid

South is the Declarer; West must lead a card of his choice; North will table his cards as dummy, with Hearts on his right; South will have the responsibility of playing the cards from his own hand when it is his turn, and to call for cards to be played from the dummy when it is dummy's turn.

6. Provided each player adheres to the rule that he must follow suit if he can, no player is under any compulsion to win a trick. He may play higher or lower than a card already played according to how he wishes.

7. The tricks taken by each player belong to the side to which that player belongs, e.g. if in the hand bid above 5 tricks are taken by cards led from the dummy hand during the course of the play, and 5 are taken by cards led from the Declarer's own hand, the Declarer will have made his 10 trick contract.

Skill in the Play

Declarer play

There are many declarer techniques that a player can only learn over a period. Trial and error at the table teaches surprisingly adequately to begin with, and experienced players are always happy to advise beginners (sometimes you will think that they are too happy!). At the end of this chapter you will find some brief explanations of some of the expressions your "benefactors" will use. Most standard techniques are dealt with in the numerous books available so by the time you are eager to gain better understanding of them you will have no difficulty in reading about them elsewhere; therefore, apart from drawing your attention to the comments on skill in Whist (in Chapter 2 and particularly in Chapter 3), I will only cover one aspect now, i.e. the play to the very first trick.

The most frequent mistake made in declarer play is playing too quickly to the first trick. It is essential for the Declarer on first seeing the dummy to sit back and think. He must formulate the main elements of his plan in his own time before he plays the first card from the dummy. Now that he knows the specific cards held by the dummy, as compared with the general picture he had built up from the bidding, he must:-

1. Think again about the opponents' bidding. Did their bids give an indication of the cards each is likely to have? Did their failure to bid give any clues? For example, if they have 22 high card points between them and neither made a bid in the Auction what is the most likely distribution of those 22 points? If either had 13 points they would have bid, so the distribution must be either 11-11 or 12-10. To carry that example a little further later on, if you are satisfied that the distribution was 11-11 or 12-10 and the opponent on your left plays in succession an Ace, a King, and a Queen, can he still have an Ace left in his hand?

2. Count the winners. Given a sequence of play which is straightforward, and taking into account the cards Declarer thinks each opponent is likely to have, are the number of tricks contracted for all present and correct? Or is the

Declarer likely to fall short of his contractual target? If the latter is the case is there anything Declarer can do about it?

3. Count the losers. Although there seem to be enough tricks available could the opposition defeat the contract by taking their winners before Declarer can get to his? If so, is there anything Declarer can do?

4. Preserve your entries. If your plan calls for you to play a specific card from the dummy at a later point will you have been able to ensure that the dummy had won the previous trick? Would you have preserved a card in the dummy high enough to take the previous trick if necessary? Or, if the entry was needed in your own hand would you have preserved your entry card there? Will that affect your play to the first trick?

Let's look at an example. The bidding is:-

W	N	E	S
1 ♥	X*	3 ♥ **	3 ♠
4 ♥	4 ♠	No Bid	No Bid
No Bid			

* A Take-out Double (see page 85).
** A hand on which the response would have been 2 Hearts had it not been for North's intervening "Double".

The lead is a small Diamond.

Even before the dummy hand is laid down South is able to visualise some aspects of opponents' hands. The bidding indicated that West has 13+ points and probably has at least 5 Hearts. East has 6 or 7 points (for with more he might have bid more strongly over the Double) and he probably has at least 4 Hearts.

The cards South can see when dummy is revealed are:-

N
♠ A Q x x
♥ —
♦ A J x x
♣ K x x x

S
- ♠ K 10 x xx
- ♥ J x x
- ♦ Q 10 x x
- ♣ x

The winners seem to be 5 Spades; 2 Hearts ruffed (trumped) in dummy; and 3 Diamonds. A total of 10 tricks appear within grasp – all that is needed for the contract. The losers seem few . . . but . . .? Knowing that his partner had Hearts with him why did West lead that small Diamond to begin with? Declarer should assume the worst (that it was a singleton). If East's hand is:

- ♠ x x
- ♥ 10 x x x
- ♦ K x x x
- ♣ A x x

Declarer will be committing suicide if he plays a small Diamond from the dummy. East will win with the King and return a Diamond for his partner to ruff. Assuming that East plays his smallest Diamond and West then plays a Club, East will win with his Ace and play another Diamond for his partner to ruff again and defeat the contract. Declarer must base his plan on that possibility and play the Ace of Diamonds from the dummy immediately, followed by a small Spade, winning with the King in his own hand. He will then play a Heart for the dummy to ruff. The Ace of Spades will come next and if neither opponent started with all 4 missing trumps South will make the contract without any trouble.

Defender Play
Again I must draw your attention to the section on skill in Whist in Chapter 3, particularly to the comments on communication by signals, and to the table of opening leads. The most important elements in defence are precisely the same; in addition, in Bridge the defence has the advantages of being able to draw deductions from the bidding, and being able to see the dummy's hand.

The defence must plan just as the Declarer must. Let us take another look at the example I gave above – this time from the point of view of East, and note particularly East's "signal" of his smallest Diamond.

East must ask himself: "Why, knowing that I have some Hearts to help him, did my partner West lead that Diamond? Could it be that it is his only Diamond?" If Declarer is silly enough to play a small Diamond from dummy, East must win the trick with the King and play another Diamond, hoping that his assumption was correct and that his partner will be able to ruff.

Which Diamond? The answer is the smallest . . . because West will know that East had a choice and that therefore the low Diamond is more than likely to be a signal to play the lower ranking of the other 2 available suits, namely Clubs.

Heard at the Bridge Table
Here are the most significant terms and phrases you will be regaled with – space does not permit a full listing.

"Finesse"
Suppose South is Declarer holding xx in a suit in his own hand and A Q in North's hand (dummy). He cannot tell where the K is held but he wants dummy's Q to win a trick without falling to it. There is a 50% chance of success if South *both* leads an x *and* then plays the Q from dummy. This finesse of the K gains a trick if West has it (assuming West does not mistakenly play it). If East has it there is nothing lost by trying.

"Two way finesse"
There is sometimes a choice of possibilities for a finesse. For example A J 3 in South's hand and K 10 4 in dummy. South (Declarer) can play either the 3 from his hand and then the 10 from North (if West does not play the Queen), or the 4 from North and the Jack from his own hand (if East does not play the Queen). Either way a successful finesse gains a trick.

"Eight ever . . . Nine never"
One of the sayings that reveals a lazy mind. It means that if a Declarer has the Ace, King and Jack between his own hand and

that of the dummy but is missing the Queen then, if he has 8 cards in the suit between the 2 hands, he should "finesse the Queen", whereas if he has 9 cards he should play off the Ace and King, hoping that the Queen will fall. The saying ignores the information obtained from the bidding and/or the play. For example, West deals and bids 1 ♠; South ends in a contract of 3 NT and finds that he has 9 cards in Spades between his own hand and dummy. If the Queen is missing who has it? Will it drop if the Ace and King are played?

"Safety Plays"

These are types of play made in an attempt to avoid the dangers of unusual distributions when a contract seems to be secure. For example, South has A K 9 4 2 ♠ and North has J 8 3 ♠. As Declarer, South has ample tricks and entries available in the other suits and only needs 4 tricks from the Spade suit to guarantee his contract (whatever it might be). The safest way is to play the Ace and the 3 then, if both opponents have followed suit, to play the 2 towards the Jack. This guards against either opponent starting with Q 10 xx or all 5 of the missing Spades and guarantees at least 4 tricks.

"Danger Hand"

A hand which should be prevented from taking a trick if possible – even if it means giving the other opponent a trick he might not otherwise have made. For example West dealt and bid 3 ♠ (a pre-emptive bid showing not less than 7 Spades etc., see page 67). South has A xx ♠ and North has xxx ♠ and South becomes Declarer in 3 NT. West leads the K ♠ and South wins with the Ace.

If West is allowed to win any trick (which may still leave him with 4 or more Spades in his hand) the contract can be defeated. West's hand is the "danger hand" and South must take any finesses he needs, or make any safety plays necessary in such a way as to reduce the danger of West winning a trick. (For example if there is a "2 way finesse" possibility it should be taken so that even if it fails West will not benefit.)

"Hold Up"

This is the act of refraining from playing a winning card —
hoping to minimise the dangers of a suit. For example, after a
3 ♠ opening bid by West South plays in 3 NT with A x ♠ in his
own hand and xx ♠ in North's hand. When West leads the K ♠
South must "hold up" his Ace until the next trick, hoping (in
fact – expecting) that East will have started with only 2 Spades
and that when East wins a trick he will not be able to help West
by playing a Spade.

"Duck"

This is *not* playing a higher card over one which has just been
played. For example the dummy has Q J 9 and you have K xx;
Declarer plays the Queen from the dummy. You should
"duck", i.e. not play the King. If you work it out you will see
that if the Declarer has at least A x and your partner has the 10
and others the Declarer can make 3 tricks if you cover the Queen
with the King (he can finesse the 10 next) but can only make 2
tricks if you save your King for the Jack.

And lastly, here are some other refuges for lazy minds which
you should take with huge pinches of salt as they ignore all
genuine techniques:-

"Second hand plays low . . . third hand plays high" (i.e. if
you are the second person to play you should play a low card,
whereas if you are third you should play a high card). A very fair
saying – 50% of the time.

"Cover an honour with an honour" (for example you
shouldn't "duck"!).

And the classic of all time: "There's many a tramp on the
[London, Thames River] Embankment who is there because he
didn't draw trumps." It is just as likely that he is there because
he *did* draw trumps!

To complete this chapter on Bridge I must say, once again,
that all of the above represents little more than an introduction.
For further study I would strongly recommend "Begin Bridge"
by G. C. H. Fox, another *Right Way*. I have taught from it for
years, and it really is extremely good.

SUMMARY OF CONTRACT BRIDGE SCORING

	Not Vulnerable	Vulnerable
Scores below the line for tricks in excess of 6 (the book) for a contract bid and made:-		
Clubs or Diamonds	20	20
Hearts or Spades	30	30
No Trumps		
– the first	40	40
– subsequent	30	30

Over-tricks above contract are scored at the same rate above the line, as Bonuses (Note: over-tricks in No Trumps are 30 each).

Rubber Bonus (Scored above the line):-		
1 side only being Vulnerable		700
both sides Vulnerable		500

Honour Bonuses (above the line):-		
The 4 honour cards in one hand in a suit contract	100	100
5 in one hand	150	150
all 4 Aces in one hand in a No Trump contract	150	150

Slam Bonuses (above the line):-		
Small Slam Bonus	500	750
Grand Slam Bonus	1000	1500

Penalties awarded to opponents above the line for each under-trick:-		
undoubled	50	100
for the first doubled under-trick	100	200
for each subsequent doubled under-trick	200	300
for the first re-doubled under-trick	200	400
for each subsequent re-doubled under-trick	400	600

Bonus above the line for making a doubled contract (the "insult" bonus).	50	50

(Also the value of the score to which you are entitled below the line for making the contract is doubled.)

Bonus ("insult" bonus) above the line for making a re-doubled contract. (Also below the line the value of the score to which you are entitled for making the contract is multiplied by 4.)	50	50

Bonus above the line for each over-trick made:-

in a doubled contract	100	200
in a re-doubled contract	200	400

Bonus above the line for having the only part-score towards an incomplete first game in an unfinished rubber in which neither side is Vulnerable, or towards a second game if both sides are Vulnerable.	50	50

Bonus above the line for being Vulnerable in an unfinished Rubber.		300

6

Auction Bridge

Historically Auction Bridge preceded Contract Bridge but it is
easiest nowadays to regard it as a simplified version of Contract
Bridge. In the following descriptive comments, etc., the
assumption is made that the reader plays Contract Bridge
already, or has studied the earlier chapter on it in this book.

The basic areas of difference between the two games are in
scoring and bidding, and in the advantageous fact that it can also
be played in an enjoyable 3 handed version which I include.
Like Contract Bridge the aim is to win a Rubber, consisting of 2
Games (3 in the 3 handed version).

Scoring
In Auction Bridge a Game requires 30 points below the line. To
accumulate those points:-

1. A Club contract is worth 6 points for each trick made in
    excess of 6 (the "book' as described in Chapter 5, Part
    One), irrespective of the actual bid but provided the
    contract which has been bid is made.
2. A Diamond contract is worth 7 points, a Heart contract is
    worth 8, a Spade contract 9, and a No Trump contract 10
    points, all on the same terms.
3. Note that unlike Contract Bridge, points for extra tricks
    are added below the line.
4. Bonuses for making doubled contracts are scored by
    doubling the trick value below the line, together with an
    "insult" bonus of 50 points above the line.

5. Bonuses for making re-doubled contracts are twice those for doubled contracts with the exception of the insult bonus, which stays at 50 points.

In addition (although not counting towards Game) points above the line are earned as follows:

6. The Bonus for winning the Rubber of 2 Games is 250 points. There is no distinction between "Vulnerable" and "Non Vulnerable" situations in this or any other Bonus, or in penalties.
7. The Bonus for a small slam of 12 tricks is 50 points, and for a grand slam 100 points. Neither has to be bid in order to earn the points.
8. Bonuses for honours are 150 points if all 5, or 100 points if 4 from A K Q J 10 are all held in 1 hand; 100 points if all 5 are held, 3 by one partner and 2 by the other, or 4 and 1; or, in a No Trump contract, 150 points if all 4 Aces are held by one player.
9. Penalties are awarded to the opposition above the line at the rate of 50 points for each under-trick when not doubled; 100 if doubled; 200 if re-doubled.

The Auction
The Auction takes place in the same way as in Contract Bridge, i.e. it starts with the dealer and proceeds clockwise until 3 players in succession have each said "No Bid". To be valid a bid cannot be made unless:

1. Its point value is greater than the highest preceding bid, or,
2. Its point value is equal to that of the highest preceding bid but it requires more tricks to be made.

For example, over a bid of 3 Spades, worth 27 points if made, it would be necessary to bid 3 No Trumps (30 points), 5 Clubs (30 points), 4 Diamonds (28 points), or 4 Hearts (32 points). 5 Clubs would be a valid minimum Club bid over 3 No Trumps.

Skill in the Bidding

The fact that the number of tricks actually won (assuming the contract is made) determines the score below the line removes most of the science from the Auction. The degree of communication between the partners is very limited, and thus the Auction is little more than a gamble. Skill is confined to the players' assessment of the profit, or loss, which might arise from a particular bid.

For example, East has:-

♠ x x
♥ x x
♦ x x x
♣ A K Q J x x

North/South already have a Game, whereas East/West have not yet figured on the score sheet. The bidding proceeds:-

N	E	S	W
1 ♠	2 ♣	2 ♠	No Bid
No Bid	3 ♣	No Bid	No Bid
3 ♠	???		

If North/South actually make 10 tricks or more they will score 36 points or more below the line, plus any honour point bonuses they may have, and 250 points for the Rubber, i.e. 286+, and maybe even more if they manage to make a slam. To make it more difficult for them East will have to bid 5 Clubs. Could it be right?

It is not a clear cut decision. He thinks that he has 6 tricks in the Club suit from his own hand so that if he is unable to make a single trick from his partner's cards he will be defeated by 5 tricks. If he is doubled he will lose 500 points and gain 100 for his honour cards. A net loss of 400 points.

However, if his partner's hand cannot furnish a single trick there is a danger that North/South will make a slam. If they make a small slam they will score 54 points below the line, 50 points for the small slam, and 250 points for the Rubber, plus any points due for honours, i.e. 354+.

If partner's hand does provide 1 trick the potential loss by bidding 5 Clubs is reduced to a net of 300.

I suggest it would be right to bid 5 Clubs and try to live to fight again. Who knows, perhaps the contract will not be doubled; perhaps North/South will bid 4 Spades and find that West has been lying in wait with only 1 Club, 1 Ace, and a Spade which he will use to trump the third round of Clubs?

Rules of Play and Skill in the Play

For these I refer you back directly to the chapters on Contract Bridge, Whist, and Skill. As soon as the Auction is over the play proceeds as described in Contract Bridge and exactly the same elements of skill apply.

Three Handed Auction Bridge

This version for 3 players is played with a 4th (dummy) hand dealt as the 3rd hand by the dealer. The last 4 cards dealt to the dummy hand are dealt face upwards. Each player (except dummy!) now bids in turn in the normal way. The person who makes the highest bid in the Auction becomes the declarer. The dummy hand is then moved, if necessary, to the position opposite the declarer, the other 2 players become partners for that hand, and the play proceeds as in the normal 4 handed version.

By agreement between the players the number of cards to be dealt face up may be more or less than 4.

Scoring

The scoring differs from the 4 handed version in as much as each player has his own scoring column on the score sheet, and a Rubber is not won until 1 of the players wins 3 Games. For example, in the first 4 hands of a Rubber:-
  On hand (1) North bids 3 Clubs and makes 10 tricks
  On hand (2) South bids 2 Spades and makes 10 tricks
  On hand (3) East is doubled in 4 Hearts, making 9 tricks
  On hand (4) North bids 3 No Trumps and makes 8 tricks

North	East	South
(3) 100	(4) 50	(3) 100
		(4) 50
———————	———————	———————
(1) 24		(2) 36
———————	———————	———————

Skill

Three handed Auction Bridge is a much more chancy business than the 4 handed version as, apart from the 4 cards everyone can see, no-one knows all the cards the dummy has until after the first lead. Sometimes the sight of the 4 cards which are displayed may prompt a player to bid a suit expected to be held in strength by the dummy in preference to a suit in his own hand. Tactical bids become the order of the day. I know a player who, if he sees a couple of picture cards in the dummy often pre-empts the bidding, i.e. makes life difficult for opponents, by bidding No Trumps. I always tell him that he is not being fair to his father . . . me!

For example, assume the 4 cards displayed are A ♣, K ♥, Q ♠ and J ♠. My son, with a worthless collection of cards himself, will cheerfully bid 1 No Trump. My hand might be:-

♠ 10 3
♥ Q 10 8 2
♦ A K J 6
♣ Q 9 3

At this stage I don't know if my son is bluffing or telling the truth. *If he is* telling the truth, and if I bid 2 NT now (quite permissible – the fact that he bid No Trumps does not stop me), then in trying to make 8 tricks I could get a very bad result. On the other hand *if he is not* telling the truth then, by not bidding No Trumps myself, I could be missing a Game. It would be dangerous for me to bid in Diamonds or Hearts because the dummy might not have any more cards in the suit I might choose. For example, dummy could just as easily have (A) or (B):-

(A)		(B)	
♠	Q J 9 7 6 2	♠	Q J 9
♥	K 3	♥	A K 9 3
♦	5	♦	Q 10 4 2
♣	A 5 4 2	♣	A J

So what do I do? I would (1) bid 2NT and (2) blame my wife. He is her son and I'm quite sure he gets none of his bad habits from me.

7

Clobbiosh and Belot

CLOBBIOSH

One of the best things to come out of Eastern Europe in the last 100 years (apart from my maternal Grandmother) is the game of KALABRIASZ, otherwise known as CLOBBIOSH, a skilful and enjoyable game for two players.

Object
Clobbiosh (which is easier to say!) is a point scoring game, with the simple object of reaching a target of 500 points first, but it would not be breaking the rules to agree on a larger or smaller target.

There are 2 stages in each hand, an Auction, to decide upon the trump suit in which the hand is going to be played, and the play of the cards.

The Pack
The pack used for Clobbiosh is one of 32 cards, all cards from the 2 to the 6 inclusive in each suit being taken out and left aside.

Dealing
The two players, North and South (for my convenience) sit opposite each other and cut the cards. The player cutting the higher card (normal ranking of the cards for this purpose – page 15) shuffles the pack; his opponent cuts and the shuffler deals for the first hand. Subsequent hands are dealt by the winner of the previous hand. The cards are dealt in the following sequence:-

3 face down to opponent, 3 face down to dealer,
3 face down to opponent, 3 face down to dealer,
1 face upwards in the middle of the table,
3 face down to opponent separate from his others,
3 face down to dealer separate from his others.

The rest of the pack is then placed in a stack face down on top of the single card in the middle of the table but still leaving that card exposed to view. Each player now picks up his first 6 cards only. A simple Auction follows to decide on the final trump suit.

In Clobbiosh the prospective trump suit is initially that of the card placed face upwards during the deal (as above). As a result of the bidding in the Auction that suit or an entirely different suit may be decided upon as being the final trump suit, but before I deal with that you need to know how to score, so that your bidding will be appropriate to your objective of winning by being the first to reach the target score.

Scoring
Points towards the target may be scored in a number of different ways:-

1. By the value of certain combinations of cards held and declared as being held after the Auction and just before the play commences. In the calculation of the score at the end of each hand those declared combinations will not count unless a trick has been made by the player concerned in the course of play. This is known as "establishing" the score for the combination.

2. A player who is fortunate enough to hold both the King and Queen of the trump suit scores 20 points for BELLA irrespective of whether or not a trick is made, provided he makes the claim "Bella" when he plays the first of those two cards. He can play either first.

3. By the winner of the last trick in the play.

4. By the total of the special Clobbiosh point values of each card acquired as a result of the play – i.e. taken in a trick by one player playing a higher card than the card played

to that trick by his opponent. These tables are set out on page 111.

The total score a player can therefore achieve by the end of the play of a hand is comprised of the value of combinations which have been declared and established, plus points for the Bella, if held and claimed correctly, plus points for the last trick if taken, plus the total of the special CLOBBIOSH point values for each card he has been able to accumulate in front of him during the nine-trick play.

However, each hand that is played has a trump suit that has been decided by one of the two players having made the winning bid in the Auction; if that player does not finally achieve more points than his opponent a "Bate" or an "Abeyance" situation will arise. These will be explained and illustrated later in this chapter. All you need to know now is that they may affect the final score on the hand very considerably, so achieving the maximum possible points out of your hand is very important.

Value of Card Combinations

The combinations of cards that can be declared after the auction and before play commences are runs in ordinary ranking order of 3 or 4 cards in the same suit, e.g. A K Q J, or 9 8 7, but not 8 7 A. Ace is high and 7 low and never shall the twain meet for this purpose. The combinations are:-

Fifties:
A run of 4 cards in one suit, e.g. 10 9 8 7, is worth 50 points (known as a FIFTY), provided however:-

a. The other player does not have a Fifty headed by a higher card in any suit, or,

b. The other player does not have a Fifty headed by the same rank card in the suit that has become the trump suit (e.g. 10 9 8 7 in the trump suit out-ranks 10 9 8 7 in any other suit) and,

c. The player announcing the Fifty before play commences (which he must in order to score fifty points when counting up at the end) establishes it by winning a trick in the

107

course of the play. No trick scored in play means no 50 to take into the value of points earned. Any trick will do.

A player with two fifties, either of which out-ranks any fifty held by his opponent, scores 50 points for each, again provided he has announced both before play commences and manages to score a trick in the course of play.

Twenties:
A run of 3 cards in the same suit, e.g. 9 8 7, is worth 20 points (known as a TWENTY), provided:-

a. The other player does not have a Fifty, or a higher ranking Twenty in any suit, or an equivalent Twenty in the trump suit, and,

b. The player announcing the Twenty before play commences makes a trick, again any trick but there has to be at least 1.

A Fifty or a Twenty which has been out-ranked by a higher combination held by the other player immediately becomes valueless – even if the other player eventually fails to establish his combination, i.e. fails to take a trick in the play.

A player with the highest ranking Fifty who also has a Twenty scores both provided he announces both before the play and makes a trick in play. It need not be in the same suit as the Fifty, and will score even if the other player started with a higher ranking Twenty because the latter will have been made null and void by the highest ranking Fifty.

Declaration of Fifties and Twenties
The highest ranking combination is first identified; then the player who has it must describe it clearly, for example "Fifty in Spades headed by the King". If that player has any other combinations they must be similarly described at that time. The player with the lower ranking combination will have had to specify the value of the highest card in his combination (for example "Fifty headed by a Queen"), but not which suit it is in. The result of this is that the player with the lower combination

knows the specific cards involved which are held by his opponent, whereas his opponent only knows the value of the top card and the number of cards in the run against him. For example, with Spades as trumps:-

> North says "[I have a] Fifty"; South replies "How high?", North says "[headed by] a Jack"; South: "Mine is [headed by] the Jack of Spades."

South's Fifty, although at the same level, is the higher ranking because it is in trumps, and North does not have to describe his hand any further, i.e. he does not have to say in which suit he had held his (now valueless) Fifty.

Alternatively, if South's Fifty had been headed by the 10 of Spades, and North's by the Jack of another suit, South would not need to disclose that he had 10 9 8 7 of Spades, only that his own Fifty was headed by a 10 and not high enough to beat one headed by a Jack.

If it transpired that both players had Fifties (or Twenties) headed by the same value card, neither being in the trump suit, then neither would count in the scoring as no one suit out-ranks another. If neither run is going to count then neither player would need to state the suit in which his run was held. If the Fifties were of equal rank, neither being in the trump suit, the value of any other lesser run would also fail to count and would not be announced.

In the above hand North declared first but there is no rule or privilege about it; South could have spoken up first and the result would be the same because the higher ranking Fifty wins regardless. If South also had another Fifty, or a Twenty, he would announce and describe it precisely at this time.

Players are expected to remember the scores for these combinations which they claimed before the play commenced, and to bring them into account when adding up their scores after all the cards have been played.

Although we will return to it later, one more fact must be introduced here as it may have a bearing on your potential declaration of combinations and thus on your decisions about bidding which must be made prior to such declarations. It is that there is a special significance attached to the 7 (the lowest value card) of the suit of the card faced upwards in the course of the deal. If that suit becomes the trump suit as a result of the auction, either player having the 7 of that suit can then exchange it for the faced up card if he wishes – after the Auction and as a prelude to claiming Fifties and Twenties before play commences. The card thus obtainable can be taken into account in declaring a run. For example, South has 10 9 7 of Spades, the 8 ♠ is the faced up card and North "goes it" in Spades winning the auction and confirming Spades as trumps. South can now exchange the 7 for the 8 and is then able to claim a Twenty headed by the 10.

Bella

A player holding both the King and Queen of the final trump suit scores 20 points for "Bella" irrespective of whether or not he wins a trick in the play. To become entitled to the points he must make the statement "Bella" on playing the first of the two cards. Some "local" rules specify that the King should be played first; others that the Queen should be played first. The version of the game that I was taught at my Mother's knee left it open to the player with the Bella to make his own choice as to which of the two cards he played first, and, as Mother was always right . . . there is no rule governing which has to be played first.

Notice that the possibility of exchanging the 7 which is described above also relates to an exchange in order to acquire the King or Queen to make up the Bella.

Points for the Last Trick

The winner of the last trick earns 10 points. Since games are often evenly balanced these points can easily be of crucial importance to winning or losing a hand. (See later description and illustration of "Bate" and "Abeyance" for the effect of losing a hand after having won the Auction.)

Special Clobbiosh Card Point Values

In the play of the cards and in the subsequent scoring at the end of the play there are a number of differences in the point scoring and trick-winning abilities of individual cards from those usual in Whist. One set of values applies to the three suits which are not trumps; the other is specific to the trump suit. You will need to keep these special ranking and scoring tables beside you until you get used to them:-

Trick taking and point scoring order in Trumps

	Scoring Value
Jack (known as the "Yos" if in trumps)	20
Nine (known as the "Menel" if in trumps)	14
Ace	11
Ten	10
King	4
Queen	3
Eight	Nil
Seven	Nil

Trick taking and point scoring order in other suits

	Scoring Value
Ace	11
Ten	10
King	4
Queen	3
Jack	2
Nine	Nil
Eight	Nil
Seven	Nil

The Auction

Once the cards have been dealt the players conduct the Auction to decide on the final trump suit in which the hand is actually going to be played.

Not until after the Auction does each player pick up the three cards which were dealt separately at the commencement, and add them to the six he already holds.

Each player will bid or "Pass" partly on the strength of his original six cards, and partly in the hope that his unseen three are going to increase the scoring potential of his hand.

The card which was dealt face upwards on the table indicates the trump suit for the first round of the Auction, i.e. the first 2 bids assume that suit will be trumps in the play to follow. The dealer's opponent makes the first bid (known as a "call").

At this point the dealer's opponent has to decide whether or not he seems to have a good chance of scoring more points than the dealer if the already designated suit becomes the final trump suit. The potential score he will consider should include the value of combinations, Bella if relevant, together with the last trick (if he expects to make it), plus the Clobbiosh value of each card he hopes to be able to accumulate in front of him during the 9 trick play.

If he believes he will be able to score more points than his opponent he will say "I'll go it". If not he says "Pass". If he says "I'll go it" that ends the Auction. However, if he says "Pass" the dealer can now make his own decision . . . "Go it", or "Pass" depending upon how he fancies his own chances in the suit indicated by the face up card.

If both players decide to pass on the first round of calling a second round takes place. In this round the faced up card is no longer the trump suit. The dealer's opponent decides whether or not he might score more points than the dealer if one of the other three suits becomes the trump suit. If so he will say "I'll go it in . . .". It doesn't matter which suit he selects, once he selects a suit that suit is the new trump suit and the Auction ends. If he does not select a suit the right to do so passes back to the dealer.

If both players pass for the second time the cards are again shuffled and are re-dealt by the original dealer's opponent and a new Auction begins.

It is possible (though unusual) for the cards to be re-dealt several times before a trump suit is chosen.

Example Auctions
Here are some examples. In each one North dealt and the faced up card was a Spade:-

1. South says "I'll go it". South has elected to "go it" in the original prospective trump suit, Spades; the Auction is over, Spades are trumps and North can say nothing.

2. South says "Pass". North says "I'll go it". North is able to, and has elected to go it in Spades. The Auction is over.

3. Both pass on the first round then South "goes it" in Clubs which becomes the trump suit and the Auction is over. Although poor North may have 6 Hearts in his hand he can say nothing.

4. Both pass on the first round and South then says "I'll go it in Spades". Illegal. He missed his chance in the first round. His call must be changed to "Pass" and North "goes it" in Diamonds which now become the trumps.

Between the Auction and the Play

The Exchange with the 7 of the Trump Suit

After the Auction has ended with a trump suit being selected each player picks up his remaining 3 cards and, if able and wanting to, makes an exchange with the 7 of the trump suit. (As stated earlier, if either player has "gone it" in the original trump suit, *either* player who has the 7 of trumps amongst his 9 cards can now exchange it for the original trump card which was turned up when the cards were first dealt.)

This exchange, which must be made before claims for Fifties or Twenties are made, and before play commences, can be exceedingly important. The face up card may contribute towards a Fifty, or a Twenty, or Bella; it might have been the card, the ultimate possession of which decided the caller to go it in the first suit. But note that neither player can make the exchange if neither goes it in that first suit.

Claims for Fifties and Twenties

The claims are made as soon as the exchange with the 7 has, if desired and if appropriate, taken place. It doesn't matter which player makes his claim first as the specific cards in the higher ranking combination will not be disclosed until it is decided which of the combinations is the highest. Refer back to page 108 for the description of how these claims are actually made.

And finally . . .

At this point one more thing happens. The card at the bottom of the pack, i.e. the one touching the turned over face-up card, is now itself placed face upwards on the top of the pack, where it sits in splendour adding a bit of knowledge to each player but having no further part in the play or scoring of the hand.

The Rules of the Play

1. The dealer's opponent leads to the first trick, after which the winner of each trick leads to the next.
2. In leading to a trick a player may play any card in any suit, i.e. he does not have to play his highest in any suit.
3. In following to a card played each player *must* play a card in the same suit if he has one. The rules do not insist on the play of a higher card except in the trump suit (see below).
4. A player who cannot follow to a suit other than the trump suit *must* use a trump on the trick if he has one.
5. In following to the trump suit a higher trump *must* be played (to win the trick) if possible. The player who is unable to follow to a trump is able to discard whatever card he wishes.

An Example Game

North has dealt and the 7 ♠ has become the face-upwards card in the middle. Spades are therefore the prospective trump suit for the first round of bidding.

A bird's eye view of the first six cards in the two hands is:-

North	South
♠ 8	♠ A
♥ K	♥ J 10 7
♦ A	♦ K 10
♣ J 10 9	♣ -

South and North both pass on the first round, and South says "I'll go it in Hearts" on the second round. The Heart suit becomes the trump suit and the Auction is over. Both players now pick up their other 3 cards. The bottom card, which is the 8 of Diamonds, is faced upwards on the top of the pack.

With their last three cards the players now have:-

North	South
♠ 9 8	♠ A
♥ K Q	♥ J 10 9 8 7
♦ A	♦ K 10
♣ J 10 9 8	♣ 7

Although neither player has any special right to a priority announcement at this time North says "I have a Fifty". South replies "How high?" North says "a Jack", and South says "No good mate, mine is the Yos" (the Jack of trumps). North does not have to say any more about the cards which went to make up his now valueless Fifty.

Let play commence:-

Trick 1: South leads the J ♥ and North plays the Q ♥, saying as he does so "Bella". (Had he not said "Bella" he would have forfeited his claim to 20 points.)

Trick 2: South, having won the first trick, plays the 9 ♥, on which North plays the K ♥. Trick again to South.

Trick 3: South plays 8 ♥ and North discards the 8 ♣.

Trick 4: South plays K ♦. North takes it with A ♦.

Pause for a moment. The reasons why South played first the Yos, then the Menel are easy to see; he wished to denude North of trumps if possible, with a view to ensuring that he would eventually make the last trick.

Why did he play the 8 ♥? There are several reasons. It was possible that North still had the A ♥. To draw out the A ♥ South had a choice of Hearts he could play and chose the 8 because North already knew he had the 8 as a result of the earlier Fifty claim. The play of the 8 ♥ also served to give South a chance of obtaining more clues about the cards North might still have left, for example as a result of any discard North might make.

Why did South play the K ♦, and not the 10 ♦? Answer – because of the Ace of Diamonds. As North has already followed to the two trumps, and is known to have commenced with a Fifty headed by a Jack (which cannot be in Diamonds because of South's own 10 ♦) he can only have 3 cards in his hand which might include the A ♦. There are 12 cards left in the pack, so the odds against North having the A ♦ are 12 to 3 (4 to 1), but the odds against his having two cards in the Diamond suit, one of which is the Ace, are very much higher. South plays the K ♦ knowing that the odds of winning the trick with it are high, but that the odds of winning a second round of Diamonds with the 10 are very much higher. Winning with the 10 would be worth 10 points; winning with the King only 4 points so he plays the King first to "draw" the Ace if North has it.

Trick 5: Having won trick 4 North plays 8 ♠ and South wins with the A ♠.

Another pause. Why doesn't North play 10 ♣ at this point, in order to try to make 10 points and perhaps avoid the risk of having his best card trumped later on? The answer is that he is afraid that South might have two Clubs including the Ace. Just as South carried out his review before playing his K ♦ so now North thinks the hand through.

South is now known to have started with at least 4 Hearts and 1 Diamond. He therefore still has 4 cards which North can only guess at and it is very possible that they include the Ace and another Club.

If the Ace plus one other proves to be the case then if North plays the 10 of Clubs himself he will lose it to South's Ace, and if he plays any other Club he knows that South, who is not forced to win a trick in a suit played outside the trump suit, will play low on a small Club (e.g. North's Jack – only worth 2 points) in order to save his Ace for the 10.

Remember that although North did not have to state the suit in which he had his aborted Fifty, South has already limited it to a possibility of one of two suits only. As Spades was the original trump suit the odds seemed weighted in favour of the Fifty having been in Clubs. If South does have the Ace and another Club he will certainly not play the Ace on a small Club played by North.

But North need not despair yet! He knows that there is no point in risking the worst by playing the 10 ♣ so plays the 8 ♠ in order to ensure that South will win the trick and be the one who plays the first card in the Club suit. As it happens, in this game,

South cannot now avoid leading his 7 ♣ at some stage. Rather than give North 10 points for the last trick, South (to North's satisfaction . . .) leads it now.

Trick 6: South plays 7 ♣ and North wins with the 10 ♣.
Trick 7: North plays J ♣ which South wins with a trump (either one will do, i.e. he does not have to play his highest, it is entirely his own choice).

South wins the last 2 tricks with the 10 ♦ and the last trump.

Both players are now ready to score. The rule is that the player who has "gone it" scores second. As a result of the tricks North has taken he has in front of him the following:

A ♦, K ♦; 7 ♣, and 10 ♣. He scores 11 + 4, + 0 + 10, + 20 for the Bella. In all, 45 points.

South has:-
J ♥, Q ♥; 9 ♥, K ♥; 8 ♥, 8 ♣; A ♠, 8 ♠; J ♣, 10 ♥; 10 ♦ and 9 ♣; 7 ♥, and 9 ♠. He scores 20 for the Yos + 3, + 14 for the Menel + 4, + 0 + 0, + 11 + 0, + 2 + 10, + 10 + 0, + 0 + 0, + 50, for the Fifty he called, + 10 for the last trick, a total of 134 points.

South won that hand easily and with a large score. As the winner of that hand he must deal next. The cards are shuffled and cut as usual.

It is important to note the difference that one card would have made to the score. Imagine that South's 8 ♥ had been the 8 ♦. Now he would not have had a Fifty and the resultant Twenty of J 10 9 would have been out ranked by North's Fifty in Clubs. If both players had made the same value tricks (to be expected in a normal play sequence) North's score of 45 would have been increased to 95 by the value of his 50, whereas South's score would have fallen to 84 as a result of not having had his Fifty.

"Bate" and "Abeyance"

If a player "goes it" but fails to make as many points as his opponent he is said to be "Bate". The penalty for "being made" Bate is the loss of all the points that player scored in the hand. Not only that, his opponent adds those points to his own score. In the above example North would add to his own 95 the 84 taken in tricks etc. by South, and score 179 points to South's nil. Note that all the points are transferred, including the Fifty etc., and that North deals next having become the winner.

It sometimes happens that both players score exactly the same number of points in a hand. In that case the points of the player who had "gone it" go into "abeyance", where they sit until earned by the next player to win a hand by successfully going it, or by getting his opponent "Bate", and the deal passes across the table.

Skill

Consider the exchange with the 7. Picking up a high card by using the 7 is not always sensible, for example: North has ♠ 8 7, ♥ K 10, ♦ Q 9 7, and ♣ 10 8. South has gone it in the first suit which was Spades, and the face-up card is the ♠ A. Should North exchange the ♠ 7 with the ♠ A? No! It is very likely that South has the Yos and the Menel so that the ♠ A would probably fall to one of them. If North picks up the Ace he may well be making a present of it to South. Of course if North had a third Spade the exchange would be completely correct.

There are many opportunities to exercise a fairly simple level of skill in the play. Remembering what has been said, what has been played, and the probable odds against the other player having a particular card or cards in his hand, is not very difficult, and the play should be based on what are reasonable assumptions and what are known facts.

For example, if your opponent successfully claims a Fifty and a Twenty you immediately know 7 of his cards. If you have the 10 and the King only, in a suit other than the suit or suits in which you know about his 7 cards, the odds are heavily in favour of your trying to make 10 points by playing the 10 rather than the King. After all, you started with a pack of 32 cards, 18 of which have been dealt out and 2 have been turned over. There are only 12 left which remain unknown. The Ace could be one of those 12 or one of the 2 cards which still remain unknown in your opponent's hand. The odds are 6 to 1 in favour of the Ace still being in the pack.

Take another example, this time where opponent "goes it" in

a suit in which you have the Ace and 10 only. He plays the Yos. According to the rules you have to follow suit but can choose which card to play. Assuming your opponent started with the Menel in addition to the Yos he can take both your trumps if he plays the Menel after the Yos. Perhaps if you play the higher of the two cards on the Yos, i.e. the Ace, he will think you would not have played it if you had had a smaller card to play and may not play his Menel straightaway, thus possibly giving you a chance to score your 10 later by trumping a card in another suit.

A common situation is one in which a player announces a Twenty or a Fifty and has another undisclosed card in the same suit, e.g. a Twenty of A K Q with the 7 not disclosed. If the player is forced into a position of having to discard from that suit the correct card to throw away would be the Queen. It is unlikely to make a trick anyway, and to throw the 7 simply gives opponent more information.

It is always necessary to remember the 10 point bonus for the taking of the last trick in the play. Sometimes, if there seems to be the possibility of defeating opponent and making him Bate by taking the last trick, it may be advisable to take what otherwise might be an unjustifiable risk. For example, you only have the Ace and King left in a suit which is not the trump suit and you and opponent are both down to your last 2 cards. You do not know what opponent's cards are, because any cards disclosed by a Twenty, Fifty, or Bella call have already been played. Opponent plays a small card in the only suit you have. If his remaining card is a trump then you will lose your Ace if you do not play it immediately, but if you think that there is a good chance that opponent does not have a trump left, but instead has the 10 of your suit, then by playing the King followed by the Ace you will grab his 10 and the last trick to boot!

BELOT

A variation of Clobbiosh, Belot differs by the addition of 2 Auction calls:-

1.   "No Trumps", in which all Aces count 11 and all Tens count 10, and there is no such thing as a Yos or a Menel.

2. "All Trumps", in which all Jacks count 20 and all Nines count 14 and Jacks and Nines are the highest cards in every suit.

Effectively therefore there are two additional trick-taking and special card point value tables as below:-

Trick taking and point scoring order in "No Trumps"

	Scoring Value
All Aces	11
All 10s	10
Kings	4
Queens	3
Jacks	2
Other cards	Nil

If the hand is played in No Trumps a player who has all four Aces in his hand counts each one individually and also scores a bonus of 200 points. The bonus has to be claimed after the Auction and before play commences, together with any Fifty and/or Twenty claims.

Trick taking and special card point values in "All Trumps"

	Scoring Value
All Jacks	20
All 9s	14
Aces	11
10s	10
Kings	4
Queens	3
Other cards	Nil

In All Trumps each Jack is worth 20 points but if a player has all four in his hand there is an extra bonus of 200 points to be claimed after the Auction but before play commences, in the same manner described for Aces.

Calls of "100"

In Belot claims of Twenty and Fifty are still operative, but there is a further claim which out-ranks both, i.e. a claim of "100". This is for a run of five cards in the same suit. The rules for claiming and establishing a Hundred are the same as for the lesser calls.

Calls of Bella

The normal call of Bella exists as in Clobbiosh. In Belot it is also possible to claim 20 points for Bella for any set of both King and Queen in the same suit (even for more than one set) whenever the hand is being played in All Trumps.

The Auction

The Auction is more complex because of the additional calls that are available, either or both of which can be used as over-calls, and because a call made in a suit can be changed into a call of All Trumps if the other player over-calls in No Trumps.

Calls are made by each player in turn, starting with the one who has not dealt.

Neither player can "go it" in No Trumps or All Trumps in the first round, except as an over-call or in order to meet an over-call as explained below.

In the first round the first caller may Pass or go it in the trump suit. The second player may go it in the trump suit if the first player has said "Pass", or, if the first player has gone it in the trump suit the second may over-call him by going it either in No Trumps or All Trumps. If the over-call is in No Trumps the first player may convert his original call into All Trumps, the highest possible call.

If both players have passed in the first round the first to call in the second round may go it in a new suit, No Trumps or All Trumps. If he passes, his opponent has the same options, but if the first to call in the second round goes it in a new suit his opponent may over-call in No Trumps or All Trumps.

If a player goes it in the second round in a suit and is over-called by his opponent in No Trumps he has the option of converting his own call into All Trumps.

Three examples, each after South has dealt and a Spade has been faced up:-

> North: "I'll go it"
> South: "I'll go it in No Trumps"
> North: "In which case I'll go it in All Trumps."

And:-

> North: "Pass"
> South: "Pass"
> North: "I'll go it in Diamonds"
> South: "No Trumps"
> North: "Pass"

Finally:-

> North: "Pass"
> South: "I'll go it"
> North: "All Trumps"

Obviously, the same considerations are taken into account in the Auction as in a Clobbiosh Auction . . . expanded by the extra points available in Belot as described above.

One final point: if both players pass twice the hand is played in No Trumps, instead of being re-dealt.

8

Competitions

I know a lady who manages to put aside enough money from her weekly Whist Drive winnings to enable her to have spending money in the USA on her infrequent visits to her grandson. It isn't wholly as a result of my efforts to teach her . . . my mother was always lucky at Whist.

Whist is only one of the games which are played in competitions. There have been World Championship knock-out tournaments in Clobbiosh, and playing in tournaments in Bridge may well be more popular world wide than ordinary Rubber Bridge.

The rules and scoring of each game are the same except where changes are shown in the text below.

WHIST DRIVES

I hope you will have enjoyed my Chapter 3 devoted to Whist. The principle of Whist Drives is quite simple. Although there are a number of variations an example of a popular type should suffice.

In the village of Much Rambling on the Wash a weekly Whist Drive is held in aid of the funds of the Women's Institute. The entry is limited to 36 players and the entry fee is 25 pence per player – a total of £9.00. They play in the Church Hall, for which no charge is made, and of the £9.00 the winners share £3.00; £2.00 goes to the second pair; £1.00 to the third, and £3.00 to the W.I.

The evening starts at 7.30 and ends at 10.45, with a break for tea or coffee at 9.00.

In the 3 hours of actual play there are 10 rounds, each of 3 hands. The 1st hand of the evening is played with Spades as the trump suit; the 2nd with Hearts; the third with Diamonds; the 4th (i.e. the first of the 2nd round) is with Clubs as trumps, and the 5th with No Trumps. Thereafter the rest of the 25 hands to come follow the same order.

The players cut for deal at the start of each round. The pair in which a player has cut the highest card sit North and South, their opponents as East and West. Some evenings are known as "cut-in", when the partnerships are also decided by cut, others are played with pre-arranged partnerships. Each pair scores simply by taking the total number of tricks they make in each of the 3 hands and entering those totals on a score sheet which their opponents initial. At the end of the round the pair who occupied the East/West seats move to the next table; the North/South pair stay where they are for the whole evening. The final winners are the players with the highest total score for the evening.

Everyone seems to have a very enjoyable time and, if you happen to be in the area on a Whist Drive night, you can be sure to be very welcome. But a word of warning – the Vicar's wife and her partner win very regularly; notes have been taken by their opponents on eyebrow movements and the number and position of fingers visible at the back of the cards but there has been nothing proved conclusively as yet. In my opinion they just happen to be better players than the rest, but you know what people are.

On a more serious note, you all know of Whist Drives. They are used to raise money and to provide enjoyment for people of all ages. Regular pairs can, and should, win often if they exercise the skills available.

SOLO DRIVES

This excellent game is described in Chapter 4. When played in "Solo Drives" the basic idea is very much the same as in Whist Drives. Each separate hand is dealt and played as in the normal game of Solo; calls earn points on a scale drawn up by the organisers instead of money changing hands; individual scores are kept; the most successful player in a round moves "up" a table, the least successful in the opposite direction, and the other 2 stay where they are. In the event of a tie the cards are cut to decide who moves where. The overall winner is the player who amassed the highest number of points over the whole of the Drive.

Solo Drives are quite rare nowadays, but used to be very popular . . . especially for skilful players when money prizes were offered.

TOURNAMENT BRIDGE

This section relates to Chapter 5, which can be consulted by those unfamiliar with the game.

Bridge Drives

Again these are played in a similar way to Whist Drives. If a Rubber is not completed in the course of a round the standard bonuses are awarded:-

for the only part score in an uncompleted game – 50 points
for a game won in an uncompleted Rubber – 300 points

The players' score for each round is their net plus or minus result against their opponents for that round. For example, if N/S score 500 and E/W score 200, N/S will score a net 300 plus for the round, and E/W a net 300 minus.

"Duplicate" – the Principle

If you can picture a Bridge Drive you may come to the conclusion that the winners could owe much more to their luck in being dealt good cards than to their skill in calling and playing. Duplicate Bridge ("Duplicate") seeks to eliminate that particular element of luck by means of a system which results in each hand only being dealt once but played by every pair, so that the points won or lost by each separate North/South pair can be compared hand by hand against those won or lost by the other North/South pairs, as can the results achieved by the East/West pairs. To enable each hand to be played over and over again by different players Bridge "Boards" are used.

The "Boards"

Imagine a room with several tables of players. At each table there is the usual North/South pair and the East/West pair. Now imagine numbered containers on each table, these being designed each with 4 compartments capable of holding 13 cards apiece, and those compartments each having a label denoting a compass position. The containers are also marked to indicate which player is to be the Dealer and what the state of the game is, e.g. "Dealer N, E/W Vulnerable". A separate compartment holds a slip of paper (the "Traveller"). The card holding device that you have conjured up in your imagination is known as a Bridge "Board". Let me show you it at work in a "Pairs" Duplicate Tournament, one of several different types of Duplicate.

Duplicate – "Pairs"

A "Pairs" Tournament consists of a number of tables, each with 4 players as usual. The North/South pair at each table will play the East/West pair for a round consisting of a pre-determined number of hands from different Boards, after which the East/West pair will move in one way and the Boards in another, so that each of the hands will be played by different pairs in each round.

A Pairs Tournament will usually start with the players at each table being provided with the following:-

1. Sufficient Boards for their first round to be played;
2. Either a set of cards to be dealt for each hand/Board in the round (once these have been dealt to "initiate" a Board the first time it is played they become the established dealt cards for that Board for the rest of the tournament); or, pre-dealt cards in place for each Board within their appropriate compartments;
3. Individual record cards which may be used to keep track of personal scores, but on the cover of which the system (for example "Acol") for the partnerships and any special conventions in use must be described by each player. The cards, known as *"Convention Cards"*, can be inspected (insofar as such description is concerned) by

their opponents at any time (a partnership is free to alter its chosen system or conventions between rounds; if so the two players must alter their Convention Cards accordingly);

4. *"Travellers"* – these are score sheets which will be used as I shall be describing below;

5. Record cards (not used in many small Tournaments) on which the cards in each hand are written out after the hand is first played so that they may be checked before it is played again to ensure that the cards have been stored in their correct compartments.

Starting from the point that each player has his cards, either because they have been dealt in the first round, or when he has picked pre-dealt cards from his allotted compartment and checked that they are correct (if record cards are not being used the check will only be that there are 13 cards in the hand), each hand is bidded in the normal way, taking into account the directions on the Board as to who is the Dealer, and whether either or both pairs are Vulnerable.

The way the cards are physically played differs from Rubber Bridge. The cards are not played into the middle of the table and picked up by the winner of the trick. Instead they are kept by each player. As a card is played it is placed face upwards in front of the person playing it. When all 4 cards have been played to the trick the cards are turned face downwards (but still in front of each player), pointing to the centre of the table if the partnership has won the trick or parallel with the player's side of the table if the partnership has lost the trick. This procedure enables the number of tricks won and lost to be seen easily, and also makes it possible for each player to collect his cards together at the end of the hand, count to see that he has all 13, and place them face down in the appropriate compartment, ready for whoever will play the Board next.

After a hand has been played it is scored on the individual record cards (so that the players can have their own record of the result of each hand) and on the "Traveller". Before describing the latter we should look at the way the score is compiled for each hand.

"Pairs" tournament scoring

The score for each hand is determined by adding together the result (for example 3 Spades bid, 10 tricks won = 90 + 30 = 120) and, if the contract is made, a bonus as follows:-

for a part score contract bid and made ....50 points
for a Non Vulnerable game bid and made ....300 points
for a Vulnerable game bid and made ....500 points.

For example, 3 No Trumps bid and made when the Board states that the side concerned is Vulnerable would earn that side 600 points. In all but a few special competitions there are no bonuses for "honours". All other bonuses and penalties are the same as in Rubber Bridge except that the 4th and subsequent doubled Non Vulnerable undertricks each cost 300 points.

Completing the Traveller

The headings of the Traveller columns are:-

Board Number: ......

  (a)   (b)   (c)   (d)   (e)   (f)   (g)   (h) and (i)

N.S. Vs Cont. By Tricks N.S. + N.S. – Blank Columns

Assume that Board Number 1 is dealt by North, and that this Board, apart from stating that North is to be dealer, also states that neither side is Vulnerable. Suppose that on one table the Board is played in a contract of 3 No Trumps, and 9 tricks are made, by North/South pair number 1 against East/West pair number 14. The figure 1 is entered at the top of the Traveller against the Board Number; in column (a) the pair number of 1 is entered; in column (b) the East/West number 14 is entered; in column (c) the entry describes the contract – 3 No Trumps; column (d) is to identify the Declarer, say North; column (e) – 9 (the tricks made); in column (f) the figure is 400, i.e. 100 for 3 No Trumps and 300 for a Non Vulnerable Game bonus. No entries are made in the remaining columns; (g) would be used if North/South had a minus score (see below); (h) and (i) are reserved for later use by the Organisers to establish the overall winning partnerships (see page 129).

After the score has been entered the Traveller is folded so that it cannot be read from the outside and placed in a special compartment in the Board.

At the end of each round the sets of Boards are moved to different tables and the players also move so that partnerships are playing different opponents in each round, and the Boards are never played again by anyone who has already played them once.

Assume that after 3 rounds the Traveller for Board 1 looks like this:

Board Number 1

(a)	(b)	(c)	(d)	(e)	(f)	(g)	(h)	(i)
N.S.	Vs	Cont.	By	Tricks	N.S. +	N.S. –	Blank	Columns
1	14	3 N.T.	N	9	400			
12	24	3 N.T.	N	10	430			
11	22	3 N.T.	N	8		50		

North/South 12 has out-scored the other 2 North/South pairs, and East/West 22 has out-scored the other 2 East/West pairs. Perhaps North 12 proved better at playing that hand than the other North declarers; perhaps the defence put up by East/West 22 was superior to that of the other pairs of defenders. If prizes go to the best North/South and the best East/West pairs then, on the evidence of the above, 12 and 22 respectively must be favourites. You can now see how the element of luck in the deal has been eliminated, because the competing pairs hold the same cards – good or bad – and thus how, in a whole tournament, the best playing pairs are likely to become the overall winners.

Deciding the result of a Pairs Tournament
A "Director" is appointed to ensure that everything runs smoothly and to calculate the final results. Each Traveller is scored separately by the Director in the following manner:-

1. The number of N/S pairs competing is multiplied by 2 and 2 is deducted from the resultant figure. For example, if 9 N/S pairs are taking part the figure derived will be 9 x 2 – 2 = 16. That figure becomes the "Top", i.e. the maximum points to be awarded to any pair for that Board.
2. Starting from the Top the potential points go down in

twos, so that if, for example, 16 is the Top, 14 will be the second highest, 12 the third, and so on down to 0 for the lowest.

3. The results for each of the N/S pairs are now examined and compared. The pair with the highest score on the hand will earn the Top, the pair with the next highest will earn the second highest, and so on. If more than one pair has achieved the same result they share the points for the appropriate number of places. For example if three of nine pairs all have the same highest score they will each earn a third of 16+14+12, i.e. 14 each.

4. The Director records these scores in column (h) of the Traveller. In column (i) he records the E/W scores, calculated in exactly the same way.

In practice, for a 9 table tournament the Traveller (leaving out columns (c), (d) and (e), and merging (f) and (g) for simplicity) could look like this:-

N.S. pair	E.W. pair	N.S. result	N.S. score	E.W. score
1	10	400	8	8
2	18	430	12	4
3	17	200	6	10
4	16	460	16	0
5	15	420	10	6
6	14	450	14	2
7	13	100	4	12
8	12	50-	2	14
9	11	100-	0	16

When the Director has completed scoring all the Travellers he transfers the results to a summary sheet and adds that up to ascertain the final scores and the overall partnership placings. By this means the winning North/South and East/West partnerships – the pairs who have been most consistent in gaining points – will emerge as overall winners. In small tournaments a complex "scrambled" scoring method produces a single winning pair as opposed to a North/South and an East/West pair but you need not worry about that at this stage.

Skill in Pairs

In many respects "Pairs" is a more skilful version of Contract Bridge than straight-forward Rubber. It is quite acceptable in Rubber when no slam is biddable to stop in a game contract of 3 No Trumps, and make just 9 tricks; it is not clever in pairs if you find that every other declarer with the same cards has managed to make 10 tricks. It will earn a bottom result in Pairs; no less clever would be being in a contract of 3 No Trumps, making 12 tricks, and finding that all the others have bid and made the slam.

The bidding and the play have to be at their most precise and accurate in Pairs, more so than in any other form of Bridge. All the techniques have to be used to their utmost, and as a result the game becomes more demanding and more challenging.

The mathematics also become a little different. For example, it would be very rare to bid a contract in Rubber, knowing at the same time that it is almost certain it will be defeated and cost 1400 points; in a Pairs competition it is quite possible that such a bid could win the competition! A Vulnerable contract of 6 Spades bid and made in Pairs is worth 1430 points. That is 180 points for the contract of 6 (as if they were "below the line"), 500 points for the Vulnerable game, and 750 points for the small slam bonus. It would be better to be doubled and defeated by 5 tricks in a Vulnerable contract rather than to suffer opponents making such a slam. If you and your partner proved to be the only pair who had "sacrificed", i.e. voluntarily bid a contract expecting it to be defeated, and had lost 1400 points, whereas all the others lost 1430 points you would earn a Top.

Each hand is judged on its own merits . . . it is not as though in the next hand opponents would have another opportunity to win the Rubber. Accordingly "sacrifice" bidding is more of a feature in Pairs than it is (or should be!) in Rubber.

"Phantom" sacrifices are also more frequent; the name describes sacrifices made in the belief that opponents will score more points if allowed to play in a contract of their choice, only to find that, left alone, they would have scored less than you have just given them by your sacrifice. For example if your opponents had bid a game worth 620 and you sacrificed and lost 500, you would have made a "phantom" if it transpired that opponents' contract would have been defeated – i.e. the

Traveller showed that other pairs *had* played in that game contract but had been defeated.

In the play of the cards there is also an important difference from the declarer's point of view. Even the very best players sometimes bid to the wrong contract when everyone else succeeds in bidding to a better contract. For example it may happen when one is in a contract of 3 No Trumps with an apparently obvious 9 tricks to be taken, that you can see when dummy goes down 10 tricks which could have been taken in a major suit game contract which might have been bidded instead. Non Vulnerable or Vulnerable the No Trump game will be worth 20 points less than the major suit game, and the result – if all the other pairs made 4 Spades or 4 Hearts – will be a bottom score for you.

Such a declarer (on the assumption that the competing pairs will in normal play all make 10 major suit tricks) is in a situation where he can't do worse, even if he is beaten in his contract. He must look at the possibilities of either conjuring up an extra trick to earn another 30 points, or of gambling on the cards in opponents' hands being distributed in such a way that, if he plans his play very carefully he can achieve a score equal to or better than those who may declare in a major suit game.

A simple example of what might be necessary when in what appears to be the wrong contract is the following:-

North	South
♠ K 8 2	♠ A J
♥ A K J 9 8 3	♥ Q 10
♦ A 4	♦ J 8 7 6 2
♣ 8 3	♣ Q J 10 4

As a result of a misunderstanding in the bidding South is the declarer in a contract of 3 No Trumps. The lead by West is the 9 ♦ (probably "top of nothing", i.e. a lead indicating that the player leading has 3 small cards in the suit, headed by the card played).

South can see that the correct contract is 4 Hearts, and that 10 tricks will be made easily in that contract if, before trumps are drawn, the declarer plays as soon as possible first the A ♠ and 2 ♠, then the J ♠, overtaking it with the K ♠, and then playing the 8 ♠ which can be trumped with the 10 ♥. In the 3 No

Trumps contract the tenth trick obtainable by the ruff is not possible, although there are 9 certain tricks available, namely 2 Spades, 6 Hearts and the A ♦.

However, if declarer plays 2 ♠ from the dummy and plays the J ♠ from his own hand on a small Spade played by East he will be taking the 50% chance that the Q ♠ is still in East's hand. If his Jack wins, his winners in Spades will increase to 3 and his overall winners to 10 – equal to the tricks won by the players in the 4 Heart contracts but superior in the score by 10 points. He will earn the top score.

If the Q ♠ is in the West hand he will lose a trick which will now probably cost him the contract. But if his contract is defeated he will be no worse off than he would have been if he made it – either way the result is the bottom score.

In effect he sacrifices a 100% chance of making his contract in favour of a 50% chance of an extra trick, hoping to find the distribution of the adverse cards that will help him to turn the failure in bidding into success in the play.

Thinking about what East and West may hold, it is a statistical fact that if an odd number of cards are held between 2 hands they will be split as evenly as possible between the two hands on more occasions than they will be split in any other way, whereas an even number of cards will not be split evenly in the majority of cases. So if the declarer is in the kind of situation being considered, in what appears to be the wrong contract, he should assume that the distribution of adverse cards is against the odds and plan his play accordingly. That way, by catering for the unusual, he may succeed in making as many or more points in his "wrong" contract as others do in the "right" one.

Although this book cannot attempt to be a mathematical treatise, an inside glimpse at the statistical fact noted above may be helpful to readers not (yet) of a mathematical inclination insofar as statistics can be related to cards. Here is the analysis of the possible splits between two players of an odd number of cards and an even number of cards. When 5 cards are split between two players often enough, the frequency with which *each* player will receive cards will settle as per the table below on the left; whereas with 4 cards the table on the right will emerge:-

5 Cards			4 Cards		
no cards	1		no cards	1	
1 card	5		1 card	4	
2 cards	10	$20/32 = 62\frac{1}{2}\%$	2 cards	6	$6/16 = 37\frac{1}{2}\%$
3 cards	10	chance of a	3 cards	4	chance of
4 cards	5	near even	4 cards	1	an even
5 cards	1	split			split
	32			16	

Duplicate – "Individual"

A variation of Pairs, in which bidding, play and scoring is the same, is an "Individual". This, as its name indicates, is a tournament in which every participant competes as an individual. Partnerships change according to a predetermined movement card at the end of each round. The winner will be the player who achieves the best overall result from all his different partnerships. To save time, and to keep the proceedings flowing smoothly, it is usual for only a limited amount of system bids and special signals to be allowed. It is not easy to win an "Individual" because you are not able to choose your partners, and many serious minded players do not like Individual tournaments for that reason.

Duplicate – "Teams"

"Teams", which can be in multiple arrangements of several teams competing against each other at the same time, or a head to head battle between two teams, works on the principle that in one room half of a team of 4 will sit in the North/South positions, while the other half of the team will occupy the East/West seats in another room. The Boards will move from one room to the other as they are played.

The effect of this can be seen in the following example: in Room 1 N/S (Team "A") bid and made 3 No Trumps Non Vulnerable against the E/W of Team "B". Scored on the same basis as in Pairs (see above) this is worth 400 points. In Room 2 N/S Team "B" (against Team "A" E/W) are defeated by one trick in the same contract, losing 50 points. Team A therefore score a combined plus of 450 points, and Team B a combined minus of 450 points.

134

The final Team result may be based on the aggregate score, or on a complex conversion system of the points earned on each board calculated by using a special conversion table. If you are ever called upon to use it you will have a conversion table supplied to you at the time.

Skill in Teams

It is a feature of Team play that possible games should be bid whenever it seems that a game can be won. In a Pairs competition if one pair bids a game which is missed by the other pairs the gain they make is rarely enough to result in the winning of a tournament. However, a Team in which one pair scores 170 in a 3 Spade contract when Vulnerable (making 10 tricks – 90 for 3 Spades, 30 for the over-trick and 50 for the part score) suffers badly if the opponents of the other pair in the Team bid 4 Spades and score 620 (120, plus 500 for the Vulnerable game bid and made). An opposing team in that situation has gained 450 points, possibly enough to clinch the match for them.

Conversely the play of the cards is not quite as critical. A margin of 20 points which arises because a team has scored 600 in 3 No Trumps whereas its opposition has scored 620 in 4 Spades is rarely of sufficient importance to win or lose a match. In Pairs a declarer may fight very hard for an over-trick. In Teams it is not nearly as important; the aim should always be to ensure a plus score wherever possible. This need to register a plus score also reduces the number of times when a sacrifice bid is made, and thereby cuts out many phantom sacrifices.

Duplicate Bridge is the only card game I know where a player can hold mediocre cards all evening and yet play well and successfully! Perhaps it loses on the psychological front compared with Rubber as some people argue, but to my mind it is certainly the more skilful battle.

9

Black Maria

Black Maria is a very interesting and potentially skilful Whist derivative, which can be played by any number of players. It is probably at its most enjoyable and most skilful if played by only 3, so I intend to describe it in its 3 handed version. The game can be played one hand at a time, or over an agreed number of hands, or until a specified score has been reached. A glance at Whist and Friends, Chapter 3, may be helpful if you are rusty about the basics of Whist.

The Pack
The number of cards used depends upon the number of players taking part. The pack is going to be divided between those players, with the minimum number of cards in the Club suit being taken out, from the 2 upwards, in order to leave a total pack divisible by that of the number of players. For example, with 3 players the 2 of Clubs is taken from the pack; with 4 no cards need be taken out; with 5 the 2 and 3 of Clubs must come out; with 6 players the 2, 3, 4 and 5 must all come out.

Object
The winner is the player with the *lowest* score, either on a single hand, over an agreed number of hands, or at the time one of the other players has reached an agreed total.

136

Scoring

Each player accumulates his score as a result of the "penalty cards" he acquires amongst the tricks he wins. The penalty scoring cards are:-

    any card in the Heart suit ....penalty value 1 point
    the Ace of Spades................................penalty value 7 points
    the King of Spades ....penalty value 10 points
    the Queen of Spades...........................penalty value 13 points

That penalty of 13 for the Queen of Spades gives the game its name of Black Maria. A quick calculation will show you that a total of 43 penalty points lurks amongst the cards. The score is recorded after the play of each hand.

The Preliminaries

After cutting for deal the cards are shuffled and distributed equally. There is no rule concerning the number to be dealt at a time, only one that says that all players should end up with the same number of cards, face down.

    After the deal each player looks at his cards and chooses 3 which he places face down in front of the player on his right. When all have performed that act each must pick up the 3 cards they have been given and play is ready to commence. How do they decide which 3 cards to pass on? I'm afraid you will have to wait for the answer until the section on "Skill" below.

The Play

The play follows normal Whist procedures without a trump suit. The player to the left of the dealer leads to the first trick; thereafter the winner of each trick leads to the next. Tricks won are placed face downwards in front of the winners, all in one pile. As the score will only depend upon penalty cards in the pile at the end there is no need to distinguish between individual tricks.

Skill

There are two separate skill stages: the choice of cards to pass on to the player on your right and the actual play.

Assume that with 3 players the 17 cards that North picks up are:-

♠ A K Q 8 7 4 3 2
♥ A 7 5 4 3 2
♦ A K Q
♣ -

What cards should he pass over to West? Nought out of ten for anyone who says other than the 3 Diamonds! Why? Well, consider the play and the 3 cards North is likely to receive. The more tricks North wins the more probable it is that he will end with penalty cards, including those which may have won the tricks.

The best cards North could hope to receive would be 3 more in the Heart suit; that would mean (having passed on all his Diamonds) that in the play he would not take even 1 trick. (His Hearts would be discarded, or the low ones played under opponents' higher ones; his top Spades would likewise be thrown away on the play of the other suits.)

Perhaps North will receive high cards in Clubs or Diamonds. Whichever he has to take into his hand, and if he is subsequently forced to take a trick, he can get off lead again by playing a tiny Heart or Spade. In spite of all those Hearts and the penalty cards in Spades he has in fact got a superb hand.

To summarise the lessons in discarding:

1. Do not be afraid of a long Heart suit, provided there is little danger you will find yourself unable to avoid winning Heart tricks.
2. Do not be afraid of a long Spade suit which includes one or more of the penalty cards, again provided you are able to avoid winning the penalty cards in tricks.
3. Look for the possibility of shortening a suit so that when opponents play that suit you will be able to discard the penalty cards.

Skill in the play of the cards comes down to some memory,

some maths, and some common sense. It is essential to try to remember the cards that have been played . . . it also helps to remember what cards you gave to the player on your right! If you can carry out that great feat you should also be able to calculate how many cards your opponents have between them in the suits . . . and, if one opponent discards, you should be able to "know" the specific cards the other opponent has in that suit. The cards that your opponents play should also give you many clues regarding the remaining cards they hold, just as the cards passed to you at the beginning should provide clues as to the sort of hand the player on your left started with.

As in all Whist games, all that is needed is practice.

10

Piquet

Piquet must have originated in France. Despite being only for two players it is quite complex but is a very good game.

Object

The game is played in 6 "parties" each of which has 6 deals. The object is to become the overall winner by scoring as many points as possible in each separate partie. There are two stages in each deal, or hand: a "declaration" and the play of the cards.

The Pack

Aces rank high and all cards below the 7 in each suit are removed, so the pack used is one of 32 cards only.

The Preliminaries

The normal cut for deal takes place. In theory the player cutting the higher card has the option of dealing or requesting his opponent to deal; in practice he will, or should, elect to deal. In the terminology of the game, dealer is known as the "*Younger Hand*", and his opponent as "*Elder Hand*". The Younger Hand deals 12 cards to each player, face down, in a sequence previously agreed of either 3 at a time or 2, 3, 2, 3, and 2. The remaining 8 cards are placed face down in a stack between the players.

After the deal the Elder Hand selects up to 5 of his cards to place face down in front of him. He then takes that number of cards from the stack. The rules lay down that he must "discard" and exchange at least one card in this way. The Younger Hand may now place some cards in front of himself, however he does not have to discard and exchange any of his cards if he prefers not to.

Younger Hand can discard and exchange in this way up to the total number of cards left in the stack by Elder Hand. That could be up to 7 cards if Elder Hand only exchanged the minimum one card.

Both players have thus had the opportunity to gamble that they may pick up better cards.

The cards each player discards remain face down in front of him for the rest of the hand; he may consult them from time to time, but they do not figure in the subsequent proceedings that will soon be explained.

When you understand the scoring elements and the play you will be in a position to decide which cards are usually best discarded and exchanged.

Elder Hand now "declares" his hand with regard to any or all of the 5 categories of declaration explained below. He follows by leading his first card. Younger Hand then makes his declarations similarly, before playing his first card to the first trick.

Declarations

Piquet has a language of its own which must be used. Like "Elder Hand" and "Younger Hand" the terms may seem strange at first. Each player makes his separate potential scoring declarations using the language:

1. "*Point of . . .*". Elder Hand reveals the number of cards he has in his longest suit. Younger Hand may reply with (1) "[It's] Good" – meaning that he does *not* have a suit with as many cards in it as Elder Hand's suit, or, (2) "Not Good" – meaning that when it becomes his turn to make a declaration he will be declaring a suit longer than that held by Elder Hand. If (3) Younger Hand has the same number of cards in his longest suit he replies to Elder Hand's declaration by stating the number of "pips" in his own, equal length suit. For this purpose an Ace counts 11 pips, the King, Queen and Jack count 10 pips each. Cards below the Jack do not have "pips".

141

If there turns out to be equality in length of suit *and* the number of pips neither player scores.

This first statement made by Elder Hand constitutes his "Point" declaration. In effect it is a scoring claim which, if accepted as "Good" will be worth one point for each of the cards held in the suit. For example:-

Elder Hand has A K 9 8 7 in his longest suit; he says "Point of 5". If Younger Hand does not have a suit containing 5 cards he says "Good" and Elder Hand will earn 5 points. If Younger Hand has more cards in his longest suit he simply says "Not Good".

If Younger Hand has the same number of cards with, say, K Q J 9 7, he will reply to Elder Hand's declaration by saying "30 pips". Younger Hand will later earn the 5 points for the 5 card suit because his K, Q, J out-pips Elder Hand's A and K. If he is out-pipped Elder Hand says "Good" but if he has more pips (for example the Queen instead of the 9 – 31 pips) he will say "No Good. I have 31 [pips]".

Elder Hand now continues with any one or more of the potential scoring declarations from 2 – 5 below (in the order shown). So far as 2 and 3 are concerned Younger Hand's replies continue in Piquet language e.g. "Good" or "Not Good".

2. *Sequences*. Any sequence of 3 or more cards in a suit may also score points on the following scale:-

3 cards in a sequence	...	3 points
4 cards	...	4 points
5 cards	...	15 points
6 cards	...	16 points
7 cards	...	17 points
8 cards	...	18 points

If a player has more than one sequence he can score points for each, but the player who will earn those points is the one who proves to have a higher, or in the absence of a higher one, the longest sequence. If their best sequences are of the same length the one with the highest card is the one that decides the issue; if such longest sequences are both equal in length and in their highest card, then neither player scores for any sequence.

To declare a sequence the player says "Sequence of...", starting the number of cards and, if requested, the highest card in the sequence.

3. *"Threes and Fours"* Should you hold 3 or all 4 of the Aces, Kings, Queens, Jacks, or Tens, having 3 of a kind is worth 3 points; having all four of a kind is worth 14 points. A player with more than one such group can score points for each group, but "Threes" are out-ranked by "Fours" and equality is decided by the size of the card in the group. For example if both have 4 of a kind the scorer will be the player whose group has the higher value cards. A player could have 1 group of 4 and 2 groups of 3 and find himself earning no points because his opponent had 1 group of 4 only, but with higher value cards, e.g. Kings against Jacks.

To declare a three or a four the player announces for example, "three ... (Aces, Jacks, or whatever)".

4. *"Carte Blanche"* If a player has a hand without any King, Queen, or Jack, he can claim 10 points for Carte Blanche. He must prove it immediately by letting his opponent see his cards one at a time face upwards on the table.

5. *"Repique"* If either player scores 30 or more points as a result of declarations, and his opponent scores no points, the player with the 30 or more can claim an extra 60 points at the end of the play of the hand ... unless his opponent has claimed and proven Carte Blanche.

As has been noted – when Elder Hand completes his declarations he plays his first card. Younger Hand then makes any further declarations he may have before playing his first card. If either player neglects to make his declarations or claims at the stipulated times (including Repique at the end) he forfeits his right to their scoring value.

143

Example Declarations

North becomes Younger Hand on the cut. South is therefore Elder Hand. The 12 cards they have in their hands are:-

South	♠ A K 10 8 7	North	♠ J
(Elder)	♥ 10 9 8 7	(Younger)	♥ Q J
	♦ 10		♦ K Q J 9 8 7
	♣ 10 8		♣ A K Q

As Elder Hand it will be for South to declare first:-

South:	"Point of 5."
North:	"Not good."
South:	"Sequence of 4 to a 10."
North:	"Good."
South:	"I also have 4 Tens."
North:	"Good."
South:	"18 points. 4 for the sequence and 14 for the Tens."

South has a total so far of 18 points and, as Elder Hand, leads the first card to the play. It is now North's turn to declare. His sequences have been out-ranked as have his two Threes, so he simply declares his winning "point of 6", scoring six points.

The Play

Normal Whist rules apply to the play. (Chapter 3 will refresh your memory on that if required.) There is no trump suit and no suit out-ranks another. Players must follow suit if they can but can choose whether or not to win a trick by playing a higher card. During the play either player may glance at the cards he discarded, which should still be face down in front of him.

Points Earned During the Play

1. Automatically by Elder Hand for the original lead (as under 3 below).. 1
2. For winning a trick to which your opponent led 1

3. For leading a card to a trick 1
4. For winning the last trick, irrespective of who led 1
5. For winning 7 up to 11 tricks in all 10
6. For winning all 12 tricks 40

"Pique"

In addition to the above if Younger Hand scores zero on declarations (except as below) Elder Hand can score an extra 30 points for "Pique" provided "Repique" was not claimed earlier by him, and provided his total score from declarations and play together exceeds 30 points. If Younger Hand failed to score points just because of equality in Point or Sequence claims the claim of "Pique" cannot be made.

At the end of the hand the points scored to date in the declarations and play and following the play are all recorded. The deal then passes across the table.

Final Scoring

A partie is scored over 6 deals. At the end of those deals the totals up to that point are compared; if both players have scored over 100 points the player with the higher score earns 100 points plus the difference between the two scores, e.g. if North has 132 and South has 105 – North scores 127.

If one or both players fail to get to 100 by the end of a partie the player with the higher score wins by 100 plus the combined points earned by both players, e.g. – North has managed to get 350 and South has only 84; North scores 100 plus 350 and plus 84, i.e. 534 points.

6 Parties are played and the individual partie scores, as calculated above, are then totalled to see who is the winner.

Skill in the Exchanges

The object here must be to improve one's hand so that the maximum possible points can be earned in the 2 stages of a deal – the declaration and the play. In the latter the most that could be earned by Elder Hand would be 53 points. He could lead to all 12 tricks; winning all the way. He would earn a point for leading to each trick, plus an extra point for the last trick, and 40 points for winning all 12.

The maximum number of points he can have in the declaration is 100. His hand might be:-

♠ A K Q J 10 9 8 7
♥ A K
♦ A
♣ A

He would score 8 "points" for the 8 Spades; 18 points for the sequence of 8 in Spades; 14 points for the 4 Aces, and 60 points for the inevitable "Repique", provided Younger Hand was unable to prove "Carte Blanche".

In fact as Elder Hand would win the maximum points available in the play with the hand illustrated above he would finish with a total of 153 to Nil on that deal.

The odds against such a hand being picked up must be many millions to one but it should help to illustrate that the object when selecting cards to discard and exchange is to avoid discarding those that might later on earn points. For example, if Elder Hand's first 12 cards were:-

♠ K 10 9 8
♥ A 10 9 8
♦ 10 7
♣ A J

he should avoid discarding a Spade or a Heart; should retain his 3 Tens; and should give himself the maximum possibility of adding to his Spade or Heart holdings while at the same time keeping as much trick taking capability as possible. The best cards to discard and exchange would appear to be the 7 of Diamonds and the Jack of Clubs.

Imagine that as a result of making those discards he finds that he has taken the Jack and 7 of Spades from the stack. His hand will now be:-

♠ K J 10 9 8 7
♥ A 10 9 8
♦ 10
♣ A

146

If his Spade suit now turns out to be longer than any suit held by his opponent, or, if it is of equal length but with a higher pip count, it will be worth 6 points. If the sequence headed by the Jack ♠ is the best sequence it will be worth another 15 points, and his sequence of 3 Hearts will then bring in another 3. If his 3 Tens are the only Three or Four between the two hands they will be adding a further 3 points. That means 27 points in the declaration stage alone, and, if he is fortunate and finds Younger Hand has neither of the other two Spades or only has the Queen on its own, he is bound to make at least 8 tricks in the play. In short – an excellent hand.

Skill in the Play

With only 32 cards in the game; with knowledge of the cards which you exchanged; and with some foreknowledge of your opponent's cards because of the declarations, it is not too difficult to build up in one's mind the cards that your opponent is likely to hold, or as a result of failing to make relevant declarations, is unlikely to hold.

Your play has to be based on the assessment you build up of your opponent's hand and, as it proceeds, on remembering what cards have been played. The further play proceeds, as in all Whist games, the clearer the picture becomes of the remaining cards.

There is plenty of room for skill on the very simple bases of memory and common sense. Chapters 2 and 3 should prove useful on these counts in addition to the specific tips here.

11

Five Hundred

This is a 3 handed game which probably evolved from Clobbiosh. There are also some Bridge elements in it, so it is possible that it owes a bit to both games. (They can be found in Chapters 7 and 5.)

Object
The object of the game is to reach 500 points before either of the other 2 players. If, in the course of the same hand two players reach 500 and one is the "Declarer" (the winner of the Auction – see below), the latter is the winner. If neither of the two is the Declarer the winner is the player with the higher score, and if both have equal top scores the loser is the one who at some time or another had to catch up. As there will always be more than one hand that will be bound to have happened. If both scored the same throughout the game it would be a draw but it never happens!

The Pack
A pack of 33 cards is used – the 32 cards from the 7 upwards in each suit, plus a Joker. If you threw the Jokers away when you first opened the pack then the 2 of Clubs will do instead.

Dealing
After a normal Whist type cut for deal (Chapters 1 and 3) the cards are shuffled and dealt 3 at a time to each player in turn, face down, until each player has 9, followed by 1 each to make 10. The remaining 3 cards are dealt, each separately

face-upwards, into the middle of the table. These cards are known as the "Widow".

An "Auction" follows.

The Auction

As in Bridge the suits have a power ranking which includes No Trumps but, contrary to Bridge, the weakest suit is Spades. The pecking order is Spades the weakest, then Clubs, followed by Diamonds, Hearts and No Trumps.

The player to the left of the dealer makes the first bid. Bids start at 6, meaning an undertaking to make 6 tricks provided the suit specified is trumps, and go up to 10, i.e. 10 tricks. For example, if North bids 6 Spades he is offering to contract to make 6 tricks provided Spades are trumps. Once a player says "Pass" in the Auction he forfeits the right to make any further bid, but a player who has made a positive bid can bid again if his earlier bid is out-ranked. A typical Auction between North, East and South (West is baby-sitting and can't play . . .) might proceed after South has dealt:-

N	E	S
6 ♠	6 ♥	7 ♦
Pass	7 ♥	8 ♦
Pass*	Pass	

* North could not bid again even if he wanted to, having passed in the second round. Note that, as in Bridge, the call in the higher ranking suit (Hearts) of the same number of tricks out-bids the call in the lower ranking suit (Spades), whereas to out-bid Hearts in Diamonds it was necessary to contract to make an extra trick.

The contract is now 8 Diamonds to be played by South. As Declarer (winner of the Auction) he will lead to the first trick but before he does so he takes all 3 cards of the Widow into his hand and discards 3 cards, face down. In choosing his discards he has the right to throw away any or all of the cards he has gained from the Widow.

In the event of all 3 players passing on the first (and therefore only) round of bidding the hand is played in No Trumps and the player to the dealer's left leads to the first trick.

At the end of each hand the player to the left of the dealer of that hand, deals for the next hand.

Deciding to Make a Bid

When deciding whether or not you are able to make a bid you will need to know two things – (1) the special ranking order of the cards in 500, which will help you to judge the number of tricks you hope to be able to make, and (2) the scoring values of each of the contracts.

Ranking of the Cards

In the play of the cards there is a special ranking order in a trump suit which introduces two extra trump cards. The Joker becomes the highest trump followed by the trump suit Jack; this is followed by the second extra trump, the Jack of the other suit of the same colour. Thereafter the cards rank in their normal Whist sequence. For example, in Diamonds the cards rank –

Highest card . . . the Joker; next highest . . . the Jack of Diamonds; next . . . the Jack of Hearts, then Ace of Diamonds, King of Diamonds, Queen, 10, 9, 8, 7. The Jacks are known respectively as the *"Right Bower"* (the Jack of the actual trump suit) and the *"Left Bower"* (the Jack of the other suit of the same colour).

In No Trumps the cards rank in their normal Whist order, Ace, then King, etc., down to 7. However any player with the Joker (you don't also have to be declarer) can designate it at any time as the highest card in whichever suit he chooses, unless he has already failed to follow a card led in that suit. He does not have to play it as his first card in that suit unless he wishes to. He can select the best time.

Scoring Values

1. The values of contracts bid and made, without bonuses, are:-

Suit	*Number of tricks in contract*				
	6	**7**	**8**	**9**	**10**
Spades	40	140	240	340	440
Clubs	60	160	260	360	460
Diamonds	80	180	280	380	480
Hearts	100	200	300	400	500
No Trumps	120	220	320	420	520

2. Over-tricks do not score extra points but a player who wins all ten tricks scores 250 points or the value of the contract, whichever is the higher.
3. A player who fails to make his contract takes the value of the contract he bid as a minus score.
4. Each trick won in the play by either of the two defenders is worth 10 points to him (not to the defending side as such).

Here is an example to illustrate the above:-

		North	**East**	**South**
Hand 1	North bids 8 Diamonds. East wins 2 tricks. South none.	280	20	
Hand 2	South bids 7 No Trumps. East wins 1 trick, North wins 3.	30	10	−220
Hand 3	East bids 7 Hearts. South and North win no tricks.		250*	
Scores to date:		310	280	−220

* East scores 250 because he made all 10 tricks.

Play of the Cards

The play follows the normal Whist rules, except that the Declarer leads to the first trick in his contract. As usual, each player must follow suit if he can; may discard a card of his choice or play a trump if he is unable to follow suit; can elect to win or refuse to win a trick by playing a higher or lower card as he chooses. The winner of each trick leads to the next.

Skill in the Auction

This is entirely a matter of valuation, although it may be influenced by the score at a given time. For example, suppose North has to make his decision on the following hand:-

His cards are –		the Widow has –		If he could win
♠	A Q J	♠	–	the auction in Clubs
♥	K Q	♥	–	he would have, with
♦	9 8	♦	7	the Widow –
♣	K Q 10	♣	J	♠ A Q
			The Joker	♥ K Q
				♦ –
				♣ Joker, J J (♠)
				K Q 10

(i.e. if he takes the Widow he will discard the 9, 8 and 7 of Diamonds).

If it is the first hand of the game he might assume that he would make 6 tricks in Clubs, 1 in Spades and 1 in Hearts, and so can safely bid 8 Clubs. If he is very lucky and the King of Spades falls under the Ace, or alternatively whoever has it is forced to play it before he plays his Ace, then the Queen will provide trick 9. But that trick will not score points as an overtrick. That's O.K. in a first hand. However, if he already has 140 points but less than 240 points, then if either of the other players are standing on a score of 490 points towards the end of the game and a 9 Club contract would enable him to top 500 points himself if he made it, he should call 9 Clubs.

Skill in the Play

As Declarer, a player knows precisely what cards his opponents hold although he doesn't know how they are distributed. The Auction may have given him clues either by what the other players bid, or by what they failed to bid. If his contract appears to be unbeatable, regardless of the distribution, he must play as safely as possible and try to make sure of winning enough tricks to make his contract. If his contract seems to be very risky, e.g. as in the suggested 9 trick contract above, he must play as though the cards were distributed in his favour. He would try to keep his Spades until the end, hoping that the opponents would play "into" his Ace and Queen. For example:-

East is to lead late in the game and only has Spades.

E	S	N
leads a small Spade.	? ♠	Q ♠ (or A ♠ if ? = K ♠)

North takes care to keep his Ace ready to despatch K ♠.

The defenders base their play on a number of factors: the bidding, the lack of bidding, the cards in the Widow before play started; and last but not least – the scores of each player to date.

The defenders are playing against the Declarer and against each other, and the tactics can be very interesting. Each defender scores 10 points for every trick he wins, and it will often happen that a defender will over-take a high card which was played by his "partner", even if by so doing it helps the Declarer. For example East has a minus score of 200, South a plus of 490, and North a plus of 460. East plays a Queen in a suit in which North has the Ace and a small card; South plays the King. East, so far as North can judge, probably has the Jack and if he is allowed to win a trick with it he will make his contract. North doesn't care at all if East should make his contract; what he is after is to stop South getting to 500 points, so he over-takes South's King and, if he has no certain tricks of his own to take will play the small card in the suit to enable East to win with the Jack.

Of course, if it is the Declarer who is near to winning the game it is in the interests of both defenders to co-operate as closely as possible in the defence. This they will do on the basis of the cards they hold and the cards they expect, or hope, that their "partner" will have.

So defence is highly tactical and can be very amusing . . . unless you happen to be the defender losing tricks to your "partner"!

12

Poker

Poker is a game with many variations and is primarily a gambling game. It can be played with as few as 2 people but is best with 5, 6 or 7. In many "schools" it is usual for the first dealer to nominate the version to be played for a round of deals. After all the players have dealt in such a round (the deal moves clockwise around the table after every hand – the cards being shuffled after each hand) the next dealer (to the left of whoever nominated before) will choose whether to continue with a fresh round of the same or switch to something different; it is his privilege to choose for the next round. However, whatever the version, the object is always the same.

Object
This is to win money as a result of having or being believed to have, a combination of cards which ranks higher than any combination held by a competing player. This statements holds good for all versions of the game, so we should have a look at the possible combinations first of all. They all consist of, or are held within, 5 cards.

Card Combinations

Starting with the highest:-
A Straight Flush . .   a run of 5 cards which are in the same suit; the highest straight flush would be one headed by an Ace (a "Royal Straight").

Four of a Kind .... 4 cards having the same value, e.g. 4 Aces. These are also ranked downwards from the Aces, e.g. 4 Aces beats 4 Jacks.

A Full House ..... 3 cards having the same value together with another 2 which are a pair, e.g. 3 Queens and 2 Fives. The 3 card holding decides the rank, thus Q Q Q J J loses to K K K 2 2 (known as a Full House King high).

A Flush .... 5 cards which are all in the same suit. If there are competing Flushes the issue is decided in favour of the one headed by the highest cards. E.g. A 8 7 6 5 is the winner over K Q 10 7 2 because of the Ace but it would lose to A 9 7 6 5.

A Straight .... a run of 5 cards which are not all in one suit. The highest card determines the winning such Straight.

Three of a Kind ... 3 cards having the same value. (7s will beat 6s regardless of suits, etc.)

Two Pairs .... 4 cards, in sets of 2, each set having the same value cards in it, e.g. two 10s and two 8s. The player with the highest set wins; if both of the highest sets are the same, the winner is the player with the next highest.

A Pair .... 2 cards having the same value (ignoring suits . . . higher pairs outrank lower brethren).

A hand without any combination may still be good enough to win as a result of its highest card or cards being higher than those in another hand. Aces are always ''high'', that is they are ranked above Kings.

At this point you may well be asking yourself ''Who wins if the hands are identical, for example if one player has a Straight headed by the Ace of Hearts and another has a Straight headed by the Ace of Diamonds; or if two players each have 2 10s and their other cards are also identical?'' The answer lies in the betting . . . in brief the winner will be the one who last raised the "pot" in that round of betting. Occasionally the pot may be shared but you'll see what I mean a little later on.

Poker Variations

This chapter can only investigate a modest number of different poker games, selected for their reliance on skill rather than on luck. However, once the essence of a typical game has been grasped the task of picking up how to play any of the huge choice of variations becomes easy. Even within a particular version of poker there can be divergence as to the "house rules" but each school defines such matters as and when necessary.

In order to illustrate the mechanics of all poker games therefore, here is an example of a popular version of 5 card "Stud". It is not to be taken as a definitive statement of the 5 card Stud rules in every particular for every school; however it does reflect all the basic Poker rules.

5 CARD STUD

Some definitions of the terms used (which apply to all the variations of Poker) will help:-

The **"Pot"**. The "Pot" is in the centre of the table. It is an area of the table into which the money to be won is placed. The term is also used to describe the total amount of money to be won . . . "there was £50 in the Pot", meaning £50 on the table waiting to be won. A school may decide on a maximum amount of money which can be in the pot at any time.

"Chips". The players use "chips" i.e. small coloured disks, instead of money. There is an agreed value of the chips for each colour and everyone buys a supply of chips before the start.

The **"Ante"**. Before any cards are dealt each player has to put his "Ante" of a previously agreed value of chips into the pot. You may know the expression "ante up", meaning to "put your money up first"; it derives from Poker.

The **"Stakes"**. Another word for "Bets"; a player may "bet" or "stake" his all. In many schools the house rules govern the minimum and maximum amounts that can be staked in an individual bet by any player.

"Check". A player who says "Check" wishes to forfeit his right to make an immediate bet but to retain an option to join in the betting before the next card is dealt.

"Go out". A player who "goes out" does so by returning his cards to the dealer and takes no further part in that hand.

Before the Main Betting

All 52 cards are used. They are shuffled and the dealer for the first round is decided on a high card cut. Matters of etiquette and so forth regarding the choice of dealer and shuffling will be found in Chapter 1.

The dealer gives each player in turn 2 cards face down. They are dealt one at a time in 2 rounds of dealing. He then gives each player in turn 1 card face upwards.

The players examine the 2 concealed cards they keep in front of them. The player with the highest card which has been dealt face up is now due to start the betting. In the event of equal highest cards the lucky player nearest to the dealer's left bets first. The face up cards remain on view throughout the game.

The Betting

There are usually three rounds of betting during which the stakes in the pot accumulate and unless all bar one of the players decide to go out before the start of the third round (in which case the remaining player takes the pot) the third round decides the ultimate winner of the pot.

The Betting – first round

Assume that a rule of the school is that the first bet must be exactly double the agreed individual ante that players will already have put into the pot. (This is a common rule but not an integral part of the game). The first player due to bet has 3 options:

1. He can "go out" by giving his cards back to the dealer, to be placed (the face down ones unseen by anyone else) at the bottom of the remainder of the pack.
2. He may say "check".

3. He may stake the amount required for a first bet, i.e. double the "ante" he had to put into the pot originally. (Although it is usual to require that the first bet be double the ante, it is quite common to vary that, for example to limit the first bet to the same ante amount.)

The betting now continues clockwise around the table.

If the first player goes out the next player inherits his 3 options. If the first player checks, the next player equally inherits all his options. However, once any player makes a bet the next and subsequent players are not allowed to check; their options are reduced to going out, or betting.

The second and subsequent players who do decide to bet, unless the rules of the school are to the contrary, must always bet the same as, or double the amount bet by the previous bettor.

Thus each succeeding player in the first round has the right, either to check if all still in who preceded him did so, or to equal or exactly double the last bet subject to any house limit on individual amounts bet at any one time. For example, if player 1 has bet 2 chips, and player 2 has bet 4 chips, player 3 will be able to bet 4 or 8 chips unless the house rules stipulate that no more than 4 chips can be bet in the first round. (The rules might also state that no player can bet more than a total of "x" number of chips within a round of betting.) Remember, succeeding players can go out if they wish, but cannot check if a previous player has made a bet.

When the last player in the first round has spoken, both those who checked and those who may have bet less than a later higher bet, can opt to put in the amount required to make their stake equal to the highest bet made if they wish to stay in the game; or they can give up their cards, losing the money in the pot they have put in up to that time. They cannot increase their bet beyond the amount of the previous highest bet in this first round. Should all players decide to check, the game moves straight on to the second round of betting for which see further on.

Here is an example of the first round of betting in a game between 5 players (it could have been 2 or more; it just happened to be 5 but this was nothing to do with the name of this version of Poker.) The ante was 1 chip:-

Players	1	2	3	4	(dealer) 5
Face-up cards	2 ♣	8 ♥	4 ♦	Q ♠	Q ♥
First Round Bets				Check	Check
	Out	Bet 2	Bet 4	Bet 4	Out
		Bet 2			

Player 4 was the first to say anything, being the first player on the dealer's left with the equal highest card – a Queen. Player 2 made the first bet of double the ante and subsequently increased his bet to match the amounts bet by players 3 and 4. Players 1 and 5 will take no further part.

The Betting – second round

The dealer now deals another card face up to those players still remaining in. Another round of betting takes place, led by the player whose two face up cards taken together are the best.

The first bettor in the second round is no longer obliged to double the ante. However, apart from that the same rules apply to the betting on the second round as apply to the betting on the first round, with two exceptions:

1. If a player makes a bet which gets doubled he may, when it comes to deciding if he is going to stay in, increase his initial bet in the round by an amount which more than equals the opposing bet by any amount he chooses within the permitted maximum bet. The minimum to stay in would be to equal the opposing bet.
2. If a player does go for an additional increase then the other players have to match that increase or go out; but they are not permitted to increase the bet still further.

In the unlikely event of all players checking, the third round of betting begins forthwith.

To continue with the example above, players 1 and 5 having dropped out during the first round of betting:-

Players	2	3	4
First face-up cards	8 ♥	4 ♦	Q ♠
Second face-up cards	7 ♠	4 ♣	2 ♠
Second Bets		Bet 2*	Bet 2
	Bet 4	Bet 4	Bet 4
	Bet 2		

* Note that this bet of 2 was simply the amount Player 3 decided to bet; as explained above there is no rule to say how much he *must* bet as the opening bettor in the second round. If he had wished to he could have said "check". Notice also why he starts the 2nd round betting – he only had a lowly pair on display but no-one else had anything better on view. When Player 3 subsequently had to put more chips into the pot to match Player 2 he took the opportunity to increase his second round betting to 6; Players 4 and 2 persevered and made their bets up to the required amount. Everybody had stayed in to the tune of a total stake of 11 each.

The Betting – third round
The dealer deals a fifth and last card to each player, again face up. The stage is set for the climax of the hand.

Assuming that the player to bet first has not given up in disgust on seeing his last card, he may check or bet as before. In the event of all of the other players also checking in this the last round, each reveals his concealed cards and the one with the best 5 takes the pot. If any of the hands revealed are exactly equal the players concerned share the pot.

Should any player bet, then, if the other players all give in, the sole bettor takes the pot. The winning player in such a case does not have to show his cards; the others believed they were good enough to win without even seeing them and if they were wrong in that belief they need never know!

Indeed it is even considered to be bad etiquette for a winning player in such a case to show his cards. It is also not very sensible . . . a player may have fooled his opponents with a perfect "poker face" – revealing nothing about his thoughts – and does not have to reveal his trickery just to show how clever he was. Next time the opponents may call his bluff.

"Call"

If any of the other players decide just to match the highest bet they must put their chips into the pot and say "Call". When everyone has had an opportunity to do this (and assuming no-one raises) all the players then show their cards and the one with the best 5 takes the pot. If there are hands which are exactly equal and the player who was "called" has one of those hands he wins and takes the pot; otherwise the pot is shared between the players with the winning hands.

Thus whenever a player raises a prior bet in the third and last round the other players who previously bet less have the right in turn to give up and go out, or to match and "call", or to increase.

If there are more than 2 players still in the game a situation could arise as follows:-"A" bets 4; "B" also bets 4 and says "call"; "C" bets 6. To stay in the game both "A" and "B" must increase their bets by at least 2. "C" 's raising of the stakes has superseded "B" 's call. "A" or "B" can match or call, or attempt to grab the initiative by increasing.

In theory players could keep increasing prior bets for ever; in practice they won't do that, either because the rules of the school don't permit it, or because nobody is that rich. That school rules always allow other players to raise or call the highest bettor is fundamental; it is one of the factors that distinguishes Poker as a *gambling* game.

To end the example above – third round:

Players	2	3	4
First face-up cards	8 ♥	4 ♦	Q ♠
Second face-up cards	7 ♠	4 ♣	2 ♠
First Bets	Bet 4	Bet 4	Bet 4
Second Bets	Bet 6	Bet 6	Bet 6
Third face-up card	7 ♦	6 ♠	Q ♦
Third Bets			Check
	Bet 2	Bet 4	Bet 6
	Go out	2 & Call	

Players 3 and 4 now show their cards and the one with the best combination(s) wins all the money in the pot.

161

Assume it is player number 3 who takes the pot because one of his concealed cards is another 4, whereas the only other useful card number 4 had was another 2 . . . player number 3 winning by 3 of a kind against 2 pairs. As each player started with an ante of 1 chip the total pot is worth 49 chips, of which player number 3 put in 17, so he has won 32.

Skill

If we examine the cards that were dealt, the possibilities of each hand at the various points, and the decisions each player took, we can begin to understand some of the elements of skill that come into Poker.

Take *Player number 1* first. He took the decision to opt out whilst only 1 card (the 2 ♣) had been dealt to him face up. The inference is that his other 2 cards were low in relation to the 2 Queens he could see in front of two of the other players and that he had no cards which promised a strong possible combination.

Let's follow *Player number 2*. After 2 checks and an "out" of which he took mental note, he made the initial first round bet, and thought enough of the possibilities of his hand to increase his bet of 2 to a bet of 4 when number 3 bet higher and number 4 had also matched 3. On the second round, after adding 7 ♠ to his 8 ♥ he bet 4 with his first bet; this increased his total stake by that stage to 9. When number 3 increased it further he matched 3's increase by bringing his own total stake up to that point to the same level (11). What cards might 2 have had?

To bet as he did on the first round should have indicated at least a pair, or chances of a Straight. There are several ways that the 7 ♠ could have improved his hand for the second round of betting, depending on what his concealed cards were.

1. They might have been a 9 and a 10 – now improving his chances of a Straight.
2. Perhaps they were a 7 and an 8 – now giving him 2 pairs.
3. They might have been two 7s – now giving him 3 of a kind.

Any of those combinations would have encouraged him to bet as he did . . . or he might have been bluffing. Betting as he did

162

might lead the other players into thinking that he could have such cards, even if he didn't!

On the next round he received another 7 and bet 2. That was a low bet at that stage of the game and could have been made for one of 2 reasons: (1) he now had what he hoped would prove to be the winning hand (a Full House 7 high, or even four 7s) and, by his low bet, was trying to tempt the other players into betting higher, or, (2) his prior betting had been based on the hope of getting a Straight and he was now hoping that the other players would not call his bluff.

His final surrender could have been because he had been bluffing with an unsuccessful Straight, or because, although his cards were good, he had suffered an attack of pessimism and thought (wrongly if that were the case) that they would not out-rank those held by one or both of the other players.

Player number 3 seems to have played a simple game. The bet on the first round, i.e. the increase he made to the stake, looks like a bet being made with a promising hand. The possibility was that at that stage he already had a pair to go with the 4 that was on the table in view. The next card he received, the 4 ♣, should have improved his hand further, but he was quite modest with his betting at the beginning of the 2nd round. At that stage a high bet might have discouraged the other players and made them decide to opt out. Whereas his modest initial bet gently kept the stakes moving upwards.

The bets and the call that player 3 made on the last round were obviously justified. No player in his right senses, who either actually had a good hand, or had succeeded in giving his opponents the impression that he had a good hand, would fail to make the first of them after the check and small bet from the other two remaining players. Betting would at the very least serve to continue the impression that he had a good hand. It was in his interests to try to get the pot increased, but not by too large an amount in case he lost. So he had to bet.

His final bet and call matched his hand – which was not good enough to prompt him to raise the stakes still further but was good enough to equal player 4's bet and force the comparison of the 2 hands.

Knowing now that *player 4* had a 2 as the best of his concealed cards it is easy to see that his second round bets were on the optimistic side because one 2 (the original face up card of player 1) was not available to improve his hand, and at the time player 3 had better cards face up on the table. His gamble in the third round of betting had a certain element of bluff in it but gave him a last chance of winning if players 2 and 3 also happened to be bluffing.

The above displays three out of the four main elements of skill in Poker, i.e. common sense, logical deduction, and a bit of amateur psychology . . . who is bluffing who, and when? The other major element of skill is an appreciation of the odds against receiving any given card at any time. However, in the course of going into them in a little depth we can take the opportunity to look at another Poker variation where they are as important as they are in 5 Card Stud – "Draw" Poker.

DRAW POKER

In this (as in all other versions) the shuffle and deal etiquette is unchanged. However, rather as the name of the game implies, no cards are faced-up and each player's hand remains concealed throughout.

The players each receive 5 cards dealt one at a time face down. A round of betting takes place as in the first round of Stud, including checking, betting or going out. (See above, page 157 if you need to check these rules.) Then each player in turn discards up to 4 cards face down into the centre of the table and receives in replacement an equal number from the remainder of the pack. (Players are free incidentally, to decide that their first 5 cards are so bad that they might just as well go out without joining in the first round of betting and then exchanging cards.) All discards stay on the table face down until the end of that game.

It is not mandatory to make any discards; a player may decide to stay with the 5 cards he received originally. In fact any player who bets with 5 and then discards as many as 4 is probably a candidate for a medical examination but the right exists!

A second, and final session of betting then ensues, which can be quite protracted with some participants dropping out as the stakes rise.

Clearly the mathematics of the odds are very important in deciding which cards to replace and which to retain and we can now examine some of the most significant odds.

The Odds

It is not my purpose (even if I could!) to teach anybody to be a mathematician; the methods of calculating the odds accurately depend upon mathematical formulae which no-one has time to apply during a game. Fortunately, the popularity of the game (particularly in the USA) is such that most of the key statistics have been published, and any player who aspires to expertise in the game can easily find out the really important figures to learn by heart.

It is interesting to note (but not to learn by heart!) that the ranking order of the combinations is a reflection of the statistical frequency of such combinations. The chances of five specific cards being dealt to (or drawn by) one of 5 players all receiving cards are just under 2,600,000 to 1 against. If the cards were shuffled and dealt 2,600,000 times, each time to 5 hands, there would be approximately:-

4	Royal Straight Flushes
36	Straight Flushes
600	Four of a Kind
3700	Full Houses
5100	Flushes
10200	Straights
54900	Three of a Kind
123500	Two Pair
1098200	Pairs

So, for example, if a player is lucky enough to have a Straight Flush headed by a King the odds against any other player being able to beat him on that hand are astronomical. Such a player would have to have a Royal Straight Flush; a hand which comes only 4 times in 2,600,000.

The most important approximate figures are those setting out the odds against receiving specific cards in a draw, or of receiving them dealt in Stud, assuming none of the cards are face up on the table (in Stud). In a game for 5 players (and the relationship between the figures is the same irrespective of the number of players) the cards that a player is most likely to be optimistic with, i.e. that he hopes may prove to become the winning hand if they are improved upon in a draw or by later cards dealt in Stud, are a Pair; Two Pairs; Three of a Kind; a potential Straight; a potential Flush. The simple odds are:-

1. With a Pair, the chances of improving to 3 of a kind by drawing or being dealt 3 cards are 8 to 1 against.
2. With 3 of a kind the chances against drawing a Pair in 2 cards to complete a Full House are 15½ to 1 against.
3. With a Straight needing 1 card at either end the chances of receiving that card are 5 to 1 against.
4. With a Straight that can only be completed in the middle (an "inside straight") or by a card at one end the chances are 11 to 1 against.
5. With 4 cards of the same suit, needing 1 to complete a Flush, the chances are 4½ to 1 against. (With 3 cards needing 2 the chances are 23 to 1 against.)

Other factors can be extrapolated from the above without the aid of higher mathematics, for example trying to improve a Pair by drawing 3 cards, or to improve Three of a Kind by drawing 2 cards, each has a greater variety of chance than an attempt to fill an inside Straight by drawing one card.

Even the simple figures above show that, for example, with A A Q J 10 the chances of drawing a third Ace are better than drawing a King. (8 to 1 against as opposed to 11 to 1 against.) Drawing 3 cards to the two Aces gives the added chance that the 3 received will include a pair, thus improving the hand to 2 Pairs or even 4 Aces! Perhaps Three of a Kind will be drawn, improving the hand to a Full House.

I must stress that if you like Poker enough to want to play it well you should learn these simple odds against receiving specific cards. This should be no more difficult for you than learning all the rules of the game.

Notice that odds operate for or against *all* the players, so they must be taken into account in a comparative sense, i.e. "are my chances of improving my hand better than the chances the opposition have of improving the hands I think they may have?"

The discards made by opponents in Draw Poker also have to be carefully observed. If a player discards only 2 cards it is correct to assume, until convinced otherwise, that he is playing with the odds and that his remaining cards are Three of a Kind. If a player only discards 1 he could have a variety of hands: 2 Pairs, a potential Flush, or Straight or better. He might even have Four of a Kind, so if he stays in the betting for long you should be very cautious . . . unless of course it's Bert, who always bluffs like mad . . . but then, he could have it for once. Beware!

The odds have to be taken into account in judging how far one should go in betting against the known or assumed cards held by the other players. In theory the *size* of the pot should never come into a player's reckoning. One of the sayings Poker has given to our everyday speech is "if you can't stand the heat stay out of the kitchen!" In other words if you can't afford to bet you should not be playing; alternatively, if you are mesmerised by all the lovely money waiting to be won . . . you will probably lose! Those who play with the odds will beat you every time.

OTHER VARIATIONS

There are many other variations some of which I shall comment on very briefly.

7 Card Stud: this is a variation of 5 Card Stud (described earlier) in the course of which 7 cards each are dealt but 2 discards must be made. It is played identically up to the dealing of the fifth card to everyone still in play. Having received their fifth cards each player must discard one and the dealer distributes a replacement. If the discard is one of the concealed cards the replacement is concealed; if it is the faced-up card the replacement is faced-up. A second discard is made by all and a second replacement given; when that card is received each player has his final 5, having been dealt 7 in all. Betting only takes place after the first 3 cards have been received, after the fourth card has been received, and following the 2 exchanges.

Misère Pots: probably borrowed from Solo (see Chapter 4), this is a reverse of normal Poker in as much as the object is to have the worst hand, for example 2 4 5 6 7 not in the same suit.

Jokers wild: in this variation a Joker, or possibly more than 1, is used in addition to the 52 card pack, and can be taken by the player receiving it to represent any card he nominates.

Deuces wild: similar to Jokers wild but with all 4 Twos as "wild" cards.

Finally, a number of versions are based on the dealing of 1 or 2 cards into the middle of the table, face up, and the players betting on the best 3 out of their own 5 cards which have been dealt face down, together with the two faced up cards in the centre.

Yes, there is a lot of luck in Poker but you will find that some players win much more frequently than others, and if you analyse the reasons why, you will find that they are good at knowing when to bet, when to give up, and how to convince their opponents that they have the cards they haven't got! If they happen to be *very good* at knowing what to do and when, the best advice I can give you is to watch them but never play against them unless you feel like becoming their favourite charity . . . i.e. the one they get their money from.

13

Brag

Brag is reputed to be an ancestor of Poker, the subject of Chapter 12. In theory any number from 2 upwards can play but it is most enjoyable with 5 or 6 players. It has many similarities to Poker, not least of which is the number of variations. However, as in Poker, the object is always the same. If you are not familiar with Poker you will understand Brag better if you read Chapter 12 first.

Object
The object is to win the stakes by having or being believed to have a superior combination of cards.

The Pack, Pot and Deal
The complete pack of 52 cards is used without Jokers. The procedure for cutting for deal, shuffling and cutting the cards prior to the deal are the same as in Whist (see Chapter 1).

Before the deal the dealer places the opening bet into the "pot" (as in Poker – a place is reserved in the centre of the table into which money – or chips in lieu – can be put). He can bet any amount up to a limit agreed by the players. The other players do not have to bet yet; apart from the mandatory dealer's bet there is no general "Ante" as in Poker.

Three cards are dealt clockwise face down (one at a time in 3 rounds) to each of the players.

The other players now bet, basing their bets on the card combinations they have.

Card Combinations

In Brag the Ace of Diamonds, the Jack of Clubs, and the 9 of Diamonds are known as "Braggers". A player who holds one of the Braggers can use it either with its normal meaning or as a "Wild" card to represent any other card he chooses. *If a player has 2 of the Braggers he is only allowed to use one as a Wild card*. For example with the A ♦, Q ♥, and Q ♣ a player (as you will see below) would use the A ♦ as a third Queen, but with the A ♦, Q ♥, and 9 ♦ he would not be permitted to use 2 Braggers and would elect to nominate the 9 ♦ as an extra Ace, using the A ♦ as a normal card.

In order of rank, i.e. ability to win, with the highest first, the combinations are:-

Three Natural Aces	any 3 of the 4 Aces, one of which could be the Ace of Diamonds
Three Aces	2 Aces (one of which could be the Ace of Diamonds) together with one of the other 2 Braggers
Three Natural Kings . . .	3 of the 4 Kings
Three Kings	2 Kings and a Bragger

and so on down to Three Deuces. A complete list includes "Three Natural Jacks", one of which could be the Jack of Clubs; "Three Jacks" (one of two of which could be the Jack of Clubs) together with one of the other Braggers, "Three Natural Nines" and "Three Nines" with the Bragger Nine being used as a natural card.

From combinations of "Three" the ranking goes to Natural Pairs, i.e. 2 cards of the same rank, followed by Pairs, 2 cards one of which is a Bragger. If no-one has a combination the winning hand is that which has the highest ranked card within it. If 2 or more players have the same high card the decision depends on their next highest, and so on. If 2 or more players have winning hands with exact equality (the suits are irrelevant) they share the pot.

The Betting

Starting with the player to the left of the dealer, betting progresses round and round in a clockwise manner, including the dealer, again and again perhaps, until no player is prepared to raise the stakes higher – or to the point that an agreed limit has been reached. Each player can either give up (return his cards face down to the dealer), match the previous highest bet, or bet an amount greater than the previous highest bet. If all the players who have stayed in the game eventually bet the same amount the cards are turned face up and the holder of the best hand wins the pot or it is shared in the case of equality. If one player bets an amount which the other players are unwilling to match then they will have given up, and he wins.

Other Versions

The most popular variation is **Three Stake Brag**. In this all players are required to bet on their first card. Betting can continue round with the stakes being raised till no-one wants to go further, as in the betting stage described above. When the bets are all in, the cards are turned face up and the holder of the best card takes the first pot. If 2 or more players have the same card (it being the highest) they share the pot. In this round Braggers have their normal card meaning.

Players now leave their first card in view in front of them. Another round of betting follows dealing the second card each; again the new cards are faced up after the betting and the winner, who takes the second card stake money, is determined by the best Pair combination held according to the ranking given above. This time Braggers can be used just as laid down for ordinary Brag. If no player has a Pair the issue is decided on high cards, or shared as above.

Again the faced up cards remain on display and the final round of betting takes place after a third card each has been dealt. Instead of looking for the best combination of 3 cards as in the ordinary game, in Three Stake Brag the winning hand in the third round is that which has a total card value nearest (above or below) to 31. In calculating the total value of the cards an Ace is worth 11 points and the King, Queen and Jack are each worth 10. Braggers have their normal face value, as do all the other cards below 10. But wait for the sting in the tail! There now enters an additional gambling twist which makes Three Stake Brag even more exciting.

Starting with the player to the left of the dealer, and going clockwise from him, any player whose card points add up to less than 31 can risk taking one extra card from the top of the pack after the betting has ended and all the players' cards have been exposed but before the final winner is decided in the aforesaid manner. (Note that another player might well hit 31 thus sharing the pot with someone who hoped he had already won.)

Multi-card Brag. This is my own description of the many variations which involve players being dealt more than 3 cards and selecting their 3 best for the betting – on Brag or Three Stake Brag lines. More than 1 round of betting can take place at pre-determined stages of the deal. Invent your own version!

Skill
The element of skill in any version of Brag is quite low. Bluffing is prevalent and knowing when to bluff is often a matter of knowing one's opponents. Apart from that the most successful players are those who try to work out the odds in favour of the cards they hold.

14

Cassino

Cassino (also spelt with one ''s'') is another very good game for 2, 3 or 4 players. In its 2 and 3 handed versions each player plays for himself; 4 handed it is played on a partnership basis. It is usual for partners to sit opposite each other and for their scores to be aggregated at the end.

Object
The object of the game is to score more points than the other players.

A number of special Cassino terms are used to describe specific cards and some of the happenings during the play. Each will be explained as we go through the play, together with the manner in which the cards or events earn points; meanwhile, because you need prior knowledge of what points will be awarded for, you will find just below some of these terms and their point scores on which the game hinges.

Table of Points

The ''Great Cassino'' (the 10 of Diamonds)   2
The ''Little Cassino'' (the 2 of Spades)   1
''Taking in'' the majority of the cards   3
A ''sweep'' of the cards in the ''layout''   1
''Taking in'' any Ace   1
''Taking in'' the majority of the Spades   1

With the exception of the point for a ''sweep'', these points are all claimed at the end of the game and each player scores according to the value thus derived from the cards he has gained during the play. The point for a sweep *must* be recorded at the time it is achieved – a player is not allowed to claim it after the event. A score sheet can be a simple plain sheet of paper.

The Pack and the Deal

A full pack of 52 cards without Jokers is used. Cutting for deal, shuffling, etc., follow Whist rules (see Chapter 1). Two rounds of cards are dealt two at a time face down to each player and to a vacant position on the table known as the "layout". The layout cards are dealt face upwards and separated.

When each player including the layout has 4 cards the dealer places the rest of the pack to one side face down. In the remainder of the game he will be in charge of succeeding deals for the hand – in which the players each receive 4 more cards face down – until all the cards in the pack have come into play. (No more cards are dealt to the layout after the first deal.)

The Play

In the course of the play each player seeks to place as many cards as possible face down in front of him. Starting with the player to the dealer's left, each in turn uses ("plays" – in the somewhat unusual Cassino sense of the word) one of his cards. When everyone has played all his 4 cards the next distribution of cards will be made.

In each "play" a card must be either discarded by the player by adding it face up to those already in the layout, or used to "take in" cards (show the card to the other players and then place it and card(s) from the layout face down in front of him) in one of the 7 ways itemised below.

Although a player may be *able* to take in cards he is not compelled to do so. (An example of this in practice is given later under "Skill".)

Methods of Taking in Cards

A player may take in cards as a result of:

1.   Achieving a "*pair*". If one of his cards is of equal value

to one or more of the cards in the layout, e.g. he has a 3 and the layout also has a 3, he shows his 3 to the other players and places it face down in front of him together with the 3 he takes from the layout. If the layout had had another 3 he could have taken both.

2. Achieving a "*combine*". Combines are judged by "Pip" value. For this purpose each Ace is worth 1 pip and the pip value of the cards 10 and below inclusive matches their numerical value, e.g. an 8 and an Ace total 9. However, the court cards, i.e. King, Queen and Jack, cannot be used in any combination; they are deemed not to have a pip value, and can only be paired.

   If any *two* or more cards in the layout have a *combined* pip value equal to the pip value of a card of his of 10 or under he can play his card and take in the relevant cards from the layout. For example, he has an 8 and the layout has a 5 and a 3. He can add both to the 8 and place all 3 face down on the table in front of him.

3. Placing face down in front of him either the *Great Cassino* (eventually worth 2 points) or the *Little Cassino* (which will be worth 1 point) immediately following pairing or combining, i.e. before the next player takes his turn.

4. Achieving a "*sweep*". If all of the cards in the layout combine in groups or together to equal the pip value of a card which he has (with the exception of the Great Cassino – see below), he can take them all and thereby has a sweep to place face down in front of himself. For example if he has a 9 and in the layout are the 6, 3, 5 and 4, there are two sets of 9 to be combined with the 9 in his hand.

   He must remember to record his point score of 1 for the sweep as he takes it in.

   (Note that if all the cards in the layout have been taken with a sweep the next player is forced to discard thus starting a new layout.)

5. Achieving a "*coup*", by combining the Great Cassino with all the cards in the layout. Although all the cards in the layout are taken in, a coup does not earn an immediate

score in the same way as a sweep.

6. Achieving a "*build*". This he does by adding one of his cards to a card in the layout and announcing the total "build" value of the two cards. He places his card alongside the card in the layout and on a subsequent play expects to be able to combine those cards with one that he will then play from his hand. However, any following player can take advantage of his action and grab both cards first. For example, North, with an 8 and a 3 in his hand, sees a 5 in the layout and adds his 3 to the 5 announcing as he does so, "I build 8". Unfortunately for North, East who plays next, puts his own 8 on the table and takes in the two cards making his own combine.

Building can be cumulative. A player may only add one card at a time but can aim to make a build in two or more steps. Thus a player with a 9, a 4 and a 2 could add the 2 to a 3 in the layout and say "I build 5", and on the next round add the 4, announcing "I build 9". On the following round he would expect to take in the 3 cards in the layout with his own 9. A single card which has been nominated as part of a build cannot be taken from that build by another player but the initiator does risk that any of the other players may be able to take the whole build to date before he gets his chance to combine it.

Once a player has played a card to a build he must either combine or continue to build when it is next his turn to play. Alternatively he may convert a build to a "call", the last of the 7 methods of taking in cards.

7. "*Call*". A player "calls" by placing one of his cards into the layout together with cards already in the layout which combine to the same value and, in the next round, takes them all by playing *another* card of the same value from his hand. For example a player has two 4s, and the layout has a 3 and an Ace. He adds one of his 4s to the 3 and Ace in the layout and says "I call 4s". On the next round, unless one of the other players forestalls him and snatches the call just as he might grab a build, he plays his other 4 and takes the 3 cards from the layout.

Scoring

When the entire pack has been used the hand is over. The players now examine the cards they have taken in and claim, agree and record their scores according to the table of points given at the start of this chapter. (They add in any sweep scores already noted.) Cards left in the layout at the end of the game register no points.

The winner, or winners in a partnership game, may be decided on a hand by hand basis; on the best of an agreed number of hands, or by an agreed target score being reached first. With the latter method the game can end in the middle of a hand, for example because the scoring of a sweep enables the scorer to reach the target.

Skill

Memory, arithmetic and tactics are the main elements of skill that are involved. As each player "makes" his pair, combines, sweep or coup, his cards are placed face down in front of him. A skilful player will try to remember as many of those cards as possible in order to increase his chances of achieving a successful build or call. He will also take those cards into account when he has to contribute a card to the layout. For example, if he is thinking of discarding a 4 his thought process will be aided if he can remember that one of the other players paired with three 4s earlier in the game. If no other player has used a 4 then the longer the game goes on the more likely it becomes that one of the others is going to be able to pair if he discards his own 4, so he should hold it as long as possible.

When planning his combines, builds and calls a player must always remember the extra points he may be able to earn as a result of taking in aces or the majority of the Spades (and the extra points other players may earn as a result of his own discards of Aces or Spades into the layout – it is necessary to be particularly wary of using Aces or Spades in builds and calls unless you are happy that another player is unlikely to step in and earn the fruits of your labour).

Although it is unusual it is possible to lay a trap. For example a 2 handed game has been proceeding for several deals and no 8 or 3 has yet been played. You have taken in the majority of the cards so far and know that your opponent is getting desperate. You have an 8 and a 2 and a 3 and there is a 2 and a Jack in the layout. If your opponent also has an 8 and a 3 then, by discarding your 3 (instead of pairing your 2 with the 2) you may lure your opponent into adding his 3 and announcing "I build 8" . . .

It is also possible to judge how many points the opponents are scoring . . . not specifically, except very early in the game, but certainly in general. For example if one player has a large pile of cards in front of him and the others have small piles of cards they should have a pretty good idea who is winning up to that point. If a player believes he is behind it may be justified to start a "call", whereas a player in front by a good margin should avoid calling.

There is no such thing as an overall winning strategy – the best that a player can do is to use the cards that have been dealt to him to the best advantage, remembering the cards that have already been played, and planning "taking in" opportunities in advance whenever possible. A player who can do that and who also has average luck with the cards dealt to him should be a steady winner over a period.

Skill in the Partnership Game
The partnership game has an additional level of tactics, best illustrated by example.

North and South are playing as partners and South adds a 3 to a 4 on the table, saying "I build 7". North has a 7 in his own hand. It would be a justifiable risk early in the game to play that 7 into the layout without pairing or combining. With luck South will take all 3 with his next card; better still, South may have two 7s in his hand and subsequently add one as a call, and later take in all the cards.

15

The Rummy Family

INTRODUCTORY VERSION

All versions of Rummy are based upon the same objective, although the scoring, the number of cards dealt, and the combinations which count, may differ. Even the best known variations undergo minor changes in their character with the passage of time but the substance never alters. They are very popular amongst all ages. In this chapter I have developed an introductory version, the purpose of which is to demonstrate how Rummy can be played at a very simple level by 2 players with rules which fit the overall concepts that apply to all Rummy.

Object
The object of all Rummy games is to gain more points than your opposition. Points are earned via a process often described as "going down" in which cards are laid out face up on the table by the player or the partnership with a view to the ultimate divestment of all cards held in the hand – "going out".

Let's now look at my game for 2 players.

The Deal
The players use a full pack of 52 cards plus a Joker. The winner is going to be the first player to score 100 points.

After cutting for deal and shuffling (see Chapter 1 if you seek strictly correct procedure) each player is dealt 7 cards and a 15th is placed face upwards alongside the rest of the cards, which are left in a stack in the middle of the table, face down.

The Play

The dealer's opponent is the first to play. He may pick up the exposed card or take the next card off the top of the stack taking the chance of what he will get. The card he selects will depend upon the cards he already holds in his hand. Once he has picked up a card he can put some (or *all* – if he can) of his cards face upwards in front of him in clearly visible sets on the table.

A set constitutes 3 or 4 cards of the same denomination, or a run of 3 or 4 cards or more in the same suit. Aces may be used to head a run where the next card is a King, or at the bottom of a run where the next card is a Two. The Joker may be used to represent any card in any suit. Only complete sets (i.e. at least 3 cards) may be put down.

Unless he is able to put down all 7 of his cards immediately (''go out'') the dealer's opponent *must* make a discard face upwards on top of the exposed card (or into its earlier position should he have picked that one up). He can do this after having put down a set, or instead of putting down a set.

The dealer plays next and has the option to take a card from the stack, or to take the card his opponent has just discarded (he is not allowed to take the original exposed card if it happens still to be there). He can then put down his own sets and/or discard. Play continues in this fashion.

If either player has put down a set in a round he is allowed in subsequent rounds to add new cards to sets put down by his opponent or to his own previous sets.

There is no rule that states that either player *must* put down a set or sets or add cards to his own or his opponent's sets even though he may be in a position so to do.

Play stops whenever one or other player has ''gone out'' by disposing of the last of his cards. He does not have to make a discard at this time but can do, for example if he has 4 cards left – 3 of which are a run with the fourth an odd card.

Scoring

Scoring may take place on the basis of individual hands; over a number of hands, or when an agreed target or time has been reached.

To calculate the score the face value of the cards left in the hand of the player who didn't go out is added up. An Ace counts 11 points, picture cards 10, the others their face value, and the Joker 15. The total then becomes the score of the winner of the hand, i.e. the player who disposed of all his cards.

An alternative method of scoring is for both players to earn points for each of their sets put down (including cards they succeed in adding subsequently) during play, and for the loser to deduct the value of the remaining cards held in his own hand from his score up to that time.

Skill

In such a simple game there is very little skill involved; it is more a case of pitfalls to be avoided. For example, your opponent has only 1 card left and one of the sets on the table is the 9 8 and 7 of Diamonds; you have 3 cards left, one of which is the 6 of Diamonds; if you are good enough to remember that some time ago your opponent picked up the 5 of Diamonds you will avoid adding the 6 of Diamonds to the set on the table . . .

16

Kaluki

Kaluki – a Rummy game – can be played by any number from 2 to 6 but is at its best if played by 4 people. In the previous chapter I introduced the principles of Rummy. You may like to pause and read that first.

Object
The object is to accumulate the *lowest* number of penalty points while opponents exceed 150 penalty points 3 times. Each time a player exceeds 150 points he loses a "life". His third life is therefore his last life. After each of his first and second lives he re-enters the game for the start of the next hand with the same number of points as the live player holding the *second* highest score at that time.

The Pack and Deal
The game is played with 2 complete packs and 4 Jokers. The packs and Jokers are shuffled together and dealt, one card at a time, clockwise starting with the player on the dealer's left. Each player is dealt 13 cards, all face down. The next card is placed face up in the middle of the table and the balance of the packs is put in a stack face down alongside that card. The player to the dealer's left is the first to play.

Penalty Points
You accumulate penalty points according to the value of the cards left in your hand at the moment another player manages to dispose of all his cards ("go out"). The scale of values is:-

Each Joker	15 points
Each Ace	11 points
Each picture	10 points
Other cards	their face value

For example, a player left holding A A K K 3 would score 45 penalty points. The penalty points are recorded at the end of the play of each hand.

Sets

In order to denude oneself of penalty points it is necessary to place "sets", face-up in full view on the table. Sets comprise any 4 cards of the same value; any 3 cards of the same value; a run of 4 cards in the same suit; or a run of 3 cards in the same suit.

When making a set of cards of the same value each card must be different; thus it is not permissible to form a set of 3 Aces including 2 Aces of Hearts (remember – the game is played with 2 packs, so 2 Aces of Hearts is quite possible).

In making up a set a Joker can be used to represent any other card, in which case it assumes the value of the card it is representing.

In making runs the Ace can only be used in conjunction with King and Queen. Neither Ace 2 3, nor King Ace 2, is a run.

The Rules of Play

Each player in turn picks up a card from the table before laying down sets and/or discarding. Every turn *must* start with a pick up and end with a discard. The first set or sets that any player lays down must have a total penalty value of 40 points or more.

The first to play has the option of taking either an unknown card from the top of the stack, or the card dealt face upwards. However, if he wishes to take the card dealt face upwards he can only do so if he is able to use it immediately as part of a set or sets having a total penalty value of 40 points or more, which he must then lay down before making his first discard. If he takes the unknown card he is under no obligation to make an immediate lay down of a set or sets. His discard is made face upwards on top of the original faced up card or, if he picked that one up, into the position it had been.

The second and subsequent players have the option of picking up the card that the previous player discarded, or taking a card from the top of the stack. If they take an unknown card from the stack they can choose to lay down and then discard, or just to discard. But, a player who has not yet laid down cards is not allowed to take the exposed card unless he uses it immediately to make up the 40 or more points necessary and lay down cards which include it.

However, once a player has gone down, he becomes free thereafter to pick up the previous player's discard and hold it without playing it until he is ready to (or until suffering the penalty of being left with it when another player goes out!).

Once a player goes down with a set or sets to a minimum value of 40 points he gains a number of other options for the rest of that turn and for all subsequent turns:-

1. He can now add other cards from his hand to either or both ends of runs tabled by the previous player(s) (or tabled by himself in a previous turn).

2. If a previous player (including himself in a previous turn) used a Joker in the *middle* of a run (but not at one end) he can replace that Joker with the actual card it was intended to represent provided he uses and lays the Joker at *once* as part of a new set or to represent another card in an extension of an existing run.

   For example with 9 8 and 7 of Diamonds already on the table and the 5 of Diamonds in his own hand, if he is able to replace a Joker in another set on the table he could use it to represent the 6 of Diamonds and play it with the 5 to add to the Diamonds on the table.

3. If a Joker has been used as part of a set of only 3 cards of equal value he can replace it by playing *both* of the missing cards that would make a set of 4 and playing the Joker at once as part of a new set. Alternatively he can add just one of the missing cards and declare the set "closed". E.g., if the set is A ♠ A ♥ and a Joker he can either add A ♦ and A ♣ and take the Joker and play it in a new set, or he can simply add either of those two Aces and declare the set closed. (Once closed a set cannot be

added to by any of the players, nor can the Joker be substituted for as above.)

A card which is discarded but which could have been added by the player making the discard to a set already on the table cannot be picked up by the next to play unless the discarder was not *allowed* to add it to a set – i.e. because he had not yet laid down sets of his own. Only then can the next player pick it up and use it (or hold it provided he himself has already put down his minimum).

Going Out

Lastly, a player who is down to either 3 or less cards in his hand must announce that fact. He has to repeat the warning as the number diminishes, when (if) it goes from 3 to 2, and then again as it goes to 1.

The hand ends when one of the players discards his last card. After the scoring the cards are shuffled and the deal passes clockwise around the table for each new hand. The game continues until only one player has any lives left. He wins.

"Kaluki"

And what is Kaluki? A Kaluki occurs when a player still having 13 cards in his hand picks up one, places sets on the table (and adds to opponents' sets if he can and also wishes to), and, as a result, has only 1 card left which he discards. There is no bonus for this. It just enables the player concerned to crow a little.

There is something one might call a "Misère" Kaluki, borrowing an expression from Solo (Chapter 4). This happens if any player can play all 13 cards at once, the total value of which does not exceed 40 points. This Kaluki is an allowable exception to the 40 point rule. It is quite a rare occurrence.

Skill

It would be easy to conclude that the winner is always going to be the player with the most luck in picking up good cards. Nevertheless some players do manage to win consistently. They do so because of their skill in discarding, and when putting down sets or adding cards to existing sets. This skill inheres in the attention they pay to the face up cards the other players pick up and to the cards that other players discard. In other words success demands a practised memory.

Memory provides the key to avoiding discards or adding cards to existing sets, either or both of which are going to help the next person and/or hanging on to cards hoping to make up a set when the necessary cards were discarded along ago. Faced with a decision as to where best to use a Joker a choice could reflect knowledge of cards reckoned to be held by the opponents, using that knowledge to avoid giving them unsolicited chances. The longer a game goes on the greater the advantage the more skilful player has, with his appreciation of the possible cards that his opponents are waiting to play.

The rule about not picking up a discard which could have been added to a set already on the table, will sometimes be made use of by a player discarding a card which he feels certain other players would have loved instead to have seen out on the table (where they would then have been enabled to add more to the set themselves).

17

Gin Rummy

A version of Rummy which used to be very popular, particularly in the USA is "Gin Rummy". It is still widely played, although over-taken in popularity by Kaluki. I will describe it as a game for 2 players. In theory it can be played by more than 2 but is at its best as a game with only 2. Unless you are familiar with any other Rummy game please look at Chapter 15 first.

Object
To score more points (including the final Bonus points) than your opponent either after an agreed number of hands has been played, or after an agreed target has been reached. 100 points before Bonuses are added is the usual target.

Pack
An ordinary pack of 52 cards is used, without Jokers. The cards rank from King down to Ace, which only ranks low.

The Deal
After the usual shuffle and cut (see Chapter 1 if necessary) the dealer gives 10 cards each, 1 card at a time, all face down. He then turns the next card face up alongside the remaining cards which are left in a stack in the middle of the table. At the end of each hand the deal passes across the table.

The Play
The non-dealer plays first. The rules state that he must start this turn by picking up one card and end it by discarding one. He

may or may not "go down" with some cards as well according to the rules here following.

He first has the option of picking up the card at the side, or taking 1 unseen from the top of the stack. He can then put cards face upwards on the table in sets, and/or discard a card face upwards alongside the stack. This discard starts a "discard pile"; it goes atop the original face up card if he didn't choose to pick that one up.

Sets
Sets comprise 3 or 4 cards of the same rank, or runs of not less than 3 cards which must be all in the same suit.

Going Down
The dealer's opponent is not allowed to put any sets down unless they contain 3 cards and unless the total face value of the cards he *retains* is 10 points or less. That value is obtained by giving each court card except the Ace a value of 10 points, the Ace 1 point, and the other cards their face value in points. One exception to this is a "Gin".

Gin
If the dealer's opponent is able to put down all 10 cards at once (a discard must always be made, i.e. a player cannot put down 11 cards at once, only a maximum of 10) he tables them and announces "Gin".

Provided the non-dealer does not go down (for which see below) or have Gin, it now becomes the dealer's turn. He may pick up the card his opponent has discarded, or choose to take an unseen card. He then has the same options as his opponent had on his first play.

The End of the Play
If neither player manages to put down a set or sets in their first turn (which could be because they don't wish to) the play continues. At his turn each player selects an unseen card from the stack or chooses to take opponent's discard as before.

As soon as one player puts down a set or sets both players reveal the cards they still hold. The other player puts down whatever sets he has in his hand at that point. He gains an additional privilege; he may add cards to his opponent's sets if he can. However, he is not allowed to make a discard. The player who put down first is *not* allowed to dispose of any more cards by adding to any sets his opponent has put down. He took his chance when he put his set(s) on the table.

The play has now ended and the scoring commences.

Scoring

Points
Points are earned in 3 ways:-

1. The total face value of any of the cards left in each hand is now calculated on the same basis as mentioned above for Going Down. If the player who precipitated the end of the hand has cards left of a lower value than his opponent he scores the difference in values as points.
2. If the player who did not put down first has cards left of a lower total value he scores the difference in value, plus an additional 10. If the values are equal the player who did not put down first, merely earns 10 points.
3. If a player has called Gin he scores 20 points in addition to the value of any cards the other player is not able to put down. He gets his 20 even if the other player manages to put down all his cards. (But when that other player does manage to put down all his cards he earns 10 points notwithstanding the "Gin" as in 2 above.)

Each hand is scored individually at its end.

Bonus Points
After the agreed number of hands, or when the target has been reached or passed, each player earns bonuses:-

1. The player with the highest total points overall receives bonus points equal to the number of points he has won by.
2. Each player receives 20 bonus points for each deal won by him.

3.   100 extra points go to the player who reached the target first, or who has the higher points score (excluding bonus points) over the agreed number of hands played.

Thus the winner is decided. Then:-

4.   100 extra points go to the winner if the loser failed to score throughout the whole of the game.

The winning margin can be substantial; it can seem even more substantial if the game is played for money on the basis of the winner winning x per point of the winning margin.

A score sheet for a game ending when a player has exceeded an initial 100 points target might look like this:

| | **A** | | **B** | |
	Points	*Bonus*	*Points*	*Bonus*
Deal 1: A put down, retaining cards worth 5 points; B had 12 points.	7	20		
Deal 2: B had Gin; A had 24 points.			44	20
Deal 3: B put down retaining 6; A had 2 left.	14	20		
Deal 4: A had Gin; B had 60 left.	80	20		
	101	60	44	20
Game bonus	157**			

** The bonus of 157 equals the difference between the two scores at the end before bonuses plus 100 for reaching the target of 100 points first.

A wins by a total of 318 against 64. I hope they were not playing for money!

Skill

There is little room for skill in Gin Rummy unless a hand takes some time to end, when remembering the cards picked up by the other player from the discard pile, and what you may have thrown there which he didn't pick up, becomes a significant factor.

It will often happen that a player has a choice of sets he can make out of the cards he has. For example, after picking up, North has:-

♠ 9 8 7 6; ♥ 9 8 7 6; ♦ 9 8 6; ♣ –

(1) He can put down ♠ 9 8 7, the three 6s, the ♥ 9 8 7, retain 8 ♦ and discard 9 ♦. Or (2) he can put down 9 9 9, 8 8 8, 6 6 6, retain a 7 and discard a 7. The difference between retaining an 8 or a 7 is not great, so which alternative should he choose?

His choice should be dictated by the opportunities he may give to his opponent. He may have no idea of the cards South holds if it is very early in the game, or could know several of those cards if the game has being going on for some time.

If it is early in the game he should take into account that his sets of 3 cards of the same value can only be used by his opponent to add 1 card, whereas his runs can be used to add cards at each end. For example, if South happened to hold including his pick up:-

♠ J 10 4 3 2; ♥ J 10; ♦ 10; ♣ 4 3 2

If North chooses alternative (1) South will be able to dispose of all his cards, whereas if North puts down his cards as per alternative (2) South will not be able to get rid of both his Jacks, and North will win. (Why don't you work it out?)

In fact there is another choice . . . he can decide to keep all his cards for at least one more round, hoping to pick up a card which will give him "Gin". What would I do? Keep my cards for a round.

191

18

Canasta

Canasta is a variation of Rummy which originated in South America and was very popular for a few years. It is not played as much nowadays but is good enough to make a comeback. It can be played by 2, 3, or in a 4 handed partnership version. The latter is probably the most interesting and is the one I shall describe, although I warn you that it is quite complicated. Chapter 15 expounds the basics of Rummy and you may prefer to begin there. Conversion to 2 or 3 handed games is returned to at the end of this chapter.

Object
To score most points through going down. (Cards, laid face up in sets on the table, earn points as they are put down; those left in your hand at the end of the hand lose them.)

The Pack and the Deal
Two packs of cards are used together with the 4 Jokers. The Jokers and all eight 2s are "wild" cards.

After the partnerships have been agreed the cards are cut for deal. The dealer is the player to the right of the player cutting the highest card. The cards are then shuffled and 11 cards are dealt to every player, 1 each at a time, face down. The next card is turned face up in a position in the centre of the table. This card starts what is subsequently described as the "discard pile". It will be added to in due course as you will see.

If the faced up card is (1) a black 3, or (2) a wild card, or (3) a red 3, a 2nd card is faced up on top of it. Placing a card on the black 3 has no significance later on in the game (it's just a rule that you have to do it . . . don't ask why!); you will see the result of placing the additional card on top of a wild card or a red 3 when you get to "Stopping" and "Freezing" later.

The remainder of the cards are spread out face down in a line across the table avoiding areas of the table in front of each player but in such a way as to make it easy for any player to select any one to pick up when entitled to as the game progresses. These cards are called the "stock".

Point Scoring

At the end of each turn the player must discard one card on to the discard pile unless he is "going out" (putting all his cards down), when he is relieved of this obligation. As we shall see to make a discard may be the only thing he can do on a particular turn but if he is able to go down he can choose to do so before making the discard. Cards laid down in front of you score points at once on the following scale:

Jokers	50 points
Twos	20 points
Aces	20 points
All cards between King and 8	10 points
All cards between 7 and 4	5 points
The black 3s	5 points
Each individual red 3	100 points

Going Down

To go down initially you must be able to make at least one "*Meld*" (the Canasta word used in place of "sets" as in Rummy) containing a minimum of 3 cards and having a point scoring value of not less than 50 points. (Each card scoring according to the above scale, e.g. a Joker scores 50 points even though it may have been used to make a meld of 4s – for which see also below.)

Once one player of a partnership has gone down, the minima no longer apply to that hand and cards can be added by either partner during his turn to melds of their own already on the table, or new melds of at least 3 cards can be started. Each player normally places his own melds in front of himself for convenience but note that he can add to his partner's melds across the table.

A "Meld"

Unlike sets in other Rummy games a meld cannot be made from a run, e.g. 10 J Q etc. A meld must contain 3 or more cards of the same rank. Wild cards can be substituted to represent "natural" cards, e.g. 2 Kings and a 2 would constitute 3 Kings. This is subject to the provisos that:-

1. A meld may not include a wild card unless there are at least 2 natural rank cards in it besides.
2. No meld can contain more than 3 wild cards.
3. A meld of 3s cannot include red 3s.
4. Black 3s can only be melded at the end of a hand in the process of going out, and cannot be melded with wild cards.

A "Canasta"

A meld of 7 cards is a "*Canasta*" and earns a special bonus *if it is put down all at once* in addition to the value of the cards it contains. A natural "Canasta" (i.e. one that contains no wild cards) earns more than one with wild cards:-

Per Canasta if it includes any wild cards	300
For each natural Canasta	500

Bonuses Awarded at the End of Each Hand

Bonuses recorded at the end of each hand in addition to the totalled up point values each player scores as he lays down his melds or adds to existing melds are:-

		Points
1.	Per red 3 laid on the table provided the partnership went down	100
2.	If a side has all 4 red 3s	800
3.	To the side making the last meld	100
4.	If the player making the last meld did not at the same time add a card to a meld of his partner's	200

The Play of Each Hand

Before going into the detail of options open to each player when it becomes their turn to play there is one thing they must all do when it is their *first* turn – they must lay down in front of them any red 3s they have and replace them with cards taken (at random) from the stock. Note that a red 3 picked up from the stock at any point in the game is put down immediately, with another card being drawn to replace it.

Assume a game between 2 partnerships, North/South versus East/West. East who cuts the highest card starts the play, North having dealt.

East's options are:

1. He can pick up any unseen card (more than 1 if he needs to replace red 3s that he puts down in front of him) from the stock and discard.
2. He can pick up a card from the stock, meld and go down (provided he has the minimum required points) and then discard.
3. He can take the card which started the discard pile. If he selects that card he must be able to show two matching natural cards and he is obliged to go down, using it in the meld so formed – he is not allowed to pick up the faced up card unless he can go down immediately. He can make up the minimum points requirement (see earlier) with wild cards if necessary.
4. He can use his discard to "*freeze* the pack". He does this by placing a wild card on the discard pile at right angles to the card below.*
5. He can use a "*stop*" card as his discard. Black 3s are "stop" cards when placed on top of the discard pile.*

* As it is unlikely that (as the first to play) he would "freeze" or "stop" we can ignore both possibilities for the time being and explain them fully a little later – while bearing in mind that both are valid options open to all players.

Let's assume for this game that he just takes a card from stock and discards.

Although technically East might go out (putting down all his cards – though under the rules they would have to include a Canasta) in one turn and thus end the hand it is so unlikely that we can go on from the point where he discards; this he must do whether he decides to go down or not.

It is now South's turn as the play continues clockwise. He has the same options as East but rather than choose to pick up just the single discard he may be able to "*capture the pack*". If he has two cards of the same rank as the card on the top of the discard pile he can show them, and take *all* the cards in the pile. He must immediately go down with the meld he made with the top card and that meld must be enough to satisfy the minimum requirement. (It can contain more than just those 3 cards, e.g. it could also include a wild card to make up the points.) He can then put down other melds if he wishes before he discards (starting a new discard pile).

"*Capturing the pack*", i.e. taking the discard pile in this way is a move shared in Rummy only by Canasta and lesser known relatives – for example "Hollywood" – for which we haven't space in this book. In other games you might choose to take just the top discard; in Canasta, provided you are able to comply with the necessary requirements, that choice becomes to take the entire discard pile.

For the sake of this example let's assume that South is able to capture the pack and that he goes down with 4 cards: the card at the top of the discard pile, 2 others of the same rank and a 2. He then discards. (Again his discard could "freeze" or "stop" the pack – see below.)

West, who now plays, has exactly the same options as South, although one of the options is of no use to him as there is only one card on the discard pile now – South's discard – and there is no pack for him to capture. He can take South's discard if he wishes and meld and discard but we can ignore what he actually does and go straight to North.

North has all the options that South and West had before him with some added advantages.

As soon as one player in a partnership goes down his partner is allowed to play as though he too had gone down. In this game because South has already gone down North is able to:-

1. Meld with less than the minimum number of points.
2. Add to South's meld(s) without going down with a meld of his own.
3. Capture the pack by using only one card of the same rank as the top one together with a wild card. He must show the other players that he has the cards he needs in order to make the capture but does not have to put down any of the cards gained by the capture immediately unless he chooses to do so.

From this point the play develops following the same criteria of allowed moves in every turn, so before describing how a hand ends and how the game is won let's go back and explain "freezing" and "stopping".

"Stopping" and "Freezing"

We started by defining the object of the game as being to score the most points through going down and it should have become clear that capturing the pack thereby affords greater opportunities of scoring. However, each player in his turn is able to play a card which prevents the next player from capturing. He can:-

1. *"Stop"*, i.e. place a black 3 on top of the discard pile. This stops the next player from capturing but any following player can capture when it is his turn in the normal manner.
2. *"Freeze"*, i.e. place a wild card (a joker or a 2) at right angles across the top of the discard pile. The cards in the discard pile are frozen and cannot be captured until a meld is made using the top subsequent card on the pile with two natural cards of the same rank. The player making this meld un-freezes the cards and captures them all. (A red 3 or wild card which is the first card dealt to start the discard pile is turned at right angles where it freezes the pack at once and it has another (and thus capturable) card dealt face up on top of it. On capture of a pack frozen in this way by a red 3 the lucky player puts the red 3 down immediately, alongside any others he may already have.)

The purpose of a "freeze" is to prevent the pack being taken simply with *one* card of the top card's rank plus a wild card, as is normally the case once a partnership is down. It puts all players back in the pre-going down position of having to hold in their hands 2 natural cards matching the top card. (However no minimum points would apply if the partnership were already down.)

Any player who is unable to unfreeze the pack has no choice but to take a card from the stock. He can then meld, add to his own or his partner's melds and/or discard, but can no longer capture even if the card picked up from the stock gives him a natural pair matching the card at the top of the discard pile.

The End of a Hand

A hand ends when either:-
1. A player goes down with all of his remaining cards (with or without a discard) *provided that his side has a Canasta*; or
2. Because the stock becomes exhausted and subsequently each player in due turn, being allowed (but *not* compelled) to take the top card from the discard pile and make a fresh discard, declines either to take that card or to make a normal capture of the whole of the pile. (If any player does either and then discards without going out, the player to follow takes or declines the new discard and so on till nobody wants it – or someone goes out using it.)

Before either of the above happens it is likely that the hand will have been played around the table a few – possibly a good many – times, giving each player several turns. There are 2 other rules which come into effect: (1) any player who is left at any time with only one card after discarding must announce that fact, and (2) a player ready to go out can, if he likes to, ask his partner's permission. If he asks he must abide by the decision.

Scoring at the End of Each Hand
When the hand ends each partnership records their bonuses in accordance with the table on page 194. The values of the cards

left in any player's hand are then deducted from his partnership score according to the scale on page 193. (It is possible that a player will go out but that his partner will have cards left which penalise their side to a greater extent than the cards left in the hands of the other partnership – which is why a player should ask his partner's permission before going out.)

Changes in the Minimum Values for Melds

After the first hand the minimum number of points that an original meld must be worth in a subsequent hand may change according to the number of points scored by the partnership by the end of the immediately preceding hand. The scale that applies is:-

Total partnership score to date between 0 and 1495 . . . lowest value of meld required remains 50.
Total partnership score between 1500 and 2995 . . . requires a meld worth not less than 90.
Total partnership score between 3000 and 4995 . . . requires a meld worth not less than 120.

How Canasta Ends

The game ends at the end of a hand during which a side reaches 5,000 points, or when a side reaches 5,000 points after final bonuses and deductions have been taken into account at the end of a hand. The highest overall scoring side wins. However, note that it is possible for a side to be the first to reach 5,000 during the play of a hand but to be overtaken during or at the end of the hand.

Skill

It is permissible to have a house rule that any player may look at the cards in the discard pile when it is his turn to play. In the absence of such a rule players have to rely on their memory, remembering not only what is in the discard pile when considering capturing it, but also what cards may already have been captured – particularly by an opponent. A careless discard may cost many points if the card discarded will meld with cards already captured by an opponent.

As the game will be won or lost on the points scored there is much in favour of capturing the pack as often as possible but this must be weighed against the advantages of freezing the pack and allowing it to build up for a future capture by your side – particularly if you are rich in wild cards.

Having captured the pack it is tempting to put down as many points in melds as possible immediately but this can help your opponents by showing them which cards it is safe for them to discard. Conversely if an opponent announces that he only has 1 card left, or you can see that he has very few, it is tempting fate to hold on to melds which will score if they are put down but which will count against you if an opponent goes out.

If your opponents are first to capture a substantial pack your best tactic is to try to go out as soon as you can.

On the subject of discards you should watch carefully the discards made by all the other players. If you can match your partner's discards it is more likely that you will be retaining cards that will fit his melds when he goes down or vice versa. Matching the discards made by opponents is also a good idea as you are less likely to discard a card which they are waiting for in order to complete a meld. When in doubt it often pays to discard from cards of equal value. The more you have the less likely it is that opponents will be enabled to capture the pack. If you can subsequently pick up the pack your discards will come back to you!

Finally, because of the rule that requires a Canasta down for the partnership before you may go out, beware of reducing down to one card before you have that Canasta deployed.

2 and 3 Handed Canasta

The rules for 2 and 3 handed versions have not been agreed universally in all their permutations. The differences between the 4 handed partnership version and the simplest versions of 2 and 3 handed are that in the latter:-

1. No player can go out unless he has 2 Canastas.
2. In 2 handed each player is dealt 15 cards. In 3 handed 13 cards each are dealt.
3. In 2 handed a player taking from the stock takes 2 cards

each time. Only 1 card has to be discarded.

4. In view of the larger number of cards dealt and the tendency to capture and hold on to cards it is vital that you be born with very large hands.

These versions, especially when they have been extended to contain even more exotic rules (for example in one version of 3 handed two players play against one in each hand, the partnerships changing at the end of the hand) tend to be more hectic than the 4 handed game; tactics and skill are therefore less in evidence.

19

Cribbage

In the bad old good old days every home had its Cribbage peg board, and every Public House its coterie of players of the game. Nowadays the money-spinning fruit machines have taken over in our hostelries but that is surely no indictment of this delightful game.

The peg board is intended for two players, or for two teams of 2. However, Cribbage can be played by any number up to 9. The game is at its best with 2, 3 or 4 players. I will illustrate it with a 6 card version for 2 players although games with 5 or 7 cards each can be equally enthralling. At the end of this chapter you will find descriptions of some of the variations, together with minor changes in the rules that become necessary.

Object and the Peg Board

The winner is the player who scores 121 points first. If a Cribbage peg board is used that will mean moving the peg round in 2 complete circuits of the player's half of the board, plus one point. Boards are not mandatory, just traditional. Pencil and paper can be used.

The Pack and the Deal

A normal pack of 52 cards without Jokers is used. The cards are cut for deal. The non dealer immediately scores 3 points in 5 card Cribbage but this is not necessary in games with 6 cards or more. In our 6 card version for 2 players the dealer deals 6 cards each, two at a time, after the usual shuffle and a cut. (With

5 cards the cards would be dealt two, two and one; with 7 cards they would be dealt two at a time for the first 6.)

The "Crib"

Before anything further we must mention the Crib.

Between the 2 players is a spot on the table known as the "Crib", sometimes described as the "Box". As soon as they have their cards each player must select 2 and place them face down unseen by his opponent in the Crib. There is no order of priority governing which player does this first.

When the Crib cards have been put in, dealer's opponent cuts the remaining un-dealt cards to the dealer who takes out the top card from the lower portion. The upper portion is then put back and the pack is put into the middle of the table with that removed card placed on top face up.

Scoring

With one exception ("His Nob" – see below) scores are earned ("pegged") for combinations created during the initial Play, then during the "Show" and finally from the Crib. I will explain shortly how this comes about; meanwhile here are the combinations which score points (individual suits have no significance):-

Scoring Table

A Pair	scores	2 points
Three of a Kind	score	6 points
Four of a Kind	score	12 points
Any 2 or more cards which add up in face value to exactly 15 (for this an Ace counts 1, the court cards each count 10)		
known as a "Fifteen Two"	score	2 points
A Run of 3 cards*	scores	3 points
A Run of 4 cards*	scores	4 points
A Run of 5 cards*	scores	5 points

(* Aces rank low for all purposes in Cribbage and cannot be used with King, Queen etc., to make up a run or runs.)

"His Nob"

If the card which has been displayed on top of the stack of cards in the middle of the table is a Jack the dealer pegs 2 points straightaway for "His Nob".

"His Heels"

If the displayed card is not a Jack the player who has the Jack of the suit displayed when it comes to the Show or the Crib will peg 1 point then for "His Heels".

The Play

When both players have put away their Crib cards the dealer's opponent plays the first card face upwards in front of himself. As he plays it he announces its face value; for example if it is a court card or a 10 he says "10". The dealer now plays a card similarly, stating as he does so the combined face value of the 2 cards which have been played. For example if the card his opponent played had been a 3 and his own card was a 7 he would say "10".

The players continue to take turns in playing their cards each in front of themselves, and at the same time announcing (always) the cumulative combined face values (and scoring points – see "Scoring during the Play" below) until the "round" ends.

The maximum permitted *total* face value of all cards brought into play at any one time between the players is 31 points. Immediately a card cannot be played by a player without exceeding this limit his opponent has another turn (or turns) until he too is unable to play without exceeding the limit. When neither is able to play another card that "round" must stop and another must begin – started by the player who did *not* play the last card in the previous "round". The process continues until both players have played all the cards in their hands.

Scoring During the Play

In the course of the play the players will be playing each card with the aim of pegging points for the combinations it can create at the time according to the scoring table given above. They are pegged at once so it is up to the individual players to ensure that they don't miss any score to which they are entitled. As the play progresses the opportunities to score points increase:-

Opponent's first card
The dealer's opponent is unable to score with his first card.

Dealer's first card
The dealer may be able to score points with his first card in one of two ways:

1. If the card he plays is the same rank as the card played by his opponent he pegs 2 points for a Pair.
2. If the card he plays makes the total face value of the two cards played so far 15, he pegs 2 points for "Fifteen Two".

Opponent's second card
Opponent now has his first scoring opportunity:-

1. If the dealer has scored 2 points for a pair and opponent has another card of the same rank he can play it and score 6 points for Three of a Kind.
2. If the total face value is still below 15 the opponent may be able to increase it to exactly 15 and score 2 points for "Fifteen Two".
3. If the cards to date are such that they can be added to by playing another to make a run, that card can earn 3 points for a run. (The cards do not have to be played in sequence.)
4. He is allowed to pair with the card just played by the dealer. For example, North's first card is a 3; South (the dealer) plays a 7. North may score 2 points for a pair if he is able to play another 7.
5. He may score by playing a card which gives more than one entitlement to peg points. For example:-

The first card played is a 5; dealer plays another 5, states "10 and 2 for a pair". If his opponent has another 5 in his hand he could play it and say "Fifteen Two, and 6 for 3 fives". Or:-
The first card played is a 4; dealer plays a 6. If opponent has

a 5 he may play it and score 2 for Fifteen Two, and 3 for a run.

Dealer's second card

Before we go back to dealer for his second card you need to recall that the maximum face value of cards that can be played in a "round" is 31. Assuming first that dealer is able to play a card without exceeding that limit of 31 he has opportunities to score:

1. He may pair with the card just played by his opponent, and score 2 points.
2. If opponent has just scored 2 for a Pair he could score 6 if he was able to play a third card of the same rank, or even score 12 points if he was able to add a fourth to 3 already played, e.g. 3 sevens played to date and he had the fourth left in his hand.
3. He may score 3 for a run if the card he is able to play makes up a run with the 2 cards played immediately before; or 4 if he is able to make up a run of 3 into a run of 4.
4. He may earn a multiple score, for example:-

Opponent's first card	...6...	Announce	"6"
Dealer's first card	...3...	do	"9"
Opponent's second card	...3...	do	"12 and 2 for a Pair" (score 2)
Dealer's second card	...3...	do	"Fifteen Two and 6 for three 3s" (score 8)

If the dealer is unable to play without exceeding the maximum, his opponent can continue to play if he is able to, and inherits the dealer's opportunities to score more points in the "round".

The Last Card and its Bonus

As the 31 point maximum in a round is imminently reached neither player whose turn it is can opt out of playing if he has a playable card. The effect of this is that once *one* player has played the last card that he can, the *other* must then play all of any cards he is able to (1 at a time if he has more than 1) the total of which when added to the total to date will not put it above 31. However, if he has a choice of cards to play but is unable to play both, he can choose whichever card he likes.

(Note that if a player does play 2 or more of his cards in succession in the above situation he can score points for pairs, runs, etc., by creating combinations notwithstanding the fact that all the cards in the combination may be his own. For example the score has reached 25 and only one player can play; he has two 3s and can bring the total up to 31, scoring 2 points for the pair as he plays the second 3.)

The player who plays the last card in a "round" earns an extra 1 point bonus if the last card brings the total to less than 31. If the total is exactly 31 the bonus is 2 points. Taking the example above the second 3 scores a total of 4 points, 2 for the pair and 2 for hitting exactly 31.

The End of the Play
When the first "round" has been completed, i.e. 31 or the maximum possible has been reached, the Play continues on the same basis for another "round", with both players able to peg points in the same manner as above. The Play ends when both have played all their cards.

The "Show"
Provided that neither player reached the winning score of 121 during the Play the Show now takes place. Both players re-examine their cards, and, commencing with the dealer's opponent, peg the points they can count in the cards they were left with after contributing 2 to the Crib. In so doing they are allowed to add any extra points that can be taken by including as an additional card the card that was faced up; both players do this when it is their turn.

For the Show, cards are counted in as many scoring ways as possible. For example, for a 6, a 7, two 8s (say a Heart and a Spade) in a player's hand, together with a faced up 5, the scoring value is 14 i.e.:-

Two 8s	. . . a Pair	. . . 2 points
5, 6, 7 and 8 ♠	. . . a Run of Four	. . . 4 points
5, 6, 7 and 8 ♥	. . . a Run of Four	. . . 4 points
7 and 8 ♠	. . . Fifteen Two	. . . 2 points
7 and 8 ♥	. . . Fifteen Two	. . . 2 points

a total of 14 points. (Note how the faced up 5 added 2 points to the scoring value.)

A player entitled to 1 point for "His Heels" for having the appropriate Jack amongst his cards must remember to peg it during his "Show" turn. See page 204. (It could just be the winning point of the game – see below.)

Scoring the Crib
Provided that neither player has passed 120 points as a result of the Show the dealer now enjoys a special privilege. He reveals the cards in the Crib and, taking the cards in the Crib in conjunction with the faced up card which comes into use once more, he pegs what he can find there, counting in as many scoring ways as are available, just as both players were allowed to in the Show. Should "His Heels" be lurking in the Crib he can count one more point for that too!

The Winner
The winner of the game, as stated throughout, is the first to peg 121. Hence the value of the Cribbage peg board against paper and pencil; it makes more stark the exact moment of winning.

The game continues after the first hand for as many more hands as prove necessary, each new hand being dealt from a re-shuffled and cut pack by the players in turn. The 121st point can be scored at any stage of the game whatsoever, the winner being immediately declared.

Skill and Example of How to Play
Let's look at the first deal of an example game:

North deals with Q, 10, 9, 6, 4, Ace to himself and to South: K, 7, 7, 5, 3, 2.

North should choose his 9 and his 6 to put into the Crib, leaving Q, 10, 4 and Ace in his hand. He can score 4 points for

Fifteen Twos in the cards he retains, and has put 2 points for another in the Crib. (Remember, as long as play reaches the Crib stage – as it will, this being only the first hand – those points will be his.) He is not breaking up a valuable run, although should an 8 or Jack be turned up to go on top of the pack he will have lost the chance in the Show of an 8, 9 and 10 run, or a J, 10 and 9 run. Nevertheless the 9 and 6 he is putting into the Crib have excellent scoring potential there.

South ought to put the King and the 2 into the Crib. That leaves him with a fair score in his own hand, and the King and 2 are sufficiently wide enough apart to minimise the danger of the Crib producing a large score for dealer.

Assuming each of them takes my (unsolicited) advice we now find:-

North: Q, 10, 4, Ace; South: 7, 7, 5, 3; Crib: 9, 6, K, 2.

North faces up a Jack, which he places on top of the pack and at once pegs 2 for "His Nob".

South plays first, predictably with his 3 and announcing "3" as required by the rules. The choice of that card is inspired by his desire to reduce North's scoring potential. The play of any card with a value of 5 or over automatically gives your opponent an opportunity to register a Fifteen Two and this South can thus avoid. North ought now to play either his Queen or his 10, announcing the joint value of "13". If he plays his 4 South might have either a 2 or a 5 and thereby score 3 for a run. If he plays his Ace South could score for a run if he had a 2.

Next South plays his 5, announcing "18". It may seem that he should keep his 5 to the next "round" for a potential Fifteen Two there but South can already see that whichever card he plays, the probability is that he will have the disadvantage of having to play first on the next "round". Even with his 5 the total has already reached 18 with North to play, and any card played by North counting 7 or over will result in South not being able to play a card within the limit of 31. By keeping his two 7s he is giving himself the best chance of scoring in the next round. For all that South knows North may have to play all his other cards in the first round so that South's two 7s will be the only cards played in the next (when they would be worth 3 points – 2 for the pair and 1 for last card).

As it happens in this game North plays his other high card announcing "28", and when South is unable to play, North plays his Ace and pegs the 1 point for the last card. (Remember that North has to play the Ace in accordance with the rules.)

South now plays one of his 7s as the first card of the second "round"; North plays the only card he has left, i.e. the 4, and South pegs 1 point for the last card with his other 7.

The points scored in the Play stage are North: 3 (including the 2 for his Nob), South: 1.

Now we see the Show, with South counting first. Taking the faced up Jack into account he has:-

J, 7, 7, 5, 3.

He pegs 8 points, for 3 Fifteen Twos and the Pair. His total score on the hand is 9 points.

Again taking the faced up Jack into account North has:-

Q, J, 10, 4, Ace.

He pegs 9 points, for a run of Three and 3 Fifteen Twos. As dealer he now looks at the Crib:-

J, 9, 6, K, 2.

This is worth only 2 points for the Fifteen Two. In total his score on the hand has been 14 points. Further deals (as already explained) can now follow on the same basis until the magic 121st winning point is hit.

From the foregoing you should see that skill is largely a matter of tactics. The dealer has a slight advantage when considering which cards to put into the Crib because any points they represent come back to him unless the game is already so advanced that it is unlikely he will reach his Crib before he or his opponent reaches 121. But the choice of which cards to put into the Crib is rarely easy. When it is, it is usually because the cards are very bad or very good. For example, with K, 10, 7, 6, 3 and Ace the dealer would probably put in the 7 and 6; whereas his opponent would put away the K and 3. With Q, Q, 8, 7, 5, 5 the dealer would happily put in the 8 and 7. His unfortunate opponent may grit his teeth and do the same, or put in a 5 with the 8. This will depend on the score up to that time; if the dealer is a long way from the finish and his opponent very near then the latter need not worry about putting both the 8 and 7 away, thus giving the dealer a good Crib. With close scores he will want to avoid giving the dealer points even if it means sacrificing points he would otherwise earn in the Show.

In the play of the cards each player must look ahead and try to reduce the opportunities open to his opponent to score. Each must keep aware of the score at all times; it should influence the cards to put in the Crib and the tactics to adopt.

Other Versions

The most popular 2 player variations are 5 and 7 card games. The rules governing play remain the same but scoring differs from the 6 card game.

1. In 5 card Cribbage the non dealer in the first hand which is dealt pegs 3 points before play begins.
2. In 5 card, the winning final score is 61 points, i.e. only once around the Board.
3. In 7 card, players usually play for a winning score of 181 points, i.e. three times around, in view of the extra scoring potential of the hands.

Three handed Cribbage is scored and played similarly to two handed with each player scoring on his own behalf throughout. It is usual to deal 5 cards to each player and, before the cards are cut in order to take out the one which is placed face-up on top of the pack, one card is dealt face down into the Crib. Each player contributes one card to the Crib. The winning score is 121 points.

Four handed can be played in the same way as Three handed but is better played as a partnership game. Partners face each other and their individual scores (earned just as though they were playing 2 or 3 handed) are pegged on the partnership's side of the board as each partner plays and shows. The rendering of assistance to one's partner becomes an additional skill factor.

In all its versions Cribbage is a skilful and enjoyable game which you should hasten to add to your collection.

20

Pontoon

Pontoon, or as it is also called "Vingt-et-un", is a very popular gambling game, quite simple in principle, but capable of being played with skill and thought. In theory any number can play and in fact 6 or 7 players make for a very good game.

Object
The object is to bet successfully that the cards you receive are better than those held by the "Banker", or, if you happen to be the Banker, to win the majority in value of the bets placed against you.

The "*Banker*" is the person (decided by the highest card cut before the game starts) who will be the dealer until such time as he either has the Bank taken away from him or elects to sell it to the highest bidder.

The Pack
The complete pack of 52 cards is used without Jokers.

Card Values in the Betting
In Pontoon an Ace counts as 1 or 11 at the option of its holder; court cards count as 10 each, and all other cards count at their face value.

For one combination of cards held to be better than another their total must be nearer to 21, or be a "Five card trick" (5 cards together not exceeding 21), or be a "Pontoon", in that order. A Pontoon is defined as an Ace together with a court card or a 10.

For example 10 and 9 adding up to 19 is better than two 9s; 2, 2, 3, 5, and 6 – a Five card trick – is better than 10 and 9; Ace and Q is best of all because it is a Pontoon. (In some Pontoon "schools" a Pontoon using a 10 is ranked below a Pontoon using a court card.)

A Pontoon held by the Banker is better than any cards held by one of the other players.

The Deal and the Betting

The initial card and bets
After the cards have been shuffled and cut (by any willing player) the Banker deals one card only face down to each player in turn, starting with the player on his left and ending with himself. All the players look at their cards and, apart from the Banker, place an initial bet down in front of them. They *must* make a bet and there will be agreed house rules stipulating the minimum and maximum amounts that can be bet at this time.

Money can be used, or chips (or matchsticks if you like!) substituting for money, for example one match (intact) equals one penny.

The Banker does not bet until the others have bet and then only if he wishes to. If he does bet he has to place down in front of him double the highest initial bet placed by the other players. (The significance of this is that if any other players are still left in the game at "the Show" (see below) they will have to pay double if the Banker wins – or receive double the amount of their bets if he loses.)

Subsequent cards and bets
The Banker now deals another card face down to each player. After these cards have been dealt, and starting with the player on the Banker's left, each player in turn now has the following options:-

1. He may say "stick", i.e. he may stay with the cards that he has without taking any more and without adding anything to his initial bet. However, in order to be able to do this he must conform with the agreed house rule

214

stating the minimum total value of the cards. For example the rule may be agreed to be that no player can stick with less than 15 (a common rule), i.e. the combined value of the cards that he has must not be less than 15.

2. He may obtain more cards from the Banker by saying either "Buy" or "Twist".

"Buying": If a player elects to buy a card he must say "buy one" and increase his initial stake. He can bet up to a maximum of twice the amount of his initial bet but cannot bet less. The Banker deals him another card face *down*.

"Twisting": If a player elects to say "Twist" he cannot add to his initial bet. The Banker deals him a new card face *up*.

A player who has elected to buy a card can do so again at once for a fourth and again if he wishes for a fifth – each time adding to his total stake. The maximum bet for each additional "buy" is that amount wagered on the previous "buy". He can buy for smaller amounts but never for less than the amount of the initial bet. He can stick at any time, or can twist, although once having decided to twist he cannot buy a later card. For example he may buy a third card and then twist a fourth; if he wishes to obtain a fifth card he is only able to twist and cannot add to his total stake.

A player who has elected to twist can carry on twisting for more cards; he does not add to his stake and cannot change his mind and buy a card.

Note that if any card drawn at any time (by buying, twisting, or a combination of both) puts the total value of a player's cards over 21 he will have "bust", and *must* pay over his stake to the Banker immediately and give the Banker his cards to be placed under the others in the pack.

3. He may return his cards to the Banker to be placed under the other cards in the pack and forfeit his initial bet to the Banker (highly unlikely but a rule nevertheless).

4. He may announce and show that he has a Pontoon by putting his cards on the table with the Ace face up.

5. If his second card is exactly the same as his first then, provided the house rules permit, he may "split" the two cards. (The rules may stipulate that only Aces can be split

– this is the usual rule but is not an integral part of the game, i.e. it can be varied.)

Splitting cards involves turning them both face up and duplicating the initial stake on the second card. Each card is then played separately with each of the above options. It is rare, but within the rules, for more than one card to be split; for example, if the first 3 are all Aces, 3 separate stakes can be built up.

Note that each player completes his options before the next player can begin to exercise his.

The Show

When all the other players have exercised their options the Banker turns his two cards face up. He *cannot* now increase his bet (if he made one). His object is to obtain (if he does not already have) cards which are better than or equal to the cards (excluding any Pontoon that has been announced) that the other players who are still in the game may have.

He may decide not to take any more cards, i.e. he may announce that he intends to "stay" with the cards that he has, or he can add one or more cards, one at a time, "staying" whenever he wishes. If the value of his cards exceeds 21 he busts and has to pay each of the players who stayed in the betting the amount that each staked against him. If he doubled the initial highest bet after the first cards were dealt and busts he will have to pay each of them double their stakes.

If the Banker does not bust then as soon as he announces "stay" the other players turn their cards face up and they are compared with his. He pays any player whose cards are better than his and takes the stakes from all players whose cards are equal or worse.

For example, assume the Banker's first two cards are a 9 and an 8. If he decides to stay with those two he must pay any opponent whose cards total 18, 19, 20 or 21.

If the Banker doubled the initial highest bet earlier, his winnings vis-à-vis each of the other players who remained until the Show are doubled.

A Five Card Trick is (as stated earlier) only beaten by a Pontoon, and just as a Banker's Pontoon ranks above any other player's Pontoon so a Banker's Five Card Trick is rated highest. A winning Five Card Trick, irrespective of who holds it (the Banker or an opponent) is paid twice the stakes laid, i.e. if one of the Banker's opponents has it, the Banker pays him twice the money he staked, but if the Banker holds it, *all* players remaining in the Show who do not have a Pontoon pay *him* twice. (Note: A Banker who doubles the initial bet and subsequently achieves a Five Card Trick is only paid twice, *not* 4 times.)

Changing the Banker

If a player other than the Banker wins with a Pontoon (other than one achieved with a "split" Ace) he must take the Bank from the Banker when the hand is finished and either take over as Banker himself or offer the Bank for sale to the highest bidder (the former Banker is able to bid).

At any time between hands the Banker can offer the Bank for sale to the highest bidder.

Whenever there is a Pontoon (including one achieved with a "split" Ace) or the Banker changes, the cards are shuffled and cut (anyone can do it) before play continues.

The End of the Game

There is no prescribed ending to the game . . . it just stops when the players decide they have had enough (or when all bar one have run out of chips!). As long as one Banker holds the Bank he continues to deal. The cards are not shuffled or cut until there is a Pontoon . . . the cards from one hand always being collected together and placed under the pack before the cards for the next hand are dealt from the top.

Example

There are 6 players, Messrs A, B, C, D, E and the Banker. Let us look at a complete hand from each of their points of view.

Player A: The first card received by A is a 10. Good! It gives the possibility of a Pontoon, or if he receives another court card, the possibility of a score of 20. The maximum bet he is allowed (as agreed beforehand in this particular game) is 3 chips and he puts that amount down in front of him.

The second card he receives is a 4. That is not at all good. His total is 14 and he is not allowed to stick with less than 15. Hoping to get something like a 6 or 7 he says "twist". The Banker turns the next card face up and pushes it to him across the table. It is a 9. Bust! Over goes his stake of 3 chips to the Banker together with his cards.

Player B: His first card is a 7. Not very exciting. He bets the agreed house minimum of 1 chip. His second card is a 4. That is very much better; a 10 or a court card will give him 21. He buys another card for a further stake of 1 chip. The card is a Queen. He happily says "stick".

Player C: His first card is a 3. He bets the minimum of 1 chip. His second card is a 2. That is more promising. There is the possibility of a Five Card Trick. He buys another card – adding 2 chips to his stake. The card is a 5. Once more into the breach, he buys another card, again betting 2 chips. The new card is a 7 and he has a total of 17 and has staked 5 chips. If he decides to take another card, either by buying or twisting, he needs a 4 or lower to complete a Five Card Trick. There are nine cards in each suit which are higher than a 4 and only four cards which can help him. With odds against him of 9 to 4 discretion is the better part of valour and he sticks.

Player D: His first card is an Ace. Oh joy! A possible Pontoon. He bets the maximum initial bet of 3 chips. To his increased joy his second card is also an Ace. He turns both face up a few inches apart and places 3 chips on the second Ace.

On his first Ace he buys a card for 3 chips. It is a 9. He has the choice of using the Ace as 1 or 11, giving him totals of 10 or 20. He decides to use the Ace as 11 and says "stick".

He now turns his attention to his second Ace and buys a card for it with 3 chips. It is a Jack. He announces "Pontoon" and slips the Jack face down under the Ace. Altogether he has bet 12 chips in 2 different stakes of 6.

Player E: The first card E receives is a 6. He bets the minimum of 1 chip and then receives a King. He sticks.

Now it is the turn of the **Banker**. His first card was a 7 which did not inspire him so he left the stakes undoubled. His second card was a 6 and he turns both face up. He deals himself a 3. In theory he can stick but it seems that if he does he will be on a hiding to nothing. Quite apart from D's winning Pontoon there are still 4 potentially high value hands being sat on by the other players. He has won 3 chips from A's bust but can see himself paying out 20 chips for a net loss of 17.

He takes a chance and another card . . . a 5. Lucky him. He must pay D for his Pontoon but wins all the rest of the stakes for a net gain of 17 chips.

Skill

The odds are always weighted in favour of the Banker. For the other players to win, their cards have to be better than those held by the Banker, whereas the Banker will win if his are only as good as those held by his opponents.

Each player has to consider the odds against him with every card that he receives. In theory he should be prepared to go a little against the odds to off-set the Banker's advantage. If luck is with him this will enable him to hold his own but if luck is against him . . . so were the odds. For example, he should always make an initial maximum bet if his first card is a court card or an Ace. With a court card he has 7 chances in 13 of his next card giving him a total of 17 or better and he has one extra chance – receiving an ace for a Pontoon. The odds are quite good especially as the Banker may bust in an attempt to improve his own hand.

The Banker has an easier task. By the time he has to take decisions some of the other players may have already bust. He can review the table and see what his chances are of winning on the hand as a whole and take the appropriate action.

All players, including the Banker, see the cards that are placed under the pack during and at the end of each hand. As the cards are not reshuffled until a change in Banker or a Pontoon the cards used in one hand will not rise to the surface of the pack immediately. A good player will remember many of the cards he saw returned to the bottom of the pack and take them into account when judging his chances of being given favourable cards in the following hand. For example, if there were 2 Five Card Tricks in the previous hand it would be foolhardy to try to put together another Five Card Trick in the next hand.

Finally, bearing in mind the advantage that does accrue to the Banker, if you get a chance to take the Bank take it; as long as you watch what you are doing you will be unlucky to lose.

"Vingt-et-un" Modifications

Although there do not seem to have been rules published at any time for Vingt-et-un it is sometimes treated as a separate game in which Pontoons are called "Naturals" and the holders (other than the Banker) are paid double (three times in some "schools") the amount of their initial stake.

21

Patience

The game of Patience is known to many people; though not, I would suggest, in its many variations.

To some, it conjures up the image of staid Victorian matrons of unimpeachable morals, whiling away the evenings in innocent amusement. To others, it is a game to be played by children or invalids. These views are valid, but too narrow.

Many and varied are the people who have loved the game. Napoleon, while in exile on the island of St Helena, wrote that he passed the evenings in Patience-playing. Samuel Butler, the heretical Victorian writer, shows a softer side to his character when hunting through the British Museum Reading Room catalogues for new games to satisfy a sick friend, *his* invention and memory having been exhausted.

Tolstoy was keen to the point of obsession on playing Patience. At times he used it to decide on a course of action. (Although he was not above replaying any game that did not give the answer he wished!) He included the game in a scene from his masterpiece, *War and Peace*.

Another Russian writer, Dostoyevsky, makes his character, the siren Grushenka in *The Brothers Karamazov*, play a Russian Patience called 'Fools' at a time of great anxiety.

Today, many enjoy unwinding after a hectic day with a game that will not engender bad feeling or an empty wallet! I have even seen this being done on an InterCity train between Paddington and Bristol, not without 'help' from passers-by on their way to the buffet.

And a game that does not need a partner is a godsend to a

harassed parent with a bored child with nothing to do.

As with most card games, its origins are obscure. In America it is called Solitaire, the reason for this being obvious; the British favoured the name Patience, that being the virtue nurtured in the successful ending of a game.

It was not until the nineteenth century that books began to appear, listing the many games of Patience and their variants. Lady Mary Cadogan compiled the first book on the subject in English, in 1870. This was taken from French sources, as is shown by the titles of the games demonstrated: *Les Quatre Coin, La Fortresse, Les Quatorze, Le Cadran* and others. It would be interesting to know if any were devised by Napoleon and if it was he who made the game fashionable in France.

A great populariser of the game in the 1890's was Miss Whitmore Jones, whose volumes went from reprint to reprint for thirty years.

I come to the end of this brief comment on the game. But take heed: Patience does not *always* possess a calming quality. The frustration of a very complicated game which 'comes out' only once in ten or twenty attempts, or of the simpler *Clock Patience* being brought to a sickeningly abrupt termination by dealing oneself four kings in a row – after which one cannot even begin – has to be felt to be believed!

Still, a successful conclusion is all the more satisfying after these. So then, let us begin . . .

All Patience games are played with a standard pack of fifty-two cards, the jokers are not included.

There are four suits in each pack (clubs, diamonds, hearts and spades), the sequence running ace, two, three, four, five, six, seven, eight, nine, ten, jack (also known as 'knave'), queen and king. The latter three cards are called the 'court cards'.

When the court cards need a numerical value, the jack is valued at eleven, the queen at twelve and the king at thirteen. The ace always has a *numerical* value of one.

A 'piquet' pack is the name given to an ordinary pack with all cards below seven removed, but retaining the ace.

'Foundation' cards are the all-important base cards of the piles, on which are to be built the entire pack (or packs) in the required order. The aces often take this role, but not always.

The 'tableau' consists of cards arranged upon the table at the beginning of a game in the way the game dictates. One usually builds downwards upon an available or exposed card here until it is possible to remove them to foundation piles. A successful game will find *all* tableau cards transferred thus.

The 'reserve' holds cards on which *no* building takes place, ever!

To 'build up in suit' means to place the two of one suit onto the ace of the same suit, the three of that suit onto the two, the four onto the three, and so on, all the way to the king of that suit.

To 'play regardless of suit' is to look only at the number of the card, ignoring whether the card is a club, diamond, heart or spade, so that you play any three on any two, any four on any three, etc.

The 'heap' or 'heaps' contain the cards which cannot be played at that moment, but will be brought back into play as soon as is possible. All cards in the heap face upwards, but only the top card is available for use. There must be no rummaging through the heap for the card needed, useful as it would be on countless occasions!

It is important always to shuffle the cards thoroughly between games.

If you have known these simple rules from the cradle, I can do nothing but apologise.

The Baroness Patience

One pack of cards, with the four kings removed, is needed for this. Simple this elderly Patience may be, but it is addictive.

Deal out a row of five cards from left to right, face upwards.

Remove any two cards which total thirteen when added together, such as ace and queen, seven and six, five and eight and so on. (Now you understand why the kings, valued at thirteen, are removed before the start of play.) Do look closely at the cards which remain: there may be more pairs adding up to the number required.

Deal another row of five cards across spaces or cards not taken away and play as before.

Continue this until all the cards in your hand have been dealt.

(The final row will contain eight cards.)

A successful game will have all the cards paired and removed from the board.

Triplets Patience

One pack of cards is necessary for this venerable Patience. All cards face upwards.

Deal sixteen groups of three cards, each trio overlapping one another in the shape of a fan. Four cards remain: use these to make two fans of two.

The aim of the game is not to build on a foundation, but to eliminate all cards in numerical groups of three, ignoring suit, until just one card remains. (For example: five, six, seven; or queen, king, ace; or king, ace, two; or nine, ten, jack.)

Only the exposed card at the top of each fan, that with nothing upon it, is available for play and each card removed must be taken from a different fan. It is not permitted to dispose of an original fan in one fell swoop!

Some, of more heroic stature, make the game more difficult by removing one card from the pack before the game begins and attempt to empty the table completely.

Push-pin Patience

Two packs are needed for this very simple Patience. Shuffle the packs together very thoroughly, then deal out the cards from left to right and side by side, face upwards.

Whenever one or two cards are between two others of the same value or suit, discard them and close ranks. (Seven of clubs and three of diamonds between the queen of hearts and the queen of spades, discard the seven and three. Eight of hearts and two of spades between the five of diamonds and the jack of diamonds, discard the eight and two.)

Should there be three or *more* cards caught in this way, all can be removed *only* if they are of the same suit. (Queen, ten, six, three and two of diamonds imprisoned between the four of clubs and jack of clubs, take away all the diamonds.)

The game is won if two cards remain side by side at the end, all the others having been taken away.

(There is a second chance, however, if a line of whatever

224

length remains when all the cards have been played out. Switch any two cards in the row to revive the game.)

Drivel Patience

You will need one pack of cards for this game. It is a simple Patience, but I think the alternative title, *Idiot's Delight*, is going too far.

Shuffle the pack very thoroughly and deal four cards in a row, face upwards.

If any of the cards are of the same suit, remove those of a lower value and put them to one side. The highest card in that suit remains in its place. (Aces are of a higher value than kings in this game.)

Fill the gap, or gaps, with the next card from those held in your hand. Should *that* card be lower than another in the same suit on the table, remove that, too.

Continue until you have four cards of a different suit, then deal out four cards at a time on top of the previous four, discarding all the lower value cards in the same suit as before.

Gaps made by the removal of all the cards in a pile must be filled *at once* with the top card from one of the three other piles. This releases the card beneath, hopefully for removal. It is wise to play an ace into a gap whenever possible.

A successful conclusion to the game sees the four aces in a row, all the other cards of lower value having been removed.

Clock Patience

Only one pack of cards is needed for this. Shuffle the cards thoroughly, then deal out, face down, twelve cards in the shape of a clock face. Place a thirteenth card in the centre, also face down.

Repeat this until you have thirteen piles of four cards, then turn the top card on the thirteenth pile face up. If, for example, this is the five of diamonds, place it face up underneath the five o'clock pile on your clock face. Leave it protruding somewhat so that its number can be seen. Take the top card from the five o'clock pile and put it under its appropriate number pile.

An ace is placed at one o'clock, a jack at eleven o'clock and a queen at twelve o'clock. A king is placed under the pile in the middle.

The object of the game is to have all the cards face up in the right piles, but this happens rarely because once all the kings have turned up it is impossible to continue.

Fig. 1. Clock Patience.

Grandfather's Clock Patience

One pack of cards is needed for this Patience. The twelve foundation cards – see below – are set out in a circle before play begins. (All cards must face upwards in this game.)

Remove the following to be used as the foundation cards, putting them in the position of the corresponding hour on the clock face:

Nine of clubs – twelve o'clock; ten of hearts – one o'clock; jack of spades – two o'clock; queen of diamonds – three o'clock; king of clubs – four o'clock; two of hearts – five o'clock; three of spades – six o'clock; four of diamonds – seven o'clock; five of clubs – eight o'clock; six of hearts – nine o'clock; seven of spades – ten o'clock; and the eight of diamonds – eleven o'clock.

The object of the game is to build upwards on each card, in

The Foundation

The Tableau

Fig. 2. Grandfather's Clock Patience.
A good beginning – the five of diamonds, three of hearts *and* ace of clubs can be removed to their respective foundation piles, immediately freeing the cards above them for use. (All cards face upwards.)

suit and in sequence, until the appropriate number to its position on the clock face is reached. You will remember that the jack is valued at eleven and the queen, twelve.

After shuffling the remainder of the pack, deal out five rows of eight cards each, overlapping the rows so that the tableau resembles eight vertical columns.

The exposed, or available, card at the base of each column can be played to a foundation pile, if at all possible, or used to build downwards in sequence, but ignoring suit, on another column until needed. Only one card at a time is to be moved.

Fill a column emptied in play with any available card. A

successful ending to this game will see all cards gathered to the foundation piles and the 'hours' correct.

Carpet Patience

This simple Patience requires one pack of cards. Place upon the table four rows of five cards each, all facing upwards. This forms the 'carpet' of the title.

As the aces emerge, put two to the right and two to the left of the carpet.

Build up on the aces, in suit, to their respective king. Any of the cards in the carpet are available for use. Use the cards in your hand to build on the aces or to form a single heap of those not immediately playable. As always, the top card of the heap is available.

As 'holes' are made in the carpet, fill the gaps with cards from the heap or from those in your hand.

It is not permitted to gather up and replay the heap, neither is this often necessary.

Perpetual Motion Patience

Never was a game so well named. It is also addictive to a maddening degree.

You will need one pack, well shuffled. Begin by dealing out, face upwards, thirteen piles of four cards. Imagine that these piles are numbered from one to thirteen and line them up in whatever way helps you to remember. (As usual, the jack equals eleven, the queen twelve and the king has the value of thirteen.)

The object of the game is to eliminate the pack, in batches of thirteen, in the following way.

Take the top card from the pile numbered one, putting it beneath pile number two. Move the top card from pile number two to the bottom of pile number three, continuing in this way until you arrive at pile number thirteen. The top card from *this* pile returns to the bottom of pile number one. (The *Perpetual Motion* of the title.)

However, whenever the top card of a pile agrees with your numbering of it, do not remove it. Instead, move the card you have taken from the previous pile to the bottom of the next

Fig. 3. Perpetual Motion Patience.
The nine of spades will move to beneath the two of clubs, missing the correctly placed king of clubs.

pile which is *not* topped with its correct number. (There will be less and less of these as the game progresses.) Going back to the beginning, if there was an ace on the first pile as the game began, the first card to move would be the top of pile number two.

Hopefully, all top thirteen cards will soon be where they should be, running in sequence from the ace to the king. Then is the time to remove them, putting them to one side. They take no further part in the game.

The last card removed before the thirteen cards were taken away is now placed beneath the next pile to it (or the next available under the rules should that be already topped by its correct number) and play continues as before.

Should you have succeeded in spiriting away three sequences of thirteen, the game is won. The last layer will be correct, but do not ask me how!

Spoilt Patience

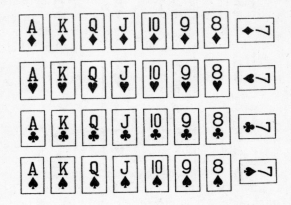

Fig. 4. A successful Spoilt Patience.

Again, a very simple Patience, but none the worse for that!

One pack of cards is required, with all the twos, threes, fours, fives and sixes removed. (This is sometimes called a piquet pack.)

Lay out four rows of seven cards each, facing downwards, with a reserve of four cards placed to one side, also face down.

The four rows represent four different suits in the following order: first diamonds, second hearts, third clubs and the fourth row is spades.

Take the first card in the reserve and put it in its correct place, face up. If it is an ace it will be first in its own row, if a king the second, if a ten the fifth and so on.

(Let us assume that the first card in the reserve is the jack of clubs. Lift the concealed card that is lying in the place where the jack of clubs *should* be and lay the jack there. Put the card thus ousted into the correct place for *it*, removing the card that is lying there. Play on in the same way, placing and removing.)

Should you discover a seven while doing this, for which there is no space available, place it horizontally at the end of the appropriate row and take a card from the reserve to continue the game.

If you turn over the *fourth* seven while there are still cards face down, there is one last chance to make the game a success. Turn one of the remaining concealed cards and, if it is in the correct place, lay it down face up and turn another. This enables you to play on.

The game has failed if the card chosen was not where it should be: a *Spoilt Patience.*

Czarina Patience

One pack of cards (well shuffled) is needed for this game.

Deal five cards on to the table, face upwards and in the shape of a cross; this is the tableau. The next card from those you hold is put, face up, into the left-hand corner. This is the first foundation card. Three other cards of the same value must be placed in the remaining corners, as soon as they emerge in play.

Fig. 5. Czarina Patience.
The first foundation card has been placed.

The object of the game is to build a thirteen card sequence, upwards and in suit, on each foundation. (Fig. 5 has the seven of hearts as an example. Thus, the sequence will run seven, eight,

nine, ten, jack, queen, king, ace, two, three, four, five, and end
with a six.) To achieve this, you will be building *downwards*,
regardless of suit, onto the cross cards until these cards can be
removed to a foundation pile.

Build any cards that can be used from the tableau onto the
foundations, filling gaps from those you hold. (Later in the
game, a gap may be filled with *any* card available; that is, the top
card of the heap, of a tableau pile or those in your hand.)

If, in the initial tableau, you are fortunate enough to deal
consecutively numbered cards, for example, a jack *and* a
queen, you can build down immediately by placing the jack
on top of the queen. Then another card can be dealt into the
space that is left. This rarely happens if the cards are well
shuffled.

Now begin to deal your cards, one by one. Play them upwards
onto the foundations, or downwards onto the cross cards until
needed. Unplayable cards are put face up onto a single heap and,
yes, the top of this is always available for you to use!

When all the cards have been used, no redeal of the heap is
permitted.

The game has succeeded if each foundation pile contains
thirteen cards, built upwards in suit, causing the central cross to
vanish silently away.

Knaves' Dial Patience

This is one of the more simple games, requiring two packs of
cards, for days when only a gentle brainteaser is needed. This
does *not* mean that a happy ending is automatic.

Begin by shuffling the two packs together, very thoroughly.
Turn the top card – this will decide the suit of the twelve
foundations.

Excluding the jack (or knave), arrange the cards of this suit in
a semicircle, as they emerge in play, running from the ace to the
king. All cards face upwards.

The eight jacks play no part in this game. They are placed in
two rows of four, inside the half circle or 'dial'.

The object of the game is to build the other seven cards, of the
same value, upon each of the corresponding cards in the semicircle, alternating the colours. (The suit being diamonds, a black

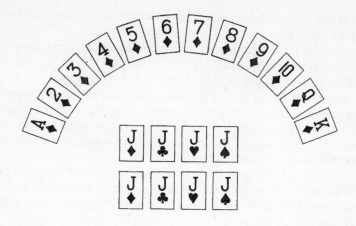

Fig. 6. Knaves' Dial Patience.
In this game, the ten of diamonds was the top card.

ace will be placed on the ace of diamonds, a red ace on the black ace and so on.) But you need *all* the foundation cards in place *before* you can put any cards of the opposing colour on top of them.

Deal out the cards in your hand one by one. If possible, play these upon the foundation cards or discard them to a single heap, the top of which remains available, as ever.

All cards having been used, turn over the heap and play it through again, once. If you have been successful, the dial will have changed colour; in *this* game from red to black.

Pas Seul Patience

One pack of cards is needed for this. *Pas Seul*, peering back through the mists of time to ballet classes, is that golden opportunity yearned for by budding Pavlovas, the solo-dance. A most suitable title for a Patience.

All cards in this game face upwards. Begin by dealing out six cards in a row for the tableau.

Your object is to take the aces as they emerge in play, building upwards upon them in suit and sequence to the king.

(Put these foundation cards, when discovered, in a line at the top of the table.)

Start by removing any aces, and cards that can be built upon them, from the tableau. Fill the resulting gaps, if any, with cards taken from those you hold.

If your tableau consists of consecutively numbered cards of alternating colours (e.g. a red seven and a black eight), build these cards downwards on each other (e.g. place the red seven onto the black eight). Again, fill any resulting gaps with cards taken from those you hold.

After this, deal out the pack one by one. Build on the foundation piles wherever possible or build downwards on the tableau cards, in sequence but alternating the colours, until they can be removed. Overlap these cards to make six columns of differing lengths.

Discard unplayable cards to a single heap. Cards available for you to use are the top card of the heap (naturally), the top card of those in your hand, the exposed card at the base of a column or any part of a downward sequence, provided that the rule about alternating colours is observed. This is very useful in extricating a vital card.

Gaps in the tableau, a column having been played off, are filled by any one available card *or* a sequence.

No second chance is given in this game as one may not redeal the heap.

Pyramid Patience

One pack of cards is needed for this simple Patience. Shuffle the pack thoroughly (absolutely vital in this game) and construct a pyramid in the following fashion.

Deal out, face upwards, five rows of cards as a reserve in the shape of a pyramid: one card in the top row, two in the second, three in the third, four in the fourth and five cards in the bottom row.

The object of the game is to remove the four aces, as they surface in play, to the top of the table, building upwards upon each in sequence and in suit to the king.

Every card in the reserve is available for use. Take away from there any aces, and cards to be built on them, filling spaces from the cards you hold.

Now deal your cards one by one, either to a foundation pile or to a single heap, remembering that the top of this yearns to be of assistance.

No redeal of the heap is permitted when all your cards are played.

A successful ending will find the pyramid vanished and four neat piles, each crowned with a king.

Les Quatorze Patience

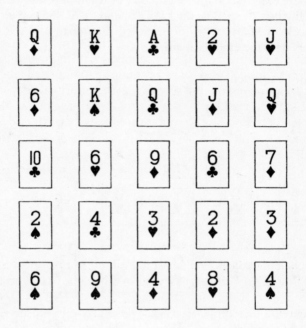

Fig. 7. Les Quatorze Patience.

Two packs of cards are needed for this game. Shuffle the cards and deal out twenty-five cards, face upwards, in five rows, each containing five cards. The object of this Patience is to make the number fourteen with any two cards, taken only from a perpendicular or from a horizontal row. The cards paired in this way are placed to one side and their places taken by the cards in your hand.

The jack counts as eleven, the queen twelve and the king thirteen.

If, during the game, the number fourteen cannot be made, one has a second chance. Any two cards may be taken from their proper position and may change places with two other cards so as to make one or more fourteens. This exchange of cards can be done only once in each playing.

If you are successful in this game, the entire pack will be paired off.

In the example given, the queen of diamonds can be paired with the two of spades, the king of hearts with the ace of clubs, the jack of hearts with the three of diamonds and the six of spades with the eight of hearts.

Picture Patience

Fig. 8. Picture Patience – ready to begin.
(All cards face upwards.)

You will need two packs of cards for this game, but do not shuffle the packs together.

To begin, take one pack and lay out nine cards in three rows (three cards in each row), facing upwards. Then play out the cards in your hand into a heap; placing the four aces, as they appear, in a perpendicular line on the left. The four kings, as *they* appear, are placed to the right. The aces are built on upwards, in suit. (Two of hearts to be placed on the ace of hearts, three of hearts to be placed on the two and so on.) The final card on these piles will be a king.

The kings are built on downwards, in suit. (Queen of hearts to be placed on the king of hearts, jack of hearts to be placed on the queen and so on.) The final card on these piles, if successfully worked out, will be an ace.

Whenever you can use a card from the centre nine, replace it with the top card from the heap. When you have worked your way through the first pack, continue with the second. The aces and kings from this pack are put on the waste heap or become one of the nine central cards until they can be correctly placed. The heap can be turned over when all the cards are used, and played through once again to give one a second chance. If all the cards are not placed in their proper sequence after this, the game is unsuccessful.

Quadrille Patience

This decorative Patience is one of several named after a dance. (Seeking always to inform, I have discovered that the quadrille was a square dance of French origin, reputed to have been introduced into England in 1813 by the Duke of Devonshire!)

Only one pack of cards is required for this. Shuffle the pack very thoroughly and deal the cards out onto a heap, removing the aces and twos as they emerge and placing them to form the figure of a quadrille.

Once all eight foundation cards are laid out, they must be built on according to suit, but not as in most of the other games in this book. This time you must build in alternate numbers: for example, on the ace is placed first a three, next a five, then seven, nine, jack and finishing with a king; on the two is placed a four, then a six, followed by eight, ten and finishing with a queen.

There is only one heap, so progress can be very difficult

Fig. 9. Quadrille Patience.

sometimes. The heap can be used twice more after all the
aces and twos have been found, but no further chances are
allowed.

Sultan Patience
You will need two packs of cards for this game, the aim of which
is to surround the sultan, or king of hearts, with his harem.

238

Remove the eight kings and one ace of hearts and place them in three rows of three, facing upwards, as follows:

Fig. 10. Sultan Patience – ready to begin.

Top row: king of clubs, ace of hearts, king of clubs.
Middle row: king of diamonds, king of hearts (the sultan), king of diamonds.
Bottom row: king of spades, king of hearts and king of spades.

Give the rest of the cards a good shuffle, then deal out eight cards and place them face upwards at right angles, four to the left and four to the right of the square. These cards are called the 'divan', the Turkish word for a long bench covered in cushions, much in evidence in Victorian paintings of the mysterious harem.

The king of hearts in the centre is not to be covered by any other card. The other kings and the ace of hearts are to be built in suit up to their respective queen. (The ace is placed on the king,

239

the two on the ace, etc. The two of hearts is placed upon the ace of hearts and so on.)

Use the cards in your hand to build if possible, or place them onto a single heap, the top card of which is always available.

When there is a suitable card in the divan, this must be used and the space filled from the top of the heap. (If there is no heap at that moment, use the next card from those you hold in your hand.)

All the cards having been used, the heap may be played twice *without reshuffling*.

If the game has come out successfully, the king of hearts is to be seen surrounded by his eight queens.

Alhambra Patience

You will need two packs of cards for this game, somewhat strangely named after the citadel and palace in Granada, built at the behest of the Moorish kings of the thirteenth century.

Remove the ace and the king of each suit from one pack, putting these eight cards at the top of the table as foundation cards.

The aim of the game is to build the aces up in sequence and in suit to the king (ace, two, three, four, five, six, seven, eight, nine, ten, jack, queen and king). The kings build downwards in sequence and suit to the ace.

Shuffle the remaining cards together very thoroughly and deal out a reserve of four rows of eight cards each, face upwards, from left to right. Overlap the rows so that the layout resembles eight upright columns, with the value of each card clearly seen.

Use any suitable exposed card (those at the base of a column with nothing upon them) to build on the foundation cards. By doing this you release the cards above for use.

When you can do no more, play out the cards in your hand one by one, building up or down wherever possible.

There is no building on the reserve. Discard useless cards to a single heap, the use of which is somewhat different from the norm. Exposed cards in the reserve can be played to the top of the heap, if their numbering is consecutive, either up or down. Suit is of no importance. For example, if the card on the top of the heap is a seven, an exposed card valued at six or eight can be moved on to it. This is very useful in unblocking trapped cards, as you will appreciate!

The heap can be turned over and played through again twice at the end of the first deal, but careful planning is needed for a successful conclusion.

A *horrible* variation of this Patience begins with the reserve dealt out in eight piles of four cards, with only the top card facing upwards. I believe this to be impossible to bring out. (Well, I can't do it . . .)

Captive Queens Patience

Fig. 11. Captive Queens Patience – ready to begin.

One pack of cards is required for this game. Remove the four queens from the pack and place them face upwards, one upon another, in the centre of the table. These are the 'captive queens'.

All the fives and all the sixes are arranged in a circle around the queens, also facing upwards. Once the opening tableau has been arranged, the Patience is ready to begin.

The fives and the sixes are the foundation cards. The object of the game is to build upwards on the sixes, in suit, to the jacks and to build downwards, in suit, on the fives to the kings. (This last runs five, four, three, two, ace, king.)

Using the cards in your hand, build on the foundation cards if possible. Place those not immediately needed face upwards on a single heap. The top card is always available for use.

You are permitted to replay the heap once, but there must be no reshuffling of the cards, however useful this might be to a happy ending!

Duchess De Luynes Patience
You will need two packs of cards for this game.

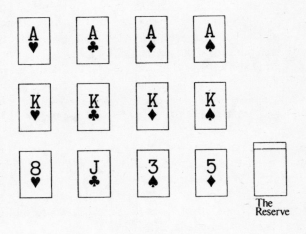

Fig. 12. Duchess de Luynes Patience – the layout.

Deal out four cards in a row side by side, facing upwards, with two more cards (called the reserve pile), one upon the other beside them, facing downwards.

The object of the game is to take one king and one ace from each suit as they appear, building upwards on the aces, in suit to the king (ace, two, three, four, five, six, seven, eight, nine, ten, jack, queen, king). The kings are built downwards, in suit to the aces (king, queen, jack, ten, nine, eight, seven, six, five, four, three, two, ace).

Remove any aces or kings there might be in the row of four and place them as shown in fig. 12; a row of four aces at the top and a row of four kings in the middle are required.

Continue dealing four cards onto the previous four and two cards onto the reserve pile. Pause between each deal to see whether there are any kings and aces to be removed or any building (up or down) that can be done.

When all the cards in your hand have been used, spread out the reserve pile and remove any cards that can be used immediately. Then check to see whether any exposed cards on the row of four can be built onto the king/ace piles. If so, build them accordingly.

After this, gather up the four piles from right to left and put the unused remnants of the reserve pile on top. Continue the game as before. Three redeals are permitted but, on the last redeal omit the reserve pile and just deal out one row of four cards.

I am told that there is a Patience game, entitled *Parisienne*, with precisely the same rules, the only difference being the removal and placing of the four kings and the four aces *before* the game begins. It makes life a little easier, I suppose . . .

Rouge et Noir Patience

You will need two packs of cards for this game. Begin by removing the eight aces from the packs and place them side by side in a row, facing upwards.

Below these foundation cards deal out a row of eight cards, also face up and side by side. This is the tableau.

The object of the game is to build upwards, in sequence, on these ace foundation cards to the king. The difference in this game is that the piles are built in alternating colours, the red and black of the title (a red two on a black ace, a black three on a red two, and so on).

Take any suitable cards from the tableau and place them on the foundations. Fill any gaps from the cards you hold in your hand.

If you have consecutively-numbered cards in the tableau of opposing colours, you can build *downwards* on them, i.e. place a black seven on a red eight. Again, fill any gaps from the cards you hold in your hand.

Begin to play, dealing one card at a time. Anything that cannot be placed immediately on the foundation cards can be built downwards on the tableau until needed or onto a single heap, the top card of which is always available for use.

Single cards can be moved from the top of each tableau pile onto the foundations, or from the top of one tableau pile to the top of another, if this is helpful; but never to fill a gap.

Gaps in the tableau line must be filled immediately from the top of the heap. If the heap has been used, fill the spaces with cards dealt from those you hold. Should *those* have been exhausted, the gap must remain a gap!

One redeal is permitted when all the cards have been dealt. Pick up the heap, turn it over and play on as before.

The game is won if all the foundation piles have been built in alternate colours up to the king.

Legitimist Patience

I remain in cheerful ignorance as to the identity of the supporter of the French royal house of Bourbon who (presumably) invented this Patience. It does not stop me playing it.

Two packs of cards are needed. Shuffle both packs together, first removing one king and placing it upon the table. (All cards are placed face upwards in this game and the suit is of no importance.)

As they emerge in play, put in a row beside the king from left to right, a queen, jack, ten, nine, eight, seven and six. These are the foundation cards (or *origines* as the French has it). There is one difficulty. Foundation cards *must* be moved into position in the order stated (the queen before the jack, eight before seven, etc.).

The object of the game is to build, in sequence, downwards on these, paying no attention to suit. Thus, in a successful game, the king finishes the thirteen card sequence topped with an ace, the queen with a king, the jack with a queen, ten with a jack, nine with a ten, eight with a nine, seven with an eight and six with a seven. But you don't have to wait until you have all the foundation cards in place before you start building.

Play the cards in your hand one by one upon any available foundation card. If they cannot be used immediately, put them in a single heap, the top card of which is always available.

The heap can be turned over and redealt twice. If you have not succeeded . . . well, 'tant pis!'

Square Patience
Two packs of cards, well shuffled together, are needed for this game.

Fig. 13. Square Patience.

Deal out twelve cards, facing upwards, to make three sides of a square: four cards at the top and four at each side. This is the tableau.

Remove the twos as they emerge in play, placing them in two rows of four inside the confines of the square, face up, naturally.

The object of the game is to build upwards, in suit and sequence, until each foundation is crowned by its respective ace. (The sequence runs two, three, four, five, six, seven, eight, nine, ten, jack, queen, king and ace.)

245

Deal out the cards you hold in your hand one by one. Build upwards on the twos, if there are any available, or build downwards in suit on any suitable card in the tableau (e.g. onto the ace of diamonds put the king, queen, jack, ten, etc. of diamonds) until these can be played to the foundation piles. (If, when you deal out the tableau at the start of the game, you have consecutively-numbered cards in the same suit, you can, of course, build downwards on them and then deal other cards into any spaces.)

Unplayable cards are discarded face up to a single heap, the top card of which is always available. A space in the tableau, caused by the removal of a card or pile, is filled with a card taken from the top of the heap.

I hope that all the foundation piles are now topped with their aces, no second deal of the heap being allowed.

A variant to this game, named *Deuces*, is a little less difficult. All the foundation twos are put in place *before* the game begins, but the columns of the tableau to the left and right have three cards in each, not four. The rest of the Patience is played in the same way, but this game *does* allow a redeal.

Herring-Bone Patience

I have a weakness for the more colourful layouts: this is one such, and the title is appropriate. Two packs are needed.

After shuffling the packs together, deal out two rows of three cards as a tableau, one above the other. (All cards in this Patience face upwards.)

If a jack is among the original six, remove it to the centre of the table, replacing it with the next card from the pack.

Put *all* the jacks, as they emerge in play, into the centre of the table to form a non-overlapping, upright column of eight. These are the foundation cards.

The aim of the game is to build downwards, in sequence and in suit, upon the jacks to the ace (jack, ten, nine, eight, seven, six, five, four, three, two and ace).

The king and the queen are of no value in this game, other than to add verisimilitude to the title. When a jack is in place, the king and queen of matching suit are put at an angle on either side of it; the 'herring-bone' takes shape in this way.

The Tableau

Foundations

The Heap

Fig. 14. Herring-Bone Patience.
A demonstration of the layout, with three jacks still to emerge.

Nothing can be built upon the king of spades in the tableau; he awaits the arrival of the second jack of spades for his removal.

The royal couple must not be placed before their jack emerges, being discarded to the solitary heap or remaining in waiting upon the tableau, if they arrive at the wrong time.

It is not necessary to have both king *and* queen before moving them into place.

Deal out the cards in your hand one by one. Play anything suitable to a foundation pile. If this is not possible, build upwards, in suit, upon the cards in the tableau until they are needed.

The whole, or part, of a tableau pile can be built upon another if the rules of upward sequence and matching suit are observed.

(Fill gaps in the tableau with the top card from your hand or from the heap.)

Do not build higher than a ten on these. If the original layout had any kings, queens or tens in it, they cannot have anything placed upon them. Your only chance is a speedy removal to a foundation pile.

Discard unplayable cards to the single heap, the top of which is always available.

All cards having been dealt, turn over the heap and play it through once again. I wish you success.

This game is one of many for which you will find a very large table, or miniature cards, helpful. The more venturesome will scorn these suggestions and sit upon the floor.

Royal Cotillion Patience

Two packs are required for this game. Originally the cotillion was a dance for four couples, in which the ladies lifted their skirts to reveal an inch or so of ornate petticoat (*cotillon* in French). Later the name was given to a fast waltz.

Shuffle the two packs together very thoroughly and deal out, face upwards and not overlapping, twelve cards, in three rows of four, to the left of the board. (The 'left wing'.)

Next deal sixteen cards in four rows of four to the right of the board – yes, the 'right wing'. These cards also do not overlap and all face upwards.

Between these wings, as they surface in play, are placed the foundation cards in two upright columns of four, comprising one ace and one two from each suit.

The aim of the game is to build upwards, in suit, on these foundations by two. Each thirteen card sequence runs as follows:

Ace, three, five, seven, nine, jack, king, two, four, six, eight, ten and queen.

Two, four, six, eight, ten, queen, ace, three, five, seven, nine, jack and king.

All the cards on the right wing are available for building onto the foundation piles, gaps being filled by the next card from those you hold or from the top of the, as yet unformed, solitary heap. (Obviously, preference must *always* be given to the heap if the

248

Fig. 15. Royal Cotillion Patience.
A demonstration of the layout.

game is to have a happy ending.) Of course, if you deal any aces or twos into the right wing at the start of the game, you can use these as foundation cards and fill the spaces they leave behind with other cards from the pack.

The cards in the left wing are not so easily caught. Only the bottom row is available, a removal from here freeing the card above for use, while spaces remain unfilled.

Play out the cards in your hand one by one, discarding useless cards to the single heap mentioned above, building on the foundation cards whenever possible.

Redealing the heap is not permitted. A successful conclusion shows the four kings partnered by their queens and ready to dance.

Octave Patience

Two packs are necessary for this most enjoyable and colourful Patience.

Remove the eight aces as foundation cards, putting them in a row at the top of the table, alternately red and black.

Shuffle the remainder of the two packs together very thoroughly and deal out three rows of eight cards each; the first two rows to face downwards and the third row to face up. Overlap the rows, so that the tableau resembles eight upright columns of three.

The object of the game is (a) to build upwards *in suit* and sequence to the tens and (b) to have beneath each foundation pile a column containing a king, queen and jack in *alternating colours*.

Available cards in the tableau are built downwards on the columns, in alternating colours, until taken to the foundations. When an exposed card is removed, turn the one above face up.

Now play out the cards in your hand one by one, either to a foundation pile or onto the tableau (remembering the colour rule). Discard unplayable cards to a single heap, the top of which is always available.

(Only one card at a time, not a sequence, can be moved about the layout.)

Fill a column, emptied in play, with any available card, but beware: remembering the second objective, it is wiser to put a king at the top of an empty column, where possible.

Having played all the cards in your hand, gather up the heap and turn it over. A second chance is given. Deal out eight cards in a line below the tableau. Use any of these eight cards for building on the foundation piles or tableau, filling up spaces with the next card from the heap.

When none of the eight can be placed, the game is practically at an end, *but* the anonymous inventor permits a last, desperate fling. Play the next card from the heap to see if this will reanimate the game. After this, you have no more chances of ending successfully (but I trust you already have).

Wheat-Ear Patience

Two packs are needed for this game. The wheat-ear was a very popular motif in Georgian and Victorian times, which certainly dates this Patience. The Crown jewellery collection includes six fine diamond brooches of this design, dating from the days of William IV; but that is by the by.

Shuffle the two packs together very thoroughly and deal out twenty cards in the shape of a wheat-ear (see fig. 16). The cards are to be placed face upwards, as are all in this game. Beside them

Fig. 16. Wheat-Ear Patience.
The four of spades, from the side reserve, and the four of clubs, at the base of the wheat-ear, can be removed to the foundation row immediately.

place a further eight cards, four to each side, as a second reserve. The next card dealt, of whatever value, is a foundation card. In the example given, it is a four. Take the other seven cards of the same rank as they emerge in play and put them in a row beside the first. The object of the game is to build upwards on these foundation cards in thirteen card sequence, disregarding suit, arriving at a card one less in value to the base card (four, five, six, seven, eight, nine, ten, jack, queen, king, ace, two, three).

Play out the cards from your hand one by one, discarding unplayable cards to a single heap. The top of this remains available, as usual.

All eight cards of the side reserves can be used at any time. Gaps here are refilled with the top card from the heap or with the next card from the pack.

The wheat-ear reserve differs slightly. The cards available for play are those nearest to you at the bottom of the layout. Removing one frees the card above. The wheat-ear is not replaced and quickly vanishes.

When all *your* cards are gone, turn over the heap and play it through again once more. A successful game will find the table empty of all save eight neat piles of thirteen cards.

Gate Patience

One pack is needed for this and all cards face upwards.

Deal out ten cards, putting five in an upright column to the left and five in an upright column to the right. These are the 'gate-posts', or reserve.

Now deal another two rows one above the other, four cards in each, between the parallel columns to represent the 'bars' of the gate. This is the tableau.

The object of the game is to remove the four aces to a line above the two bars of the gate, as they emerge in play, building upwards upon them to the kings, in sequence and suit.

Remove any foundation cards, together with anything to be built upon them, from the tableau or from the exposed cards at the base of the reserves to the side. (As always, this frees the card above for use.)

Build downwards in alternating colours on the tableau moving one card at a time and also using any suitable exposed cards from the base of the reserves.

Spaces made in the tableau are refilled with the next available

Fig. 17. Gate Patience.
The two of clubs is to be removed to its ace pile. If the eight of hearts is taken to fill the gap, the two of spades above is freed to be built upon the ace of spades.

card taken from the posts. When the gateposts have vanished – and this can happen very quickly at times, because the reserve is not replenished – use the top card from the, as yet non-existent, heap.

Begin to play out your cards one by one; to a foundation pile if you can, otherwise building downwards on the tableau until they can be removed. (Do remember the rule of alternating colour.) *Sequences* must not be transferred between columns.

Discard unplayable cards to that good old solitary heap, the top of which is available.

There is no second chance in the guise of a redeal of the heap.

Snail Patience
You will need two packs for this imaginative game. All cards face upwards.

Begin by extricating all fives, sixes and jacks from both packs and place them on the table, coiled round to represent a snail's shell. Begin with the jacks, spiralling them inwards, afterwards

Fig. 18. Snail Patience.
The layout – the seven of diamonds can be removed to a foundation card immediately, and replaced.

using the sixes and ending with the fives.

Shuffle the remainder of the two packs together and deal four cards, horizontally, beneath the layout as a reserve. (See fig. 18.) The snail is now complete.

The object of the game is (a) to build downwards in suit on the fives to the king (five, four, three, two, ace and king) and (b) to build upwards in suit on the sixes, but ignoring the jack, to the queen (six, seven, eight, nine, ten and queen).

The reserve quartet can be used at any time. Deal the cards in your hand one by one, building on a foundation pile, hopefully.

Discard unplayable cards to a single heap, the top of which remains available.

Gaps made in the reserve are filled with either the next card taken from your hand or the top of that ever present heap.

One redeal is permitted. A successful game will show a snail shell made entirely of court cards. But if you find this game too easy, deal the cards only once.

(I have just been told that the Old English word for 'snail' is 'snaegel'. I didn't know that!)

Windmill Patience

Fig. 19. Windmill Patience.
The layout. Only two of the four kings have emerged so far. The two of diamonds can be moved directly to the centre ace and the gap refilled from the heap.

Two packs are needed for this classic Patience.

Take an ace, of any suit, placing it in the middle of the table.

255

This is the first foundation card.

Shuffle the two packs together and deal a reserve of eight cards (face upwards, as are all the cards in this game): put two above, two below, two to the right and two to the left of the ace, representing the sails of the windmill.

As four kings, of any suit, emerge in play, place one diagonally between each of the sails as foundation cards. (See fig. 19.)

The object of the game is (a) to build four sequences of thirteen cards upon the ace in the centre, ignoring suit, to finish with a king (ace, two, three, four, five, six, seven, eight, nine, ten, jack, queen, king, ace, two, three and so on; the numbering is continuous). And (b) to build downwards on each of the four kings, ignoring suit, to the ace (king, queen, jack, ten, nine, eight, seven, six, five, four, three, two and ace).

Fig. 20. Windmill Patience.
The happy ending.

Begin to play out the cards in your hand one by one, building wherever possible. Discard useless cards to a solitary heap, the top of which is there to be removed at any time.

All eight cards in the reserve are available. Spaces made here are to be filled from the top of the heap or, if that is exhausted or not yet begun, with the next card from the pack.

It is permissible to transfer the top card of a king foundation pile to the ace foundation pile, if you consider it advantageous, but *never* remove the base card. I am afraid the opposite is not allowed: cards placed upon the centre ace are not removed.

No redeal of the heap is allowed. If you have been successful, the final layout will look like fig. 20.

Queen of Italy Patience

Fig. 21. Queen of Italy Patience.
(a) The six of hearts can be built upon the five of spades, seven of spades upon the six of hearts and the eight of hearts upon the seven of spades. The exposed card from the terrace – the nine of clubs – is placed upon the eight of hearts.

(b) Place the two of spades upon the three of hearts in the tableau.

As there is, as yet, no heap, fill the gaps with the next cards from the pack in your hand and play on.

Two packs are needed for this most interesting Patience. Good decisions on your part will help to bring this game to a successful conclusion. (Another name given to this is *Terrace*, a self-explanatory title, as you will see.) All cards face upwards.

When you have shuffled the packs together very thoroughly, deal a row of eleven cards at the top of the table as a reserve, overlapping them from left to right. (This is the Terrace.)

Below these deal a second row of four cards. Choose *one* of these as the first foundation card. The object of the game is to remove the other seven cards of the same value to the foundation row as they emerge in play. One must then attempt to build upwards, in sequence and in *alternating colours*, until each pile contains thirteen cards with the top card being one lower in value than the base card. The value of the cards is continuous, the ace being above the king and below the two.

Before deciding on your foundation card, look at the reserve to see what it contains. This row can be built *only* to a foundation pile, so think carefully. (In the example, I chose the five of spades as the first foundation. As you can see, the nine of clubs is the exposed card on the terrace; had I chosen either the two of spades, ace of spades or jack of diamonds as foundations, the cards in the terrace would have remained, unmoving, for a long time.)

If you deal two (three, or even all four) cards of the same value among these four cards, you will probably decide to keep both (or all) as foundation cards.

Take the rejected cards to begin a third row beneath the second and deal some more cards to bring the total number of cards in the bottom row to nine. This is the tableau.

Play what you can from the tableau to the foundations, building upwards in sequence and in alternating colours. In fig. 21, the foundation card is a black five. The sequence there will run thus: black five (five of spades), red six (six of hearts), black seven (seven of spades), red eight (eight of hearts) and so on until you reach a black four.

If you cannot play the cards in the tableau directly onto a foundation pile, play them on each other, building downwards in sequence and alternating colours until needed. Again, the value of cards is continuous so that if you have a red ace and a black king in the tableau, you can put the king on top of the ace. When building down on the tableau, it is better to place the cards in such a way that the value of all of them can be seen. Unfortunately, only single cards can be moved when building down, not sequences of cards.

The exposed card to the right of the reserve, or terrace, is built onto a foundation pile and nowhere else, as I have already said. Using this card frees the one beside it for use.

Spaces made in the tableau are to be filled from the heap if this is already in existence, from the top of the cards you hold if not.

Now deal out the pack one by one, building upwards on foundation piles where you can. Sheer impossibility? Then build downwards on a suitable card in the tableau.

Unplayable cards must be abandoned to a single heap, the top of which remains available throughout. There is no redeal.

If you were fortunate in your choice of foundation, the end of the game will find eight piles of thirteen cards beaming back at you, while the terrace has long since crumbled away!

Waning Moon Patience

Fig. 22. Waning Moon Patience.
(a) The four of hearts can be placed on top of the five of hearts in the tableau.
(b) The three of spades is placed on top of the four of spades.

Two packs are needed for this most appropriately named game. All cards are to be dealt face upwards.

Shuffle the packs together very thoroughly and deal out thirteen piles in the shape of a semicircle, three cards to each pile. This tableau represents the crescent moon.

Any aces found during this deal are taken out (replaced by the next card in the pack) and used to form a curved row beneath the tableau. (The remaining aces will take their places later as they emerge in play.) These are the foundation cards.

The object of the game is to build upwards, in sequence and in suit on the foundations, to the king.

The top card of each pile in the tableau is available for use and removing cards frees those beneath.

When all available cards in the original layout have been removed to the foundations, build *downwards* on the tableau, in suit, until they can be played off. (For example, seven of hearts upon the eight of hearts, four of diamonds on the five of diamonds and so on.) But please remember to keep the tableau piles meticulously tidy. You don't wish to see the cards beneath the top card and cheat inadvertently, do you?

Now deal out the cards in your hand one by one; either to the foundation piles or to the tableau. Discard unplayable cards to a single heap, the top of which always remains available.

Move cards singly, not in groups, between piles. A gap in the tableau is filled by any exposed card. You must decide whether it is wiser to choose the top card of the heap or the top card of a tableau pile for this.

As it is not permitted to play through the heap again, all cards having been dealt, a great deal of thought is needed to bring this game out. Should you have built correctly on each foundation pile to the king, the crescent tableau will have disappeared . . . the moon has waned.

One Foundation Patience

One pack of cards is needed for this game. This Patience differs from most in having only one foundation, and beware . . . it is not as simple as it first appears!

Shuffle the pack and deal a row of seven cards side by side, face upwards. Deal a second row in the same way, overlapping the first; continue this until five rows have been dealt. This has the appearance of seven columns, the bases of each being the exposed cards.

Deal the next card, face up, onto the table. This is the foundation card. The object of the game is to gather all cards to it.

The peculiarity of this game is that one may build, in

Fig. 23. One Foundation Patience.
The beginning. (All cards are facing upwards.)

sequence and regardless of suit, upwards *or* downwards, changing direction at any time. Exposed cards at the foot of the seven columns are used to build. Each time a card is used, the card above it becomes available for use. (If you use up all the cards from one column you don't replace them, but leave an empty space.)

For example: the foundation card in fig. 23 is a six. Either a five or a seven can be built upon it. One must plan ahead to avoid becoming blocked too soon. And here is the difficulty. An ace must *not* be placed upon a king, a king cannot be played upon an ace. (A queen is the only card permitted to be dealt upon a king and a two upon an ace.)

When further play from the columns is impossible, deal the next card from those held in your hand onto the pile. This is a new foundation.

Play available cards onto this until you become stuck, yet again. Deal another new foundation from those cards you hold and continue until all have been used.

The game is won if all fifty-two cards sit one upon another on the foundation.

Deauville Patience

Why this game is named after the French coastal town I do not know; but I am positive that two packs of cards are required to

play this excellent Patience. A great deal of thought is needed to
bring it to a successful conclusion.

Fig. 24. Deauville Patience.

After the two packs have been well shuffled together, deal
three overlapping rows with ten cards in each. All these cards
face downwards. Deal a fourth row of ten cards to overlap the
third, *this* row to face upwards. These are the 'exposed' cards.

Remove any aces that are immediately available in the
exposed cards, placing them in a row below the tableau. The
others will emerge in the course of play to join them. These are
the foundation cards.

The object of the game is to build upwards, in suit and
sequence, on each ace to the king.

When an exposed card has been removed, turn the card
beneath over, so that it becomes available for use.

You can build downwards on exposed cards in the tableau in
sequence but in alternating colours (red five on black six, black
four on red five, and so on). When you do so, place the cards in
such a way that the tops of any other cards there can be seen.
This helps to plan the best move possible.

Play the cards in your hand one at a time. These, and all the
exposed cards in the tableau, can be played in the following way:

(a) Immediately onto the foundation cards, hopefully . . .

(b) If this is not possible, build downwards in sequence in alternating colours on the tableau until these can be moved to the foundations.

(c) Any exposed card can be used to fill a gap caused by the removal of all the cards in one column. This is very useful when a card is blocking play.

Cards played from those held in your hand can be discarded onto a single heap if they cannot be used. The top card of the heap is always available.

Resist the temptation to move sequences into a space or onto other exposed cards in the tableau. Each card must be moved singly.

There is no redeal of the heap. The game is won if each foundation runs upwards, in suit and sequence, to the king.

Demon Patience

One pack is needed for this; a rarity among Patience games in that it is known to many.

Deal out a neat pile of thirteen cards, face down, to the left of the table. Turn the top card face upwards. This reserve is the 'Demon' of the title.

Take the next card from those you hold, putting it face upwards at the top of the table as the first foundation card.

Beneath this deal a row of four cards as the tableau. Again, these must face upwards.

The object of the game is to take the other three cards, of equal value to the first, to the foundation row as they emerge in play: building upwards upon each, in sequence and suit, until each pile contains thirteen cards, thus absorbing every card in the pack. The top card will be one lower in value to the base. (As the example given is the seven of hearts, a successful sequence will run as follows: seven, eight, nine, ten, jack, queen, king, ace, two, three, four, five and six of hearts.)

You can build in a downward direction on the tableau, in sequence but alternating colours (e.g. red ace on black two, black king on red ace, and so on). Spread each column towards you; it helps!

The Foundation Row
– three more Foundation cards to find

The "Demon"
Reserve

The Tableau

Fig. 25. Demon Patience.
The layout.

A space in the tableau is filled with the top card of the reserve. The face-down card below it is then turned upwards for use.

Deal the cards from your hand in groups of three to a single heap, face upwards. When you have dealt the trio, look at the top card. Remove it, if possible, to a foundation pile (either founding it or building on it). Otherwise, build it downwards on the tableau until required.

If you *are* able to play the heap's top card, the one *below* is free and the game continues in the same way.

Pausė to consider what is to be done between each deal of three. (The last group will, of course, only consist of one card.)

The top of the demon reserve is always available. (Remember to turn the face-down card upwards when the one above is removed.) So, too, is each exposed card of the tableau. These can transfer singly between the columns, or in any length of sequence, provided the 'join' complies with the rules of downward sequence and alternating colour.

Should the demon vanish, fill the gap with the top card from the heap *only*.

When the pack is dealt, turn the heap over and play it through again, redealing in batches of three as before.

This is done until the game is successful, or it becomes vividly apparent that the game is hopelessly blocked.

If the latter, there is nothing to be done but to gather up the entire pack and accept defeat gracefully. (Sweeping the cards before one onto the floor with muttered execrations is frowned on by most players!)

I wonder why this infuriating and aptly named game is so popular.

Napoleon at St Helena Patience

The apparent simplicity of this Patience masks the difficulty of bringing it out successfully. (Like life, I suppose.)

It possesses several titles, *Forty Thieves* and *Big Forty* among them, but *Napoleon at St Helena* seems to be the most popular.

Two packs are required and all cards must face upwards; one needs the addition of no *further* difficulty, goodness knows!

Begin by shuffling the two packs together and deal out four rows of ten cards as the tableau. Overlap them so that they resemble ten columns, with the value of each card clearly visible. If you deal any aces in these rows, remove them to use as foundation cards and replace them with the next cards in the pack.

The aim of the game is to take the eight aces, when they emerge, building upwards upon them in sequence and in suit to the king (ace, two, three, four, five, six, seven, eight, nine, ten, jack, queen and king). When found, put these foundation cards in a row above the tableau.

The card at the base of each column, having nothing upon it, is exposed and available for play and removing a card frees the one above.

Move any suitable card to the foundation row. Otherwise build downwards on other columns of the tableau in sequence *and in suit* (this is the stumbling block) until needed (eight of hearts upon the nine of hearts, seven of hearts upon the eight of hearts and so on). Move single cards only, not sequences.

When you have done all you can, deal out the cards you hold one by one, to the foundation piles or to the tableau. Discard unplayable cards to a solitary heap, the top of which is always available.

A space in the tableau, caused by the removal of a column, is filled with *any* available card.

No second chance in the way of a redeal is allowed.

Limited Patience

Two packs are needed for this difficult game. Shuffle the cards together very thoroughly and deal out three rows of twelve, all cards to face upwards. These tableau cards must not overlap.

Take away any aces in the bottom row and put them in a line at the top of the table. (Hopefully, any other aces *will* emerge – or be freed from the top two rows – during play!) The object of the game is to build upwards, in sequence and in suit, upon these foundation cards to the king.

The base card of each of the twelve 'columns' of the tableau is exposed and free for use. Removing a card frees the one above it. Do any building possible onto the foundations, then begin to play out the cards in your hand.

Those unable to be placed can be discarded to a single heap or built downwards on any exposed card in the layout, but it is here that the difficulty begins. One is very 'limited' in the way this is to be done. Only a single card, of the same suit and one lower in value, can be put upon another, taken either from those you hold, the top of the heap or another exposed card in the tableau (four of diamonds upon the five of diamonds, ten of clubs upon the jack of clubs and so on).

And here is the tricky part . . . This pair are now *totally* immovable until they can be played to their foundation pile. They must not be built upon further or, even worse, removed to a space. A space made by the emptying of a column is filled by any available card, if that is what you wish. But beware, it is sometimes wiser to leave the gap empty.

When all the cards have been dealt, there is a second chance for success. Turn the heap over and take the top four cards from it. Place the four cards in a line facing upwards and, if possible, play them to a foundation pile or pair with another on the tableau or put them into a space. (Now you see how useful spaces can be.) This will set the game moving once more, if luck is with you.

Anything taken from this reserve of four cards is to be replaced by the next card (or cards) from the heap. When *no* card of this quartet can be moved, the game has ended. No further helps are permitted.

Triple Line Patience

Two packs are needed for this plain, no-nonsense game. Begin by shuffling the packs together, afterwards dealing out, face upwards, three rows of twelve cards each, from left to right, as the tableau. Overlap the rows so that the layout resembles twelve upright columns of three.

The object of the game is to take the eight aces as they surface in play (putting them in a row at the top of the table), building upwards on these foundation cards, in sequence and in suit, to the king.

Remove all aces in the exposed cards (those in the bottom row of the tableau with no other card upon them) and anything that can be built on them. Yes, this releases the card above for use!

Any *single* exposed card in the tableau can be built downwards in suit onto another column until needed (seven of hearts onto the eight of hearts, six of hearts onto the seven and so on . . .). The removal of *sequences* of cards would make this game easier, but is not allowed.

When nothing more can be done, play out the cards in your hand one by one, hopefully to a foundation pile, otherwise building downwards in suit on the tableau.

Discard useless cards to a single heap, the top of which remains available.

Should all the cards in a column have disappeared, fill the gap with a single card, taken either from the top of the heap or the next card from those in your hand.

The heap can be turned over and played through once more when all your cards are dealt. Despite this grudging second chance, the game is surprisingly difficult to bring out.

Sir Tommy Patience

This is supposed to be the first Patience ever invented, but who Sir Tommy was I do not know. (Many people who think that Patience has only *one* game know this one.)

The object of the game is the usual one – to build on the aces up to the king – but it is not necessary to follow suit, i.e. diamonds on diamonds, clubs on clubs, as with some games of Patience. The number on the card is the only thing of importance.

You will need one pack of cards. Shuffle these well and begin to lay out four piles facing upwards. You can place the cards on whichever pile you like as the piles do not have to contain an equal number of cards – see below. Remove the four aces as they appear. The aces are placed in a line below the four piles and if there are any twos, place these on the aces, followed by threes and fours and so on, as far as possible.

If the cards cannot be placed on an ace pile, put them on the ordinary piles above as you please. But take care. It is a good idea to put the court cards on one pile so that the low cards, so necessary to be immediately available if the game is to be successful, are not blocked.

You must not transfer a card from one ordinary pile to another. It must stay in the pile chosen until it can be placed on an ace foundation pile in the usual way.

If you have not been able to place all the cards on an ace foundation by the time all the cards have been dealt, the game has been a failure. (Shuffle again and better luck next time!)

Colours Patience
One pack of cards is needed for this simple, but aggravating, game.

Fig. 26.

Begin by dealing out the pack, face upwards, into up to six heaps. Pile these as you please; the top cards are always available for use.

You are looking for a two, three, four and five to become the foundation cards. The two and four must be one colour (suit is not important) and the three and five the other. Obviously, the first foundation card to emerge dictates the colour of the others.

When found, put these cards in numerical order, and side by side, at the top of the table.

The object of the game is to build upwards on these, in colour and in thirteen-card sequence, to a card of a value one below the foundation card.

Build from the cards you hold and watch the tops of the heaps with an eagle eye. (Discard cards with some care, or you will find yourself becoming hopelessly blocked.) One must *not* move a card from heap to heap, only to a foundation pile.

Redealing the heaps is not allowed. A successful game shows the four foundation piles topped by an ace, two, three and four, respectively.

Double Pyramid Patience

Two packs of cards are necessary for this game. (All cards are dealt facing upwards.)

Begin by building a pyramid the easy way. Put one card at the summit and deal ten cards on either side of it. (The cards can overlap if space is a consideration.) You now have a pyramid as the tableau (see overleaf).

The next card of those in your hand will be the first foundation card and is placed inside the tableau. In fig. 27, this is a five, but it could be *anything!*

The other seven cards of the same value are placed as they emerge in play. Put them inside the pyramid, beneath the first foundation pile, in a row of three and a row of four. The 'double pyramid' of the title is thus explained.

The aim of the game is to build upwards in suit and sequence upon the foundations, ending with a card one less in value to the card at the bottom of the pile (for example, five, six, seven, eight, nine, ten, jack, queen, king, ace, two, three and four).

Use any suitable card in the tableau for building, at any time. A card removed from here is never replaced.

Play out the cards in your hands one by one. If they are of no immediate use, pile them as you choose onto one of four heaps

Fig. 27. Double Pyramid Patience.
A demonstration of the layout. (The six of diamonds and the six of clubs can be played onto the foundations from the tableau.)

that form the base of the pyramid. The top cards of these remain ever available for moving to a foundation pile; they may not, however, be moved from one heap to another.

No redeal is allowed. A successful game will find each of the eight foundation piles containing thirteen cards and the large, outer pyramid gone.

Gemini Patience

Two packs of cards are needed for this game. As with all games in this book, *shuffle the cards well* before beginning. Take the first four cards of different values and place them face up on the table. Leave a space between them as twin cards, of any suit, must be placed beside each as they turn up.

Fig. 28. Gemini Patience.

Deal out the cards in your hand onto one of the five heaps, piling them as you please. When you deal a card of the same value (of any suit) as one of those first four cards (its twin), place it in the space left for it. Then, when a card one degree higher (of any suit) than this twin pair emerges, place it above the pair. Once you have *that* card's twin placed beside it, you then build upwards, again not paying any attention to suit (any four on any three, any five on any four, etc.). In each case, before further building upwards is allowed, cards placed above the original twins must also have their twins beside

271

them (e.g. in the example shown in fig. 28 you would need a three on top of both the two of hearts and the two of diamonds before you could put a four on either of them).

Only the top card of each heap is available for use (which must not be transferred between heaps) so great care must be taken in laying out cards on the heaps, otherwise one becomes hopelessly stuck.

A successful end to the Patience shows the original twins, each with a pile above it crowned with the card next *below* it in value. If one is not successful immediately, a second chance is given by gathering up the heaps, unshuffled, and playing these cards off again; only two heaps may be formed this time and no further attempt is allowed.

This game can be made even more perplexing by playing one of the twin cards upwards and the other downwards. The end result is the same, but very difficult to achieve. Do not try it if there is anybody 'helping' you!

The Lady of The Manor Patience

Fig. 29.   The Lady of the Manor Patience.

You will need two packs of cards for this game. Remove the eight aces, putting them to one side momentarily. Shuffle the remaining cards, then count out four piles of twelve cards each, laying them in a row face upwards. See fig. 29.

Now place the eight aces in a row beneath these piles. The remaining cards are arranged in a semicircle above the four piles, according to their value, from the two to the king. Now begin to build on the aces (two, three, four, five and so on) without regarding suits. Take the cards from the semicircle to do this until an appropriate one appears on one of the four piles. This must be taken in preference to those in the semicircle, the object of the game being to use all the cards in the four piles. If you do not succeed in this, the game has failed.

Missing-Link Patience

One pack of cards is needed for this. It is important to shuffle the cards very thoroughly before attempting it.

Cut the pack and remove one card from the middle *without looking at it*. Put it to one side, face down; this is the 'missing-link' of the title.

The object of the game is to remove the four aces, as they emerge in play, and to build upwards upon each in sequence and suit to the king.

Deal the cards in your hand one by one, all facing upwards, to an ace pile (if you are lucky) or discarding unplayable cards to one of up to seven heaps. These heaps are to be formed as you think best. (Obviously it is not wise to put a high card upon one of lower value and same suit, if this can be avoided.) The top of each heap remains available for use throughout the game but cannot be transferred to another heap.

A vacancy caused by the removal of an entire heap is filled by any exposed card or the next card from the pack.

When you can play nothing more, turn the 'missing-link'. Hopefully this will revive the game. There is no redeal.

A successful game will show four piles of thirteen cards, each topped with a king.

Wheel of Fortune Patience

Two packs of cards are required for this game, but they must not be shuffled together.

Begin by dealing out a circle of sixteen cards from the first

Fig. 30. Wheel of Fortune Patience.
A demonstration of the tableau, all the foundation cards have emerged.

pack. (All cards in this Patience face upwards.)

If there are any kings or aces, remove them to the centre of the circle, putting them in two parallel lines as foundation cards. Immediately fill any gaps made with the next cards from the pack. The other kings and aces are to be placed correctly as and when they emerge.

The object of the game is to build upwards on the four aces, in sequence and in suit, to the kings and to build downwards on the four kings, in sequence and in suit, to the aces.

Move whatever else you can from the tableau to the foundation cards, always refilling spaces from the cards in your hand.

When there is no more to be done, deal a second complete

circle of sixteen cards upon the first. Use these cards to build upwards or downwards as before, remembering to remove aces or kings to the centre. The taking of a card frees the one beneath for use. Again, a space made in the layout must be filled by the next card from those you hold.

Now deal out another complete circle of sixteen cards, continuing with the second pack when the first is exhausted, and play on in the same way. (Obviously, the kings and aces in the new pack are not to be placed in the centre until needed to crown their respective foundation piles.) Probably the very last deal will not have sixteen cards, but we will excuse it.

At the end two further chances are given, should the game not have worked out.

Cards can be transferred between foundation piles *if* they agree in suit and sequence. For example, if the ace of hearts' pile has been built up to the eight and the king of hearts' pile has been built down to the seven, one pile can build on to the other, if this means that the cards left in the wheel become of use.

Spaces caused by this play can be filled by *any* available card left in the tableau. Hopefully this will free any blockage.

British Blockade Patience

Two packs are needed for this game, a more modern and less interesting title of which is *Parallels*. All cards must face upwards.

Shuffle the two packs together very thoroughly. Remove one ace and one king from each suit, putting the four kings in a vertical column to your left and the four aces, in the same fashion, to your right. Allow plenty of space between the two. These are the foundation cards.

The object of the game is to build upwards, in sequence and suit, upon the aces to the appropriate king and downwards, in sequence and suit, upon the kings to the appropriate ace.

Deal ten cards in a row between the parallel kings and aces as a reserve. Pause to consider whether any of these can be used for building. Fill any spaces made with the next cards to be dealt from the pack.

When nothing further can be done, deal a second row of ten cards below the first, but do not overlap them.

275

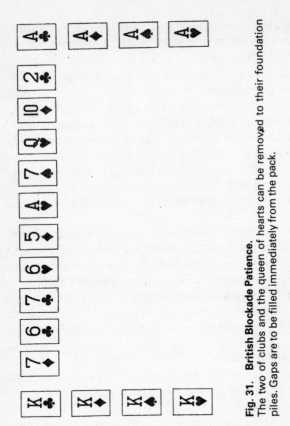

Fig. 31. British Blockade Patience.
The two of clubs and the queen of hearts can be removed to their foundation piles. Gaps are to be filled immediately from the pack.

The cards in both rows are now available for play to the foundation piles. Continue to fill the gaps with the next cards taken from those you hold.

Deal a third row of ten cards below the second, play having come to a standstill.

Now only the top and bottom rows are available. The second row finds itself blockaded, the title of the Patience is vindicated, and a card here is only freed for use when the card immediately above or below it is taken away. Build everything possible, refilling gaps as before.

Blocked again? Deal a fourth row of ten below the previous three. Now there are *two* inner rows awaiting the order of release. Play on, remembering that cards in the inner rows must have a free edge above or below (or both) before you can use them.

No redeal of the reserve is allowed when the pack is exhausted.

Running a blockade has its difficulties, so too has this game – although it's not as frightening!

A truly horrible variation does not allow the top row to possess *any* available cards until all the pack has been dealt. The less said about *that* the better.

Grandfather's Patience

Two packs are necessary for this most venerable of games. All cards are to face upwards.

Shuffle the packs together and deal out two rows of ten cards each, horizontally, parallel to each other, as a reserve. Remove any kings or aces as foundation cards (but only one from each suit, the duplicates are treated in the same cavalier fashion as any other value). Put the kings in a line above the reserve and the aces in a line below the reserve. Also take anything that can be built on them. Fill gaps, as throughout this game, with the next cards from the pack.

The object of the game is to take the kings and aces as they emerge in play; building upwards in sequence and suit upon the aces to the king and building downwards on the kings, in sequence and suit, to the ace.

Deal the cards you hold one by one, building on a foundation pile if possible. Unplayable cards can be placed in one of two ways: either discarded to a single heap, the top of which is always available or, if you choose, played to the reserve, *not more* than one card upon each of the twenty. If you do this, only the uppermost card can be used.

This *can* be most helpful in bringing the game to a successful conclusion, but great care must be taken in avoiding the inadvertent blocking of vitally needed cards.

The heap can be turned over and played through once more, when all the cards have been dealt.

If, near the end of the game, you have used up all the heap and you have spaces in the reserve, you may fill these spaces with top cards of the reserve.

A successful game will find four piles in the row above, each topped by an ace, while the four piles below are crowned with a king. And the reserve has vanished away . . .

Imaginary Thirteen Patience

Fig. 32. Imaginary Thirteen Patience.
The game now ready to begin.

I like this Patience very much, although it appears rather complicated at first. It is very satisfying when it ends well.

You will need two packs of cards for this game. Place on the table eight cards of any suit, running in sequence from the ace to the eight. Below these put a card of any suit which is double the value of the card above. (The jack is valued at eleven, the queen at twelve and the king at thirteen.) So put a two below the ace, an eight below the four, a queen below the six, and so on. A brief difficulty, speedily resolved, is caused by the doubling of the seven and the eight. This is where the *Imaginary Thirteen* of the title is used. Two sevens are fourteen, for which no card exists. If you deduct the imaginary thirteen from fourteen, you are left with one. Therefore place an ace beneath the seven. The same thing happens with the eight. Two eights are sixteen; the imaginary thirteen is deducted and so a three of any suit is placed below the eight.

Begin to deal out the pack in your hand. If you deal a card with a value equal to the total of the upper and lower cards, place

278

it on the card in the lower row. For example, place a three (one plus two) below the ace, a six (two plus four) below the two, a queen (four plus eight) below the four, and so on. Again, when the combined value of the upper and lower cards exceeds thirteen, deduct the imaginary thirteen and use a card to the value of the amount left over. A queen and a five would total seventeen, so deduct thirteen and place a four on the lower card.

If a card cannot immediately be placed onto one of the lower cards, place it on one of four heaps, reserving one of these heaps solely for the kings.

Take the cards for the lower row from the heaps whenever possible before taking from the cards you hold; in that way, you have more chance of bringing the game to a successful conclusion.

Continue adding to the lower row until the upper and lower cards together total thirteen, and place the king on the lower card. If you can do this on each of the eight piles, the game has been worked out correctly.

Jubilee Patience

Two packs of cards are required for this game. It was in 1887 that Queen Victoria celebrated her Golden Jubilee. Today a similar occasion would be marked by the sale of lurid T-shirts, souvenir tea-towels and colour supplements galore. *Then* a loyal populace devised games of Patience in her honour, of a difficulty to make one tear one's hair!

If you are feeling strong enough to make the attempt, begin as follows.

Remove all eight kings and put them, facing upwards, in a row at the top of the table.

The aim of the game is to build upwards on the kings to the queen, in suit, in the following way: king, ace, jack, two, ten, three, nine, four, eight, five, seven, six, queen.

Begin to deal the cards in your hand; either onto the king piles if you can, or to one of four heaps. (I think it wiser to reserve one of the heaps for the queens alone and beware of blocking cards soon needed.) As always in these games, the top card of each heap is available for use. But, you are not allowed to move it from heap to heap – only to a king pile.

When you have played all your cards, turn over and gather up the heaps, without shuffling them, and redeal. This can be done twice.

That doyene of Victorian writers on the game, Miss Mary Whitmore Jones, has the last word: '. . . Success is difficult to attain; it is not the lot of every queen to have a Jubilee.'

Miss Milligan Patience

Two packs are required for this classic game. No collection is complete without the maddening Miss Milligan, although some might be happy to see her go!

Shuffle the two packs together very thoroughly and deal out a row of eight cards, facing upwards, from left to right. This is the beginning of the tableau.

The aim of the game is to move the eight aces, or foundation cards, into a line at the top of the table as they emerge in play, building upwards upon them, in sequence and in suit to the king.

Remove any aces, together with any cards that can be built upon them, from the first row of the tableau. Follow this by dealing a second row of eight cards upon the first, all the cards in this Patience facing upwards.

Overlap the cards which remain, or any spaces made, ensuring that the values of all cards can be easily seen. View the tableau as eight upright columns.

Pause to consider what is to be done. The exposed cards in the tableau can be built downwards in sequence and *alternating* colours upon exposed cards in another column until they can be removed to the foundation piles (red seven on black eight, black six on red seven and so on).

There is no limit to the number of cards in a sequence which can be removed from one column to another, provided that the rule of alternating colour and downward numbering is observed.

An empty column can be filled only by a king, or a sequence of which the king is the beginning.

Deal another row of eight cards as before and play on. (Obviously, the columns will be of unequal length.)

No move is to be made until each deal of eight cards is set down.

An unusual help, called 'waiving', is permitted when the last eight cards have been placed. Any one exposed card at the base of a column can be put to one side, thus permitting the removal of cards trapped above it. The card taken must eventually be played back into the game, either to the tableau or a foundation pile.

'Waiving' can be done as many times as you wish, but the card removed must find a new home; you cannot 'waive' a second card if the first is 'homeless'. If it cannot be replaced, the game is a failure, because the eight foundation piles will not have gathered all the cards to themselves beneath the king.

Interregnum Patience

This game requires two packs of cards, and some thought to bring out! Even the title is something of a puzzle. The only historical Interregnum I know in English history is the gap between the execution of Charles I in 1649 and the accession of Charles II in 1660, so gloomily filled by Cromwell.

Begin by shuffling the two packs together very thoroughly and deal out eight cards, in a row from left to right, at the top of the table. They are called the indicator cards and face upwards, as do all the cards in this game.

Leave sufficient space beneath these for the foundation cards to be placed as they emerge during play. Then deal out a bottom row of eight cards.

Your aim is to find the card one step higher in value than each indicator card.

Building upwards on each one, ignoring suit, in thirteen card sequence until its respective indicator card can be used to crown the pile. (These elusive eight foundation cards take up their position as the second, or middle, row directly below their appropriate indicator cards.)

For example, should the first card in the top row be a two, the foundation card beneath will be a three. The sequence will run as follows: three, four, five, six, seven, eight, nine, ten, jack, queen, king, ace and, finally, the indicator card two.

All eight cards in the bottom row are available for use, either as a foundation card or for building.

When you can do no more, deal out another eight cards upon the bottom row, covering remaining cards or spaces, and play as before. (To remove a card frees the one beneath for use.)

Continue, pausing between each deal of eight cards to build upon the foundation piles whenever possible, until all the cards in your hand have been exhausted.

No redeal is permitted. A successful game will find you able to play out all the cards in the bottom row onto the foundations, and permit yourself a pat on the back.

Squaring the Circle Patience

You will need two packs of cards for this game, together with a clear head. (At least all the cards face upwards . . .)

Fig. 33.   Squaring the Circle Patience.
The layout. The king of spades is to be built upon the ace of spades, the space being filled by any top card from a heap.

Remove the four aces from one pack – one of each suit – and put them in a square upon the table. These are the foundation cards.

Now shuffle the two packs together very thoroughly and deal out a reserve of twelve cards, encircling the aces.

Your object is to build simultaneously upwards *and* downwards upon each ace, in suit, until the pile is topped by its twin, the second ace. The sequence runs as follows; ace, king, two, queen, three, jack, four, ten, five, nine, six, eight, seven, seven, eight, six, nine, five, ten, four, jack, three, queen, two, king and ace.

Begin by removing anything suitable in the twelve card reserve to a foundation, filling spaces with the next card from those you hold.

When there is nothing more to be done (although the reserve cards are always eager to be used, throughout the game), play out your cards one by one. Hopefully, *some* will find a home on the foundation piles immediately. Discard unplayable cards to one of four heaps, piling these as you choose in the most judicious manner. The top card of each is available for use, but cannot be moved from heap to heap.

Fill any gap you make in the reserve from now on with the top card from a heap. If you are in the happy position of having made the heaps disappear in play, fill spaces again from the cards you hold.

Having exhausted the packs, gather up the four heaps from left to right and turn them over, dealing them out again as before. This is your last chance to square the circle . . . a mathematical conundrum which the ancient Greeks proved impossible, but not in our case.

Martha Patience

One pack is needed for this satisfying game. After shuffling the pack very thoroughly – absolutely vital – remove the four aces and put them in a line, face upwards, at the top of the table.

These aces are the foundation cards and the object of the game is to build upwards, in sequence and in suit, until a king crowns each pile.

Deal out four rows of twelve cards: the first and third rows are to face downwards, the second and bottom rows to face up. Overlap these cards (the tableau) so that they look like twelve vertical columns.

The card at the base of each column, having nothing upon it, is 'exposed' and available for use. Removing a card frees the one above. (If *that* faces downwards, turn it over with a nonchalant air and play on!)

Move all possible exposed cards to the foundation aces, then build downwards in sequence and alternating colours onto the tableau columns until they can be played off (black five on red six, red four on black five and so on).

Any one exposed card, or a sequence of whatever length, can be played to another column *if* the rule of alternating colours is remembered.

A gap in the tableau, caused by the removal of a vertical line, is not to be filled in quite so lax a fashion. Only *one* available card is placed there – not a sequence – as a new beginning.

With careful consideration, this game should end well.

Mount Olympus Patience

In the prosaic world, Mount Olympus is a trifle under 10,000 feet in height and situated in the north-east of Greece. To most of us, as to the unknown Victorian composer of this game, it is the home of the ancient Greek gods and goddesses. The layout of the game shows this very well.

Two packs of cards are needed and the cards face upwards.

Begin by removing all the aces and all the twos from both packs. Put them in a semicircle, alternately, at the top of the table. These sixteen foundation cards represent the cloud which shrouds Mount Olympus.

The object of the game is to build upwards, in suit, on these in the following way:

ace, three, five, seven, nine, jack and king;
two, four, six, eight, ten and queen.

Shuffle the remainder of the two packs together and deal out a triangular tableau of nine cards beneath the arc of the foundation row: one card in the top row, three in the second row and five in the third row. (This symbolises Mount Olympus.) *Do* allow plenty of space between the nine cards.

Remove suitable cards in the layout to the foundations; otherwise, build downwards on the tableau cards, in suit and by twos (seven of diamonds on the nine of diamonds and so on). Make a downward column of each so that you can see the values.

Fig. 34. Mount Olympus Patience.
The beginning – the three of diamonds can be placed on the ace of diamonds immediately, and the four of clubs on the two of clubs. The gaps will be filled by the next cards from those in your hand.

Exposed cards can be moved singly between tableau piles, or in any length of sequence provided the 'join' is correct, until they can be played to the foundation piles.

Gaps must be filled immediately by the next card from those *in your hand*. Don't be tempted to do anything else, whatever the provocation from blocked cards!

When the game has stuck, deal another nine cards, one to each tableau pile, and play on.

There is no second chance, in the shape of a redeal, when all the cards have been played. But, if when you have dealt out all the cards you are left with gaps in the tableau, you can move the top card from another pile to fill the spaces.

A successful ending will show the foundation piles topped by kings and queens – gods and goddesses peering benignly from their home.

La Belle Lucie Patience
One pack is needed for this unusual and visually pleasing Victorian Patience. As it also requires thought and planning to

bring it to a happy ending, one cannot ask for more!

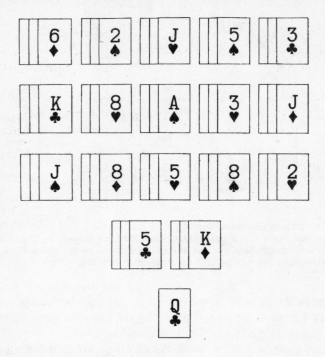

Fig. 35. La Belle Lucie Patience.
The ace of spades is immediately available, together with the two of spades to be built upon it. (All cards face upwards.)

(*Do* allow yourself plenty of room in which to play this charming survivor from more spacious days.)

Play out the cards, face upwards, in groups of three, each trio overlapping one another in the form of a fan. (There will be eighteen in these groups in the tableau, but the last 'fan' will have one card only.)

The object of the game is to take the four aces as they emerge in play, building upwards on them in sequence and suit to the king.

In this game, the 'exposed' card is that card uncovered at the end of a fan. Should any aces be seated there, desperate to catch your eye, put them in a line at the bottom of the table. These are the foundations. (The removal of a card releases the one beneath for play.)

Build any suitable exposed card onto a foundation pile. If this cannot be done, build downwards in sequence *and* suit, which adds greatly to the difficulty, upon the end of another fan until needed. (A fan removed during play is not replaced.)

Should the game become stuck, pick up all the cards not yet correctly placed on a foundation pile and shuffle them thoroughly. Redeal this 'new' pack into fans of three, as before. (Obviously, the last fan of this redeal may consist of only one or two cards.)

You may replay the cards twice, but no *further* chances are given.

An easier version of this game, named *Trefoil*, begins with the four aces placed as foundation cards at the start of the game. The tableau comprises sixteen fans, with three cards in each.

Intelligence Patience

Two packs and a large table are needed for this colourful Patience.

Fig. 36. Intelligence Patience.

Shuffle the two packs together very thoroughly, then deal out eighteen groups of three cards (face upwards, overlapping one another) in the shape of a fan. This is the tableau. If any aces emerge in this deal, remove them and replace them with the next card from your hand.

The object of the game is to take all aces to a row at the top of the table, as they emerge in play, and to build upwards upon them in sequence and in suit to the king.

The exposed card of each fan (that with nothing covering it) is available for use. These can be transferred to another fan pile if suitable, freeing those beneath. Build up or down *in suit* as you please on the tableau piles, even changing direction on the same pile, until it is possible to transfer to a foundation.

A fan removed in play is replaced by the next three cards taken from the pack.

Should you have exhausted the entire pack or, nerves stretched to breaking point, can do nothing more, gather up all cards not yet placed on a foundation pile and shuffle them together. Now deal out as many fans of three as the new pack will allow – obviously, the last fan may have a meagre one or two cards in it – and play on. (Do not forget to extricate any aces from the redeal.) This can be done twice in all.

Eight Off Patience

One pack of cards is necessary for this game. All cards face upwards.

Shuffle the pack thoroughly, then deal six rows of eight cards each. Overlap the rows so that the tableau resembles eight vertical columns.

Place the four remaining cards in a line beneath the layout. These are your reserve.

The object of the game is to remove the four aces to the top of the table as they emerge in play, building upwards upon each, in sequence and suit, to the king.

The exposed card at the base of each column, together with all in the reserve, are there for you to use. (As usual, the removal of a card frees the one beneath.)

Take anything possible to the foundation row; or build downwards in sequence *and suit* upon the tableau until needed. Move cards singly, never a lengthy sequence however tempting.

A column removed in play must be replaced by a king, no other value will do. (And this does not mean that you can extricate the royal personage from the obscurity of cards awaiting release; the space remains until he becomes available.)

This is followed by a helpful rule. *Any* exposed card can be transferred to the reserve row as you choose, provided the quantity of cards here does not exceed eight (as in the title). Good luck!